The Goals of Universities

Other titles recently published under the SRHE/Open University Press imprint:

The Goals of Universities

Michael Allen

The Society for Research into Higher Education
& Open University Press

Published by SRHE and
Open University Press
Open University Educational Enterprises Limited
12 Cofferidge Close
Stony Stratford
Milton Keynes MK11 1BY

and
242 Cherry Street
Philadelphia, PA 19106, USA

First Published 1988

British Library Cataloguing in Publication Data

Allen, Michael
  The goals of universities.
  1. Great Britain. Universities
  I. Title
  378.41

  ISBN 0-335-09504-6

Library of Congress Cataloging-in-Publication Data

Allen, Michael.
  The goals of universities/Michael Allen.
    p.   cm.
  Bibliography: p.
  Includes index.
  ISBN 0-335-09504-6
    1. Higher education and state – Great Britain.   2. Higher education
and state – United States.   3. Education, Higher – Great Britain – Aims
and objectives.   4. Education, Higher – United States – Aims and
objectives.   I. Title
  LC178.G7A44   1988
  378'.01'0941—dc19   88-17997 CIP

Typeset by Rowland Phototypesetting Limited
Bury St Edmunds, Suffolk
Printed in Great Britain by
St Edmundsbury Press Limited, Bury St Edmunds, Suffolk

Contents

Foreword

The universities of this country, as elsewhere, have benefited greatly from their rise in importance to the societies and economies that they serve. There are more of them, they are bigger in size and funded on a scale beyond the dreams of only a few decades ago. But there has been a price to be paid and not only because of the usual refrain about the piper and the tune. Ever since the late 1960s, governments in the western world have kept a politically wary eye on the universities. But they have also become increasingly impatient to get a faster and bigger economic return for the money that they have poured into the universities. They want a higher yield from the cow and they want it now, or at least before the next election. Universities, operating on a different timescale and with many and diverse functions, have not found it easy to cope with demands for a particular kind of performance. Governments have therefore been inclined to give instructions about husbandry or even to try their hand at it themselves.

British universities were long protected from direct assaults by governments and came perhaps to believe too readily in an autonomy hedged about by the divinity of their charters. In reality, their good fortune was to be the heirs of a Liberal age in which the State, with Mr Gladstone as its patron, deliberately limited its own powers. The University Grants Committee (UGC), one of the last exemplars of that age, was designed, in the words of the Croham Committee, as 'a body intended to protect universities from the danger of political interference'. The tradition was strong enough, underpinned as it was by the Robbins Report, to set the framework for the development of the modern university system in this country, the beginning of which can be dated at or about the election of 1959.

As Michael Allen so graphically reminds us, the consequence was that universities, fortified by what seemed an overwhelming vote of confidence, got on with the practical tasks of development and expansion. When asked about their role, the usual reply was a quotation of the Robbins definitions which were already looking more than a little tired even when they appeared. To give one example: 'the advancement of learning' always had an archaic ring in a definition which did not include the word 'research' or have anything to say about its application.

believed that they were doing, or thought that they ought to be doing, in their basic tasks of teaching and research. Philosophical debate about the purposes of higher education was confined to a small coterie which included very few of those who were doing the job of running a university. The government would wish to claim that the financial pressures and constant interference of the past decade have been an engine of fruitful change in the universities. But the evidence the other way is at least as great, that experiment and innovation have been stifled and that it would now be very hard to claim that students have as good a deal as they did a decade ago or that our research performance compares as favourably as it once did with that of other leading countries.

It is in the nature of governments to blame failures on others and to take credit to themselves for success. Universities have to learn to live with that and to rise above it. They know that good, and *a fortiori* great, universities can only be made by those on the spot, whose working lives are devoted to establishing academic reputations and the support of the institution to which they belong. That is a large claim. If it is to be made good in the modern world, it also involves a willingness to take on the responsibilities of accountability for performance and finance and acceptance of the penalties that should follow inefficiency and timidity.

That is why Michael Allen's book is so timely. For whatever the future may hold for universities, between the extremes of a new golden age under the beneficent eye of the UFC and dark years of government-inspired interference and continuing parsimony, there is no doubt that they would be well advised to speak more precisely about their aims and purposes than they have previously done in the too private world of the past. However the dice fall, they will need all the self-confidence and assurance they can muster and awareness and certainty about their role and aims are essential for that. In spite of a good deal of recent heart-searching by the President of Harvard and others, we have much to learn from American universities, as Michael Allen well illustrates. One reason why this is so is the extraordinary diversity of the American system, 'college' and 'university' meaning little or nothing without more precise definition. We are going the same way, if on a smaller scale, with the effective creation of a single system for higher education and the prospect of much greater differentiation of type and function among the universities. It is already evident that the universities will increasingly be under external pressure to produce statements and goals, but that may well be less significant than their own impulse to establish their own identities in the public mind. Those who are called upon to do the thinking and the drafting will be well advised to use what Michael Allen has produced as a handbook.

Maurice Shock

Acknowledgements

Many colleagues at the University of Bath gave me advice and assistance while I was writing this book. I am particularly grateful to Professor K. Austwick, Professor R. E. Thomas, Mr R. M. Mawditt, Dr B. J. R. Taylor and Dr T. J. Harvey. Final responsibility for all statements of fact and opinion rests, of course, with me.

I would like to record my thanks to the Fulbright Commission, which provided a grant for my study visit to Northeastern University, Boston, in the autumn term of 1986. Several months away from the day-to-day pressure of work gave me time to do some (further) thinking about the purposes of universities.

I am grateful to Professor Howard R. Bowen of Claremont Graduate School for allowing me to use his catalogue of goals (in Chapter 8) as the basis for my own catalogue.

Finally, I must thank Mrs Monida Harris for typing and retyping the manuscript with meticulous care.

Abbreviations

Terms which are frequently abbreviated in discussions of higher education, such as University Grants Committee (UGC) are written in full when used for the first time in the main body of the text, with the abbreviated form in brackets, as in this sentence. A key to the abbreviations used in the text is as follows:

ABRC = Advisory Board for the Research Councils
AUT = Association of University Teachers
CBI = Confederation of British Industry
CVCP = Committee of Vice-Chancellors and Principals
DES = Department of Education and Science
ETS = Educational Testing Service
IGI = Institutional Goals Inventory
MBO = Management by Objectives
MPs = Members of Parliament
NAB = National Advisory Body
PI   = Performance Indicator(s)
PPBS = Planning, Programming and Budgeting Systems
SDP = Social Democratic Party
UFC = Universities Funding Council
UGC = University Grants Committee

Readers are asked to note that the words 'he' or 'his' etc. are used throughout the book in preference to 'he/she' or 'his/her'. This convention is adopted for reasons of brevity and is not intended to imply that lecturers, students, etc. are always male. These days, whatever procedure is adopted in this respect seems certain to cause offence to someone, but no offence is intended.

References to 'the Government' are normally references to the Conservative Government elected in 1983, which was in power during the period when this book was written. Exceptions to this rule will be made plain by the context.

Introduction

The aim of this book is to assist readers to decide what the goals of a university should be. The book is not prescriptive: I do not argue that certain goals should be adopted and others rejected (although of course I do have certain preferences); my intention rather is to provide readers with the resources to form their own conclusions.

The text deals mainly with British universities, but there are frequent references to American practice, and much of what I have to say is applicable to universities everywhere. I have tried to ensure that the book will be of value to many lay readers rather than to just a few academics. After all, universities in most countries, and particularly in the United Kingdom, consume large volumes of public money; the taxpayer has every reason to be concerned about what universities are doing. I very much hope that the book will be read by parents, students, industrialists and politicians: I would particularly like to think that every lay member of a university Council will at least glance at it. Over the next few years there certainly ought to be a lively debate about the purposes of universities (and of higher education as a whole); I have therefore tried to provide some of the information which participants in the debate will need.

My interest in the goals of universities began some years ago. In the 1970s my work as a university administrator involved me in the problem of resource allocation, and in 1979 I visited a number of American universities to compare their procedures with those used in the United Kingdom. I discovered that many American universities publish mission statements: that is to say, they issue booklets which set out their aims and objectives, often at considerable length. This practice was so different from what I had experienced in the British system that I decided to investigate the subject in detail: this book is the result.

As most readers will guess, the book is based on my Ph.D. thesis. Most theses are unpublishable without extensive revision, and my own is no exception. In revising the text for publication in book form, what I have tried to do is to make it reader-friendly: I have tried to retain some rigour while eliminating *rigor mortis*. Where necessary I have not hesitated to use the first person, to distinguish what is my own opinion from what is established fact.

The book is arranged in three parts. Part 1 is intended to provide the philosophical and historical frame of reference which is needed by anyone who wishes to consider university goals seriously. In the first chapter, terms such as goals, aims and objectives are defined; and it is probably worth pointing out, right at the beginning, that many British readers will feel uncomfortable in the presence of some of these words. 'Mission' reminds us of Cape Kennedy and the space shuttle; it is at best a piece of American jargon which, like all jargon, we avoid if possible. 'Goal' has overtones of the soccer field, and that particular form of football has never been regarded as a game for gentlemen. So, from the outset, discussions of university purpose are complicated by the vocabulary which we are obliged to use. In Chapter 2, the philosophy of education is reviewed in order to extract ideas about what the goals of universities should be. The third chapter examines three further topics to see what light they shed on the purposes of universities; the topics are organisation theory, the concept of universities as an investment, and manpower-planning techniques. Finally in Part 1, the historical development of British universities is reviewed, in Chapter 4. The aims of this review are (1) to identify the goals which were envisaged for British universities by their founders, and (2) to identify the major events which have influenced the universities' choice of goals subsequently. This chapter, like the rest of the book, takes into account developments up to the end of December 1987, but events are moving fast in higher education at present and it would be futile to try to present an up-to-the-minute report.

The main aims of Part 2 are (1) to determine the extent to which the groups which may be regarded as the main 'stakeholders' in the British university system have formally considered what the goals of universities should be; and (2) to identify areas of actual or potential disagreement on goals, both within and between groups. Chapter 5 reviews the American approach to the whole issue of university goals; the aim of this review is to identify good practice, and I include a brief overview of the important American research into the measurement of opinions on goals. By way of contrast, Chapter 6 describes the British approach to consideration of the purposes of universities. Details are given of British universities' responses to my request for a copy of any formal statement of aims which they had issued; the few attempts to measure British opinions on the goals of higher education are also described. Chapter 7 records the views of the principal British stakeholder groups on what the goals of universities should be, and Chapter 8 provides a classified list of goals. This list, or 'catalogue', offers a means by which individuals or groups can familiarise themselves with the range of possible goals and can select those which they believe should be given the greatest emphasis. Chapter 9 builds on the material contained in earlier chapters: six controversial aspects of university activity are discussed in order to clarify the underlying issues. These six areas of controversy are the ones which I consider to be the most important (in terms of goals) in the late 1980s; arguments about them have persisted over many decades, and in a time of shrinking resources the debate is likely to become increasingly acute. The results of my own research into attitudes towards the six issues are briefly described.

Part 3 is concerned with practical matters. Chapter 10 reviews the environment of British universities in the late 1980s; publications such as the Jarratt Report and the Green and White Papers on higher education are discussed, and key factors which are likely to influence a university's choice of goals in the late 1980s are identified. Chapter 11 summarises a number of ways in which the goals of universities can be clarified at an organisational level: the process can be carried out either through decentralised planning, or through a centralised system, or through a compromise between the two. In Chapter 12, the reader is provided with a method of inquiry. By using this method any reader who is possessed of sufficient energy and determination can investigate (1) the attitudes towards university goals which exist in higher education's environment at any given time, and (2) the goals which are actually being pursued within a particular university. After examining the data which this method of inquiry produces, a reader who has absorbed the material contained in earlier parts of the book will be in a position to decide whether the goals preferred at a particular time and in a particular university are ones which he is prepared to support. Chapter 13 provides an example of what a mission statement for a university might look like; and the book ends, in Chapter 14, with a summary of the conclusions and recommendations which have been drawn from the work as a whole.

The usual references section gives details of the books, periodicals and other material referred to in the notes at the end of each chapter; there is also a supplementary bibliography and an index.

While preparing this book I have talked to some very distinguished officers of British universities, and they have treated me with unfailing kindness and patience. When I suggest to such men that Senates and Councils might usefully devote more thought to the purposes of higher education, the officers usually smile at me benignly over the top of their reading glasses and say something which might be translated as follows: 'My dear fellow, we're *much* too sophisticated for that.'

Well, are we? Reading this book may help you to decide. My own view is that in the matter of goals we are not sophisticated at all: I fear, in fact, that in some respects we are still in the bronze age.

Part 1

1

Definitions of Terms

This chapter provides working definitions of terms which occur frequently in the text. This clarification is necessary because there are a number of respectable authorities whose usage differs;[1] however, the definitions offered here are those most commonly used in the literature on universities.[2]

Mission

The word 'mission' is the broadest in meaning of the various terms used to denote purpose; it is often found in an American context. The mission of a university is its basic reason for existence, the reason or reasons why society supports it financially and morally. Mission can be described as 'an overall concept which attempts to catch the essence of the enterprise and to characterise it.'[3] For example, it has been usefully said that the three basic missions of universities are to transmit, to extend, and to apply knowledge:[4] the activities associated with these missions are teaching, research and public service. Another example of a mission might be 'To meet the needs of a particular locality for an educated citizenry, for trained personnel, and for community services.'[5] You will notice from this example that there is an unfortunate tendency for statements of mission to sound both pompous and obvious.

Many American universities have published 'mission statements' which often encompass goals as well as mission. So far as I am aware, only one British university has produced a mission statement (the University of Ulster) and most British universities can produce little in the way of formal statements of purpose. This point will be considered in detail in Chapter 6.

Aim

The word 'aim' is one which occurs more often in British contexts than in American, as in the phrase 'aims and objectives'. The Department of Education and Science (DES) defines an aim as 'a general statement of intent';[6] an aim is thus very similar to a mission. Statements of aims are often pious and exhortatory;[7] they almost invariably indicate that a high value is placed upon the activities they describe.

Goal

A catalogue of possible goals for universities is provided in Chapter 8, and perhaps the quickest way to gain an understanding of what this book is about is to glance through that catalogue now.

In educational terms a goal is an intermediate step in a hierarchy ranging from 'mission' on the one hand to 'objectives' on the other. Goals are more specific than missions, and they often include reference to a clientele, a process, and an outcome.[8]

Achieving a goal involves achieving a desired condition;[9] in a university the desired condition is mostly one pertaining to students, but goals can relate to staff, the institution, or to society as a whole. Goals are sometimes considered as applying to the entire university,[10] while objectives will normally differ from department to department. Two examples of goal statements are 'To create in students an ability to think critically', and 'To provide students with direct experience of industry and commerce'.[11]

Goals can be either explicit, that is to say written down, or implicit, in the sense that they can be discerned in what the organisation actually does; however, as more than one commentator has noted, what an organisation says it is trying to do may be at variance with what it actually is doing.[12]

Objective

Objectives are more specific than goals; it is often suggested[13] that they should be measurable and verifiable, perhaps with a completion date. Just as an institution's goals should logically be consistent with its mission, so the objectives should be consistent with, and indeed derived from, the goals. They carry the implication that certain action will be taken to achieve the objective. An example of an objective is: 'To enable a student to make engineering drawings in accordance with BS308'; another example is: 'Given a list of 35 chemical elements, the student must be able to recall and write the valences of at least 30'.

More has been written about objectives than about any other term associated with the concept of purpose in education, particularly in the period since 1945. Tyler first introduced the idea that objectives should be defined in terms of specific behaviour,[14] and the term 'behavioural objective' denotes a statement of what the learner will be able to do after a particular course of instruction.

In the 1950s the interest in objectives which had been aroused by Tyler's work was intensified by three developments.[15] First, a large group of academics under the leadership of Bloom produced the now famous classification system called the *Taxonomy of educational objectives*; this is known colloquially as Bloom's taxonomy. A second development was the method of task analysis which was developed by psychologists employed by the United States Air Force. The third and most powerful influence was the programmed learning movement; the programme writer has little chance of producing an effective programme unless the desired result is clear to him at the outset.

Bloom's taxonomy became 'a prodigious success'.[16] The first part, covering the so-called cognitive domain and dealing with the acquisition of knowledge, was published in 1956. A second part, produced under the leadership of Krathwohl, appeared in 1964 and dealt with the affective domain (i.e. feelings and attitudes). Simpson's work on the psychomotor domain (1966) is sometimes held to have filled the gap left by the first two parts of Bloom's taxonomy.[17]

It has been argued[18] that the enthusiasm with which Bloom's taxonomy was received indicates the existence of a deeply felt need to rationalise the process of education. The years since the publication of the taxonomy have shown, however, that applying rational analysis and measurement to the world of education is not an easy process. It is not easy to define, for example, what we mean when we say that we want a child to appreciate art;[19] nor is it easy to design a means of measuring the extent of that appreciation. It is not surprising, perhaps, that in recent years the concept of the behavioural objective has come under severe attack,[20] in the sense that the limitations of the approach have been systematically laid bare.

University

Defining the term 'university', in a British context, is surprisingly difficult. If, for example, we define a university in financial terms, as an institution of higher education in receipt of Treasury grants through the University Grants Committee (UGC), that immediately excludes the Open University, which receives its funding direct from the DES; it also excludes the universities of Northern Ireland.[21] Perhaps the best definition of British universities is that they are institutions with the power to award their own degrees, and are pre-eminent in the field of research.[22]

The power to grant degrees is conferred on universities by Royal Charter or by Act of Parliament, and the granting of a Charter or Act for this purpose gives a university a distinct legal entity. Most charters grant a wide range of powers,[23] which means that universities have, in theory at any rate, a considerable degree of autonomy over financial and academic matters. This independent legal status, together with the emphasis on research, is what chiefly distinguishes British universities from the thirty polytechnics which have been set up since 1966. (More will be said about the emergence and role of the polytechnics in Chapter 4.) It should be noted, however, that the independence and autonomy of universities are not intended to lead to variations in academic standards: the practice of appointing external examiners is designed to ensure that all degrees are of equal academic merit.

It is also worth noting that there is a conceptual problem in relation to the term 'university', particularly when associated with a discussion of goals. There are those who argue[24] that to make such statements as 'The university believes that . . .' is to commit the sin of reification, i.e. to speak of a collection of individuals as if they were a single entity. A university is an organisation, and while people can have goals, organisations, strictly speaking, cannot.

There is undeniably logic in this argument, and it is only right that the point should be made from time to time. In practice, however, most people understand very clearly that when we speak of 'the goals of the University of Newtown' we are in fact referring to the goals of that particular group of people who are in positions of influence within the university. For that reason no great attempt to avoid reification will be made in this book.

Higher education

'Higher education' is another phrase which is widely used but which proves difficult to define neatly. It will suffice for present purposes to say that, by any definition, higher education in the United Kingdom covers a wide diversity of types of institution: universities, polytechnics, and colleges of higher education among them. The definition of higher education which was adopted by the Leverhulme Inquiry covered about 450 institutions in all.[25] The point which needs emphasising, regardless of the definition chosen, is that higher education does not begin and end with the universities; this book, on the other hand, does concentrate on the universities, and no attempt will be made to cover other forms of higher education except incidentally and for purposes of comparison.

The definition of the word 'education' will be discussed in Chapter 2.

Teaching

It may be thought unnecessary to discuss the definition of 'teaching' at all. There is, however, one point which is worth making. The layman regards teaching as the process of passing on a body of factual knowledge. A university teacher, on the other hand, is well aware that the 'facts' which were established fifty years ago have in many cases been successfully challenged, and that today's certainties may also come to be questioned; consequently teachers are often just as concerned with developing skills as with imparting information.[26]

Some controversial aspects of teaching will be considered in Chapter 9.

Research

'Research' is a term which can usefully be distinguished from scholarship. Research is any form of investigation which leads to new knowledge, that is to say knowledge which has never previously been available to anyone. Scholarship, on the other hand, is the pursuit and mastery of existing knowledge, however obscure.[27]

It is also useful to distinguish between pure and applied research. Pure research is the pursuit of knowledge for its own sake; applied research is directed at solving specific problems, often in an industrial or commercial context. Pure research is sometimes called basic or fundamental.

Again, some controversial aspects of research will be discussed in Chapter 9.

Stakeholders

Stakeholders are all those individuals or bodies inside or outside an organisation who are directly affected by what the organisation does.[28] It is usually convenient to think of stakeholders as groups, and in the university context the stakeholders include students, employers, academic staff, non-academic staff, firms which do business with the university, etc. Stakeholder analysis will be further discussed in Chapter 3.

General comments on definitions

Before leaving the question of definitions, there are a number of points to be made about the linkages between the concepts of mission, goals and objectives. An institution's mission might be 'To transmit knowledge'; a goal might be 'To prepare students for a career as an engineer'; and a related objective might be 'To enable a student to make engineering drawings in accordance with BS308'.[29] This suggests that there is a simple and smooth progression from the abstract mission to the concrete objective, and indeed some authorities have argued in precisely that way.[30] The truth, however, is more complex. Missions may translate into goals relatively easily, but the problem of converting goals into measurable objectives is one which sometimes presents difficulties.[31] Suppose, for example, your goal is to improve a student's ability to cope with change: how do you measure that?

Finally, it should not be forgotten that the process of deciding on the mission, goals and objectives of a university is only an early stage in the university's work. (If, indeed, it is consciously undertaken at all.) The next stages are to select the means to achieve the goals, to carry out the necessary functions, and (preferably) to evaluate the outcomes. These processes will be further discussed in Part 3.

Notes

1 For example, the definitions of the words 'goal' and 'aim' given in this chapter differ from the definitions laid down by the International Bureau of Education in the text on *Educational goals* which was published by the United Nations Educational, Scientific and Cultural Organisation in 1980. Writing in the field of corporate

planning, Ackoff (1981) also offers definitions of 'goals' and 'objectives' which differ from those in general use in the world of education.

2 This is confirmed by Fenske (1981), page 178, in respect of the terms 'mission', 'goal' and 'objective' specifically.

3 Hutton (1972), page 57.

4 Lee, quoted by Fenske (1981), page 179.

5 Suggested by Fenske (1978), page 19.

6 Department of Education and Science (1983a), page 27.

7 A point made by Pickup (1976), page 301.

8 Fenske (1981), page 179.

9 Peterson and Uhl (1977), page 5. Etzioni offered a similar definition which was endorsed by Gross and Grambsch (1968), page 5.

10 Peterson and Uhl (1977), page 36.

11 The ability to think critically is highly valued by British academics. See Entwistle, Percy and Nisbet (1971), page 23.

12 Gross and Grambsch were among the first to point this out; see Gross and Grambsch (1968), pages 16 and 17.

13 Principally in the system known as Management by Objectives (MBO); see Chapter 5.

14 Verma and Beard (1981), page 23. Earlier writers on objectives were Franklin Bobbitt and F. W. (Speedy) Taylor: see Taylor (1984), page 85.

15 The source for the remainder of this paragraph is Pickup (1976), page 302. The use of objectives in education was also popularised by writers such as Mager, whose book on preparing instructional objectives first appeared in 1962.

16 For example by De Landsheere (1977), page 97.

17 Ibid., page 78.

18 Ibid., page 97.

19 A point made by Krathwohl, quoted by De Landsheere (1977), page 130.

20 Verma and Beard (1981), page 48.

21 Committee of Vice-Chancellors and Principals (1978), paragraph 20.01.

22 This is the definition offered by the Robbins Report; see Robbins (1963), page 22. The Latin word *universitas* simply means 'a whole': Jarman (1963), page 98. A. H. Halsey tells us that it is not known why the word university came into use in mediaeval times, adding that in Roman law it meant a corporation: Halsey (1985), page 119.

23 According to Burgess (1972), page 40, the Robbins Committee, much to its own surprise, discovered that the independence of universities was such that they could even do things which were expressly forbidden by their charters.

24 See Thomas and Taylor (1974), pages 10 and 41.

25 Ball (1983), page 12.

26 These points are made by Urwin (1969), pages 24 and 25, among others.

27 Urwin (1969), for example, states that in one year there were 226 books and papers published which related to just one aspect of one course which he taught.

28 Ackoff (1981), page 30.

29 Examples adapted from Fenske (1981), page 179.

30 For example, Laughlin and Chamberlain, quoted by Fenske (1981), page 195.

31 See, for instance, Premfors and Ostergren (1975), page 55.33.

2

Philosophy as a Source of Ideas about University Goals

This chapter considers briefly two aspects of philosophy: first, the philosophy of education in general, and secondly the philosophy of higher education in particular. The purpose of considering these aspects of philosophy is to discover what they tell us about what the goals of universities could or should be; some conclusions on this point are offered at the end of the chapter.

The philosophy of education

It seems to be generally agreed that the philosophy of education is in a confused state. It has been variously described as being 'in the doldrums', as 'a discipline in search of direction', and as being 'clearly inadequate'.[1] However, in general terms the philosophy of education can be said to consist of attempts to answer two basic questions: 'What is education?'; and 'What is education for?'[2]

The word 'education' is one to which many meanings are given.[3] One useful definition is that offered by the United Nations Educational, Scientific and Cultural Organisation, which states that education is 'organised and sustained instruction designed to communicate a combination of knowledge, skills and understanding valuable for all the activities of life.'[4] Some writers prefer not to use the word education at all, on the grounds that it is 'an emotive term lacking a precise connotation'.[5] The word is derived from the Latin verb *educare*, meaning to rear or bring up, and ultimately from the verb *educere*, meaning to lead forth.[6] The process of rearing or leading forth implies some sort of guidance, and so to educate essentially means to guide. The concept of guiding inevitably involves a destination, or an end in view;[7] thus the concept of education appears to be inseparable from a concept of purpose.

The idea of purpose in turn seems inseparably linked with value. Peters, in a frequently quoted passage, points out that the term education 'implies that something worthwhile is being or has been intentionally transmitted in a morally acceptable manner. It would be a logical contradiction to say that a man has been educated but that he had in no way changed for the better. . . .'[8]

Unfortunately, what is 'worthwhile' to Peters is not necessarily worthwhile to anyone else, and disputes about which particular set of objectives the process of education ought to be designed to achieve are at least as old as Plato.[9] Peters and his 'London School' of educational philosophers, for example, argue that education must be seen as valuable for its own sake and not as instrumental to something else.[10] On the other hand, those who favour a 'vocational' approach believe that education should be more akin to training. This link between purpose and values is further complicated by the fact that science cannot help us to resolve disputes about values;[11] and so if anything at all may be said to be historically inevitable, it is that the debate on the question 'What is education for?' is one which will continue.

The philosophy of higher education

It has already been stated, in the previous chapter, that any definition of higher education in the United Kingdom must include many other institutions in addition to the universities. However, the first point to be made about the philosophy of higher education is that it is chiefly concerned with universities; indeed many of the most important works on the subject include the word 'university' in their title.

The total number of books on the philosophy of higher education is small: a three-foot bookshelf would accommodate all the key volumes without difficulty. Considering the numbers of students who have passed through the British system of higher education in the post-war period, let alone those in any other system, and considering the rapid growth of public expenditure on higher education in those same decades, the lack of philosophical analyses of the subject is surprising. It is not just that the general public is uninterested: there is little sign of any academic enthusiasm either. Some of the books which at first sight appear promising are not so much original contributions to the subject as summaries and discussions of what has already been written.[12] Cohen and March summed up the state of the art when they pointed out that 'Almost any educated person can deliver a lecture entitled "The goals of the university". Almost no one will listen to the lecture voluntarily.'[13]

The result of this situation is that the major issues which have been raised as the philosophy of higher education has developed can be briefly described by reference to the work of a comparatively small number of writers. That is not to say, however, that the short summaries which follow give a full account of the ideas of the writers concerned. There are two reasons for this: the first is that a few paragraphs can never adequately reflect the many facets of a work which may have taken decades to complete; but secondly, it is often difficult to decide precisely what the thinkers themselves actually mean. Entwistle and Percy undertook a review of this field of philosophy some years ago and came to the conclusion that 'Throughout the range of comment there is a wealth of superficial statement and conceptual confusion. The task of extracting sense and structure from this area is formidable.'[14]

Finally, before embarking on a survey of higher educational theory, readers may find it helpful to note that an account of the actual historical development of universities will be provided in Chapter 4. It should also be noted that the criterion adopted for selecting the philosophers to be discussed in this chapter is that of influence. The philosophers referred to below are those whose ideas I judge to be those most frequently cited in the literature on higher education. Other judges might well make a different selection, and would include perhaps such writers as Sir Walter Moberley, 'Bruce Truscot' and Thorstein Veblen.

The earliest philosophers

It has been suggested that the beginnings of the philosophy of higher education are to be found in the civilisation of India in the fourth century B.C.[15] For present purposes, however, it is more fruitful to consider the ideas of two Chinese philosophers, Confucius and Lao-tse (sixth century B.C.), because their ideas embodied two potentially conflicting educational theories which have found supporters ever since.

Confucius argued that education is a process for integrating individuals into society and that knowledge should be acquired for the sake of harmony in society. Lao-tse, on the other hand, emphasised the cultivation of the individual, and argued that learning is for the sake of understanding.[16] These attitudes in some ways constitute the earliest expression of two views which later became categorised by the terms 'vocational' and 'liberal', and by a host of similar definitions.

In the western world, the first comprehensive philosophy of education is to be found in the writings of Plato. Higher education was perceived by Plato as the cultivation of the individual for the sake of the ideal society; the individual was to be helped to achieve inner happiness, which would allow the state to benefit from the harmony of satisfied citizens fulfilling their proper roles. Thus Plato's thought in some ways parallels that of Confucius.[17]

Aristotle, on the other hand, was very critical of 'vocational' education.[18] He emphasised reason as the guiding principle for human conduct, and claimed that the ultimate aim of education was to prepare the individual for the active enjoyment of leisure. Aristotle was convinced that the activity best suited to leisure was *theoria*, or the disinterested search for truth.[19] He thus disapproved of occupational studies as being thoroughly unworthy of a freeman.[20] He did, however, accept that there might be two views on the matter. His statement that 'At present, opinion is divided about the subjects of education', was quoted, evidently with feeling, by the Carnegie Commission some 2,300 years later.[21]

Philosophy between Aristotle and Newman

Aristotle lived in the fourth century B.C., J. H. Newman in the nineteenth century A.D. There is a long gap between them, and in the intervening centuries a number of philosophical ideas emerged which need to be mentioned, even if only briefly.[22]

As the classical world gave way to mediaeval Christianity, the concept of the importance of life on earth was largely replaced by a belief in the life to come; education was seen as a means of attaining salvation through the inculcation of faith, hope and charity. Later in the middle ages the belief arose that the goal of higher education is the pursuit of truth and learning, and the universities became viewed as institutions dedicated to the advancement of knowledge and the training of scholars.

At the time of the Renaissance, humanist philosophy revived the claims that learning is for the express purpose of life in this world and that the goal of education is the well-rounded development of the individual. It was argued that the training of the mind, not the teaching of vocational skills, is the central concern of education; humanist thought was therefore the direct ancestor of the liberal arts philosophy which is still influential today.

Another challenge to mediaeval concepts of education came from the Protestant Reformation. Martin Luther, for example, encouraged the individual to follow his own worldly vocation; for Luther, the purpose of advanced education was therefore to meet the needs of an individual's vocation. Erasmus also stressed the importance of living a good and worthwhile life.

Later in the sixteenth century Montaigne began to put forward a secular view of man as an autonomous being. This attitude towards education was developed by such key thinkers as Bacon and Galileo, with their emphasis on observation and experimentation. Bacon was particularly influential; he held that knowledge is necessary to attain mastery over nature and thus improve the human condition. In the seventeenth century the scientific revolution further undermined the role of tradition and revelation, and in their place came mathematical demonstration and empirical evidence.

Other influential thinkers in the seventeenth century were Comenius and Locke. Comenius argued the case for training a student to cope with any eventuality with intelligence and good judgement. This point was taken up by Locke, who agreed with Comenius in opposing specialisation.

Locke's ideas possibly influenced Rousseau. In any event, Rousseau emphasised the importance of the growth and development of the individual as opposed to the creation of a good citizen. This conflict of ideas was first noted in the ancient Chinese philosophies of Confucius and Lao-tse, and it recurs periodically throughout history.

Thus we come, very rapidly, to the nineteenth century. The philosophy of higher education in the nineteenth century has a direct bearing upon our own times, and it is most conveniently discussed in terms of its most famous practitioner, John Henry Newman; Newman's work is therefore considered in a section of its own.

J. H. Newman

Newman's book *The idea of a university* first appeared in 1852.[23] Newman was a convert to Roman Catholicism who in 1851 became the Rector of the newly created Catholic University of Ireland.[24] *The idea of a university*, which expounded the virtues of 'liberal education', was based on a series of lectures on the scope and nature of university education; these were delivered in an obscure Dublin hall to an audience of Irish bishops.[25] The greater part of Newman's book deals with matters closely related to the time and place of its origins. The modern reader should bear in mind that Newman was anxious to persuade his audience to ignore the attractions of two views of higher education which were then current. The first of these was the utilitarian view. Exponents of the utilitarian philosophy wrote in the *Edinburgh Review*. They believed, like Bentham and Mill, that all men are subject to the principle of utility, that is to say they believed that human actions are determined through the consequences of pleasure and pain; hence actions are right insofar as they are useful in increasing pleasure and diminishing pain. The principle of utility was a powerful concept in the educational philosophy of the nineteenth century, but Newman rejected it entirely.[26]

The second concept which Newman was anxious to discredit was the German model of a university, which subordinated all other functions to the extension of knowledge, i.e. research.[27] Newman was strongly opposed to the idea that research is an essential activity for a university. In the very first paragraph of the preface to his book there is a statement to the effect that a university is concerned with the diffusion of knowledge rather than with its advancement.[28] Later in the book he declared himself unequivocally in favour of a separate academy or research institute in which knowledge would be advanced. He held this view because he considered that the ability to undertake teaching and research were separate gifts, 'not commonly found in the same person'.[29]

If Newman was against both utilitarianism and the concept of the university as a centre of research, he was undoubtedly in favour of 'liberal education'. When we try to determine *precisely* what Newman meant by a liberal education, 'a number of great difficulties present themselves',[30] but the following summary includes the major points.

A liberal education is designed to develop the individual intellect as broadly as possible, with the 'liberal arts' as the core subjects in the broadening process.[31] In Greco-Roman times the liberal arts were a *trivium* of grammar, logic and rhetoric, and a *quadrivium* of arithmetic, geometry, astronomy and music.[32] Newman, however, did not imply that those seven subjects were appropriate for a modern curriculum, and he certainly did not wish to confine the curriculum to them.[33] His basic concern seems to have been with literature and science, fused by philosophy;[34] music and art were peripheral for Newman, though today's supporters of the liberal arts philosophy would probably be concerned with such aesthetic matters.[35]

Whatever the curriculum, the purpose of liberal education is clear: it is to train the mind. Through this kind of education 'a habit of mind is formed which lasts through life, of which the attributes are freedom, equitableness, calmness, moderation and wisdom.'[36] Newman claimed that individuals who have been educated in this way will be able to 'fill their respective posts in life better' and be 'more intelligent, capable, active members of society'.[37]

Before leaving Newman, we must not forget that his concept of a university, and the actual universities of his day, were closely linked to religion. 'When the Church founds a university', wrote Newman, 'she is not cherishing talent, genius, or knowledge, for their own sake, but for the sake of her children, with a view to their spiritual welfare. . . .'[38] The massive secularisation of higher education which has occurred over the past hundred years is surely one of the most significant changes, not least at Oxford and Cambridge. Until the late nineteenth century, the idea of the university as the imposer of a single version of religious belief was one which seemed very natural to the average Oxford or Cambridge don.[39] But it would surely be a brave don today who tried to enforce a rule that his students should have any religious belief, much less a belief of one specific variety.

Newman's ideas did not have the immediate effect which is often attributed to them:[40] in other words he did not succeed in banishing all talk of 'utility', and universities grew increasingly interested in research. Newman's long-term influence, however, was substantial, and continues to the present day.[41] This is particularly true in America, where 'an important aim of a liberal arts education is to engender broad intellectual and aesthetic interests.'[42] An educated person, in Newman's terms, could almost be defined today as someone who has heard of Newman; for better or for worse, very few people today appear to have actually read what Newman wrote.

Ortega y Gasset

Ortega y Gasset was a Spanish professor of metaphysics. His book *Mission of the university* was developed in 1930 from a series of lectures and newspaper articles, but it appeared in English for the first time in 1946.[43] It is frequently quoted in debates on the philosophy of higher education[44] and appears to have been influential in the post-war period.

At the time when Ortega wrote his book, the Spanish university had two accepted functions: to prepare students for the professions and to carry out scientific research. Ortega argued that the research function should be eliminated: research and teaching, in his view, were not necessarily or ideally linked; in that respect he echoed Newman. Ortega argued that the basic function of the university was the teaching of 'culture'. Culture, however, he defined much more broadly than the term is often understood:[45] Ortega's definition covered physics, biology, history, sociology and philosophy. Culture was viewed as that which 'enables a man to live a life which is something above meaningless or inward disgrace.'[46] It provides 'a way through the chaos of the tangled and confused jungle in which man is lost.'[47] These statements are very similar to many of Newman's in that they convey a strong sense of the author's conviction; yet they are bafflingly imprecise, and for many readers who live in the age of the behavioural objective, unacceptably so.

Ortega's importance is that he gave fresh impetus to Newmanesque ideas in the immediate post-war period. He also provides some encouragement today to those who wish to see a few universities, or perhaps some departments within all universities, having no research function at all.

Karl Jaspers

Jaspers's book *The idea of the university* was first published in 1923; it was extensively revised in 1946, and was translated into English (from German) in 1960.[48] Like Ortega, Jaspers wrote very much for his time and place,[49] but his importance lies in the fact that, in direct contrast to Ortega and Newman, he held that research is central to the university; perhaps for this reason his work is often referred to with approval in discussions of purpose in British higher education.

In the very first sentence of the introduction to his book, Jaspers states that 'The university is a community of scholars and students engaged in the task of seeking truth.'[50] It is impossible, Jaspers tells us, 'to put readily into words what truth is and how it is acquired',[51] but because 'truth is accessible to systematic search, research is the foremost concern of the university. . . . The university's second concern is teaching, because truth must also be transmitted.'[52] In the process of transmitting truth, university teachers 'must aim for the formation of the whole man, for education in the broadest sense of the term.'[53] There is a third function for a university, which is culture,[54] but culture in Jaspers's terminology has a meaning which is much closer to the general understanding of the word than to Ortega's definition. Each of these three functions is 'clearly inseparable from the other two'.[55]

Jaspers fully recognises a vocational role for the university. 'The university is simultaneously a professional school, a cultural centre and a research institute.'[56] These three are 'indissolubly united. One cannot be cut off from the others without destroying the intellectual substance of the university.'[57]

Jaspers thus differs from Newman and Ortega in his attitude to research; he insists that no one who is not carrying out research can fully educate students at a university.[58] However, he echoes a substantial part of Newman's case for liberal education in his emphasis on 'the whole man'.[59] He stresses the importance of giving technology a central place in the university structure so that it may achieve a 'genuine relation with the Humanities'.[60]

Jaspers's work first appeared in England at a time when higher education was passing through a period of rapid growth, and a number of academics regarded it as profound.[61] His chief attraction today is as a source of ideas for those who seek to defend the link between teaching, research, and the education of that mysterious being, 'the whole man'.

Clark Kerr

Kerr's book *The uses of the university* was based on his 1963 Godkin lectures at Harvard University; a revised edition appeared in 1973. Kerr is famous among the cynical for having stated that he sometimes viewed the university as 'a series of individual faculty entrepreneurs held together by a common grievance over parking'.[62] This statement must not, however, be taken as his final word on the nature of universities.

Kerr's influence has been considerable. According to the editor of *The Times Higher Education Supplement*, 'Newman was the household god of the traditional university, and Clark Kerr occupies the same icon-like position for the modern university.'[63]

Kerr began his book by pointing out that 'The university has been a remarkably unstudied institution until very recently.'[64] Having paid due tribute to such writers as Newman and Flexner, he went on to put forward the idea of a multiversity. This was essentially a concept of the university as having a multiplicity of purposes. (It might, or might not, have a multiplicity of campuses.) It is important to understand that in outlining this concept Kerr was not speaking of that vast and varied body, American higher education as a whole, but of a limited number of so-called 'research universities'.[65] It is also important to note that the danger associated with the multiversity was that it might come to mean so many different things to so many different people that it would be perpetually at war with itself.[66]

The very title of Kerr's lectures indicated a considerable shift, at least in America, from traditional perceptions of the role of the university; the implication was that the university should be useful, in many practical ways, to the society in which it existed.[67] And yet, even in America, universities change only very slowly. As late as 1978, the President of Harvard reported that 'The assumption that liberal education is the paradigm of higher education, is perhaps for the first time being seriously questioned.'[68]

Some conclusions about the philosophy of higher education

Most readers will by now agree with the writers quoted at the beginning of the chapter, who said that the task of extracting sense and structure from the philosophy of higher education is a formidable one. However, it seems to me that a number of broad conclusions may be drawn from this limited survey.

The first conclusion is that philosophy is not prescriptive: it does not prove, with the aid of logic or science, that universities must inevitably have certain stated goals. Secondly, there is no universally accepted view of the purpose of higher education. Nowadays the functions of teaching and research (functions as distinct from purposes) are common to almost all universities; indeed in many of the 'leading' universities research is paramount. Other functions, such as 'public service' (however defined) and 'the transmission of higher culture',[69] are more controversial. However, it is worth drawing attention once again to the two contrasting views of the function of teaching in higher education which have surfaced and resurfaced over the centuries. These, for the sake of convenience, I will call the liberal arts philosophy and the vocational philosophy.

The term 'liberal arts' (*eleutherai technai*) first occurred in Greece in the fourth century B.C. In that context it meant the skills that a free man ought to have,[70] and traditionally the liberal arts have been considered suitable educational fare for the potential leaders of society. Liberal arts philosophers hold that education should serve the needs of the individual;[71] they believe that people seek to understand the world they live in simply as a matter of curiosity;[72] the pursuit of truth is the highest virtue, and it may be found, usually, through the exercise of reason. A liberal education is said to enhance the capacity to lead a full life.[73]

Vocational studies, on the other hand, have often been considered more suitable for followers than for potential leaders. Those who favour vocational studies tend to hold the view that education should serve the needs of society rather than the needs of the individual.[74] Professional expertise should be developed not as a matter of idle curiosity but because of its enormous significance for the community; the nation needs trained manpower.[75] The truth, to supporters of the vocational principle, is perhaps not an absolute, unchanging verity but something which is always being discovered and tested and applied anew;[76] the purpose of education is essentially to improve man's lot and to travel further along the road called Progress.[77]

Both the liberal and vocational philosophies have appeared under a host of other names, a practice which has done little to clarify the ideas involved in them. Some of the better known alternative names are listed in Table 2.1, together with the authors who have devised the various terms.[78]

Whatever the terminology used, it seems clear that these two philosophies represent broad divisions of view which are difficult to reconcile. The liberal philosophy finds its greatest support in theology, in the humanities, and in the liberal arts college; it emphasises the library and the discussion group.[79] The vocational view finds its advocates, broadly speaking, in the sciences and the professions; its home is the laboratory. (The contrast between the liberal and vocational philosophies will be discussed in more detail in Chapter 9.)

The sensitive antennae of the Carnegie Commission detected a third philosophy, which has only recently emerged; this is variously described as the political, reconstructionist or transformational view.[80] The essence of this philosophical approach is an envisioned perfect state, whether it be anarchy, democracy, the 'cultural revolution triumphant', or whatever.[81] While there are

Table 2.1 *Synonyms for liberal and vocational philosophy*

Author	Term used to describe liberal philosophy	Term used to describe vocational philosophy
Harvard Report on the Nature and Purposes of the University	Classical	Pragmatic
Butts and Cremin	Intellectualist	Experimentalist
Carnegie Commission	Restorationist	Utilitarian
Burgess	Autonomous	Service
Brubacher	Epistemological	Political

undoubtedly members of most universities who could be characterised as belonging to this school of thought, there does not seem to be, as yet, any university in the western world which has adopted this approach officially or wholeheartedly. Even in the People's Republic of China the higher education policy might best be described as one of vocational–technical training.[82]

Each of the two broad philosophical approaches has been dominant at various times and in various places. The liberal arts philosophy gradually rose to dominance, in both Britain and America, in the late nineteenth century;[83] and although it is difficult to judge precisely, the vocational approach seems to be in ascendance in the United Kingdom today. The position is difficult to judge because neither universities nor governments seem to be able to take up a clear, unambiguous position. The 1972 White Paper on Education, for example, was determined to face both ways at once:

> The Government consider higher education valuable for its contribution to the personal development of those who pursue it; at the same time they value its continued expansion as an investment in the nation's human talent in a time of rapid social change and technological development. . . . The Government hope that those who contemplate entering higher education – and those advising them – will the more carefully examine their motives and their requirements; and be sure that they form their judgment on a realistic assessment of its usefulness to their interests and career intentions.[84]

The main conclusion which I draw from the material in this chapter is that the question of the purpose of a university is essentially a matter of judgement; it is not something which can be determined by science, in the same way that a dispute over the length of a piece of string can be resolved. Nevertheless, as later chapters will make clear, systematic methods of inquiry may be able to offer some assistance in determining goals, in that they may clarify and inform the debate.

Notes

1 Statements quoted by Pritchard (1983), page 119.
2 Meynell (1976), page 79.
3 Verma and Beard (1981), page 41.
4 Source: Page and Thomas (1977).
5 Beard, Healey and Holloway (1970), page 1.
6 Source: the *Oxford English Dictionary* (1961), volume III.
7 A point made by De Landsheere (1977), page 79.
8 This statement by Peters is quoted by De Landsheere (1977), page 79, and by Woods and Barrow (1975), page 10.
9 Ebel, Noll and Bauer (1969), page 908.
10 Hobson (1982), page 232.
11 For a discussion of why science cannot determine values see Brecht (1959).
12 See, for instance, Brubacher (1978).

13 Cohen and March (1974), page 195.
14 Entwistle and Percy (1970), page 31.
15 Chaplin (1978), page 3204.
16 Ibid., page 3205.
17 Ibid.
18 Brubacher (1978), page 74.
19 Chaplin (1978), page 3206.
20 Brubacher (1978), page 74.
21 Carnegie Commission (1973), prefatory page.
22 For a useful summary of this period see Chaplin (1978).
23 It has been reprinted many times, often with an introduction to set it in context. The version used for this book was Newman (1959).
24 Shuster, in the introduction to Newman (1959), page 21.
25 Kearney (1973), page 6.
26 Chaplin (1978), page 3214.
27 Beard, Healey and Holloway (1970), pages 21 and 27.
28 Newman (1959), preface.
29 Beard, Healey and Holloway (1970), page 28.
30 Shuster, in the introduction to Newman (1959), page 33.
31 Beard, Healey and Holloway (1970), page 28.
32 Brubacher (1978), page 72.
33 Shuster, in the introduction to Newman (1959), page 35.
34 Ibid., page 36.
35 Ibid., page 41.
36 Ibid., pages 30 and 31.
37 Newman (1959), page 9.
38 Ibid.
39 Kearney (1973), page 17.
40 Ibid., page 6.
41 Beard, Healey and Holloway (1970), page 40, claim that Newman's ideas had considerable influence on the academic planning of certain of the newer universities.
42 Bok (1973), page 3. Bowen, the President of Princeton University, devoted his Report of March 1977 to a staunch defence of liberal education. See Bowen (1977b).
43 Wyatt (1981), page 59. The summary of Ortega's ideas in this section is largely derived from Wyatt's paper.
44 Beard, Healey and Holloway (1970), page 38.
45 More broadly, for example, than in the reference to culture in the Robbins report. See Robbins (1963), page 7.
46 Quoted by Wyatt (1981), page 62.
47 Ibid.
48 Wyatt (1982), page 21.
49 Deutsch, in the Editor's Note to Jaspers (1965), page 16.
50 Jaspers (1965), page 19.
51 Ibid., page 20.
52 Ibid., page 21.
53 Ibid.
54 Ibid., page 51.
55 Ibid.
56 Ibid., page 53.
57 Ibid., page 54.

58 Deutsch, in the Editor's Note to Jaspers (1965), page 16.
59 Zangwill, in the preface to Jaspers (1965), page 9.
60 Ibid., page 10.
61 For example, Ashby – cited by Wyatt (1982), page 21.
62 Kerr (1973), page 20.
63 Scott (1981b).
64 Kerr (1973), page vii.
65 Kwiatowski (1983), page 464.
66 A point made by David (1982).
67 Ross (1976), page 141.
68 A statement by the Dean of the University of California Business School, quoted by Bok (1978), page 3.
69 Trow, quoted by Ross (1976), page 142.
70 Bowen (1977b), page 4. Bowen is quoting Connor, the then Chairman of the Classics Department at Princeton.
71 Nash (1975), pages 410 and 412.
72 Brubacher (1978), page 12.
73 Bowen (1977b), page 36.
74 Nash (1975), pages 410 and 412.
75 Brubacher (1978), page 13.
76 Carnegie Commission (1973), page 84.
77 Ibid.
78 The principal source for this list is the Carnegie Commission (1973), page 83. See also Burgess (1979) and Brubacher (1978).
79 Carnegie Commission (1973), page 87.
80 Ibid., page 83.
81 Ibid., page 85.
82 Chaplin (1978), page 3217.
83 Carnegie Commission (1973), page 90.
84 Quoted by Morris, Woodhall and Westoby (1977), page 90.

3

Organisation Theory, the Concept of Universities as an Investment, and Manpower Planning

The previous chapter considered the insights into university goals which may be obtained from the philosophy of education. The present chapter examines some further approaches to the analysis of universities and their purposes. The first of these is the study of universities as organisations; the second is the economic concept of universities as an investment – an investment both for society and for the individual student; the third approach is that of manpower planning. The reason for examining these issues is once again to discover what light they shed on the possible goals of universities.

Universities and organisation theory

There are, in fact, a variety of organisation theories rather than one generally accepted theory, but one of the few things which organisational theorists agree on is the necessity of defining an organisation's goals.[1] Indeed, the traditional view of organisation theorists is that an organisation is, by definition, a social unit which has been explicitly established for the achievement of specific goals.[2] However, as has already been noted in Chapter 1, to say that an organisation has a goal is to indulge in reification; the statement attributes the power of thought and action to a 'social construct'.[3] It must therefore be remembered that what appear to be 'organisational goals' are actually the common goals of the people who are members of the organisation. These goals are the result of 'shifting compromises among the individuals within the organisation and the demands made by the environment'.[4] Compromise leads to agreement, however reluctant; and therein lies the rub for universities, because many authorities suggest that it is difficult to persuade the members of a university to agree on anything. This may, however, be an unnecessarily pessimistic view.

Universities are sometimes considered to be among the class of organisations which may be called environment-serving;[5] this class includes hospitals, the post office, and the church.[6] Other authorities argue that universities cannot properly be compared with any other form of organisation. Universities are said to be unique, for two principal reasons; first, because they have a multiplicity of missions, and secondly, because no one has absolute authority within the organisation;[7] universities are at least partial industrial democracies. 'Universities are clearly a genus apart', declares Perkins.[8] 'A university is, in many ways, a non organisation', says Fenske.[9]

What then, in organisational terms, is a university? It may be an organised anarchy. This is a description which originated with Cohen and March in 1974[10] but which has found favour elsewhere.[11] According to Cohen and March, universities are organised anarchies because their goals are vague or in dispute, because the members of the university do not understand the internal governmental processes, and because the participants in the organisation change from time to time and vary in the effort they devote to the organisation. Ambiguity is alleged to be the dominant characteristic of universities.[12] Cohen and March say flatly (of the American university) that 'it does not know what it is doing'.[13]

Organisation theorists do not offer much hope that the situation is likely to be resolved even after the diagnosis of organised anarchy has been made. Cohen and March conclude that 'there are only modest signs that universities or other organised anarchies respond to a revelation of ambiguity of purpose by reducing the ambiguity.'[14] Universities are held to be peculiarly resistant to change,[15] and indeed Rice argues that 'there is in the majority of universities massive unconscious agreement to maintain organisational confusion in order to avoid recognition of the conflict of cultural values.'[16]

The picture of universities which is painted by organisation theorists is thus scarcely favourable. But to declare that an organisation is an organised anarchy is not to say that it is illegitimate, immoral or ineffective; it is simply to say that it is difficult to lead and to control.[17] Furthermore, the fact that universities have carried out their business in much the same way for very long periods of time should give them considerable credibility even if it does not provide a complete defence against the charge of irrationality. For there are at least two other procedures for choice in addition to pure reason: intuition, which causes people to act without fully understanding why; and tradition, in response to which people do things in a way which has proved satisfactory through long experience.[18]

This discussion of organisation theory could not be concluded without some reference to the 'systems approach'. In the 1960s a vast amount of literature was produced, largely in America, which compared organisations with systems of one kind or another: biological, mechanical, administrative and other varieties.[19] For some years the journals were full of systems analyses which involved inputs, outputs, black boxes, sub-systems, concepts such as homeostasis, negative feedback, and transformation; many were the diagrams which were drawn to illustrate these processes.[20] At first, much was expected of the systems approach; in fact too much was expected of it, and by 1972 Kraft and Latta labelled it an 'out' term which just a year ago had been an 'in' term.[21] Systems analysis did provide a large number of useful insights, however, and still does. What it did not do was to provide any magic answers to such difficult questions as what it is that universities should be trying to achieve, and the amount of resources which should be devoted to each particular goal. Systems

Table 3.1   *Stakeholder analysis*

Stakeholder group	Input	Output
Central government	Money	Services (chiefly graduates)
Employees	Labour	Money
Industry/commerce/ other employers	Research contracts, sponsorship	Employees, research findings
Local government	Money	Services
Professional institutions	Advice, money	Members, courses
Research Councils	Money	Research findings
Students	Money, effort	Education
Suppliers	Goods and services	Money

thinking often clarified the questions and focused attention more precisely on the issues: but it did not provide a substitute for judgement.

Another approach which has been of some value is that of stakeholder analysis. Stakeholders are all those inside or outside an organisation who are directly affected by what the organisation does;[22] they are involved, consciously or unconsciously, in a series of exchanges with the organisation. If we apply this type of analysis to a typical British university, the principal stakeholders, together with what they put in and what they take out of the organisation, can be listed as shown in Table 3.1. The stakeholders are not listed in any order of importance. In terms of stakeholder analysis, the proper aim of an organisation is not to serve any one of its stakeholder groups to the exclusion of any of the others: it is to serve all of them by increasing their ability to pursue their own aims more efficiently and effectively.[23]

To conclude, then, organisation theory offers a number of interesting and valuable ways of analysing a university's relationship with its environment; what it cannot do, any more than educational philosophy can, is to offer a definitive answer to the question of what a university's goals should be. It can only offer pointers to possible goals. It is therefore appropriate to look next at a type of analysis which conveys heavy hints as to what the goals of an institution ought to be: that is the economic concept of universities as an investment both for the community and for the individual. It will also be useful to consider the concomitant of the investment approach, which is the concept of manpower planning.

Universities as an investment

Teaching is clearly a major function of a university, and it has been suggested[24] that teaching can be viewed as having three possible effects. In the first place it can act as a process which 'matures' students; secondly, it can identify talent by filtering out the more able students from the average; and thirdly, it can increase the nation's human capital by endowing students with knowledge and skills. All of these potential outcomes imply that teaching has a value for society.

Governments have also placed a high value on research. In his speech to the Committee of Vice-Chancellors and Principals (CVCP), given immediately before he retired as Chairman of the UGC, Sir Edward Parkes commented that 'governments still hope that somehow scientific discovery is going to lead us out of world recession.'[25]

In view of the apparent benefits of teaching and research, governments have tended to regard higher education as a sound investment of public funds,[26] in the post-war period particularly. Indeed, the view has often been expressed that increasing the volume of higher education not only results in an increased rate of economic growth, but is the key to survival in an increasingly technological age.[27] The Robbins Report of 1963 argued that 'Unless higher education is speedily reformed ... there is little hope of this densely populated island maintaining an adequate position in the fiercely competitive world of the future.'[28]

By the 1970s, however, the rising cost of the expansion of universities, both in the United Kingdom and elsewhere, began to come under increasingly close scrutiny.[29] One of the major themes of a German study of 1976, prepared for the International Labour Office, was the widespread disappointment with the consequences of an expansion of higher education, at least as far as economic growth was concerned.[30] In 1980 Robbins himself stated that he simply could not take seriously 'any attempt to trace any obvious correlation between rates of growth of gross national product ... and the proportion of the relevant age-groups receiving higher education'. The variables, he said, 'are so numerous and the connections are often so indirect.'[31] A number of other commentators argued that economic expansion depends partly upon the growth of knowledge but also upon the ability of governments and industrialists to apply it, and that in the United Kingdom such ability was sadly lacking.[32]

Nevertheless, the belief that universities contribute greatly to the economic well-being of a nation clearly remains strong. In the United States, the President of Princeton University stated in his 1979 Report that 'While precise calculations of economic effects are not possible, careful studies suggest that advances in knowledge have accounted for roughly one quarter to one third of the increase in national income in the United States since 1929.'[33] The major conclusion of a lengthy American study published in 1978 was that the sum of the benefits of higher education exceeded the total cost by a factor of three or more.[34] In the United Kingdom, Robin Marris, a Professor of Economics in London University, declared in 1984 that 'the economic return to the nation from university education is so high, that there is in fact an overwhelming case for a new massive expansion; for, in effect, a "new Robbins".'[35]

The evidence suggests that, despite some lowering of expectation in recent years, there is a consensus that teaching, research and other university activities provide a sound return on investment for society as a whole; certainly that view is accepted by the Government's Green Paper of 1985 (annex B, paragraph B12). But what of the individual's investment? Anyone who embarks on a university degree course must inevitably commit a considerable period of time, and time is a finite resource; the student must also forgo the earnings which could have been generated in that time. Is the investment worthwhile?

Most authorities agree that it is.[36] The American Carnegie Council concluded in 1980 that although the return on a degree, expressed in life earnings, had fallen in the mid 1960s and mid 1970s, it was now rising again.[37] Marris is also convinced that graduates have greater earning power than non-graduates.[38] There are, of course, other benefits conferred on graduates in addition to enhanced earnings: and Bowen's study declares that 'These non-monetary benefits surely are far greater than the monetary benefits.'[39] Whatever the balance of the various advantages, it does seem clear from the relatively steady demand for admission to British universities that most young people who are qualified to take a degree believe that it is in their best interests to do so. Once again, the Green Paper of 1985 concurs, stating that the private rate of return is higher than that for society as a whole (annex B, paragraph B12).

Manpower planning

There are two principal stages in manpower planning. The first stage involves forecasting the numbers of persons with certain specified skills (engineers, teachers etc.) which are required at a future date; the second stage involves taking the action which is necessary to ensure that the required manpower is available at the target date.[40] Although manpower planning is a process which can be confined to a particular industry or profession, it is normally considered as operating at national level; one survey revealed that by the mid 1970s some sixty nations had drawn up an educational plan based on an investigation of manpower needs.[41] This kind of planning is a relatively recent innovation: the major international review of manpower forecasting cites no references earlier than 1949,[42] though the Soviet Union was certainly using manpower-planning techniques in the 1920s.[43]

Manpower planning, on a national level, must inevitably start by taking note of the goals of the nation's economic plan; the goals provide a set of required final outputs of goods and services. From these goals a calculation can be made of the future manpower requirements of the society in question. This calculation is far from straightforward. Suppose, for example, a nation wishes to calculate its need for medical staff. The planners have to begin with such facts as the age, training and positions of present personnel; they need to calculate losses due to death, retirement, emigration and other factors; they must consider the birth-rate. Once a calculation has been made of future needs, the planners have to consider how the personnel are to be trained, for how long and by whom. New institutions may be necessary; in some cases incentives may have to be devised to encourage volunteers for training to come forward. Once made, the calculations cannot be assumed to hold good for ever; they have to be kept under continual review. It will therefore be immediately apparent that manpower planning is a process which itself consumes resources on a significant scale.[44]

No matter how large the resources devoted to manpower planning, and no matter how centralised the society, there have proved to be great practical difficulties involved. Ideally, forecasts need to be made for very long periods – 15 or 20 years. But in many countries there are problems in obtaining the most basic statistics: in Nigeria, for example, even the figure for the total population was so uncertain in 1963 that the two most authoritative estimates were as far apart as 37,400,000 and 55,700,000.[45] In countries such as India and Pakistan, manpower planning in the 1960s resulted in considerable unemployment and under-utilisation of professional and technical staff in the 1970s, despite the assistance of foreign experts.[46] Even in countries such as Canada, France, Great Britain and Sweden, case histories show that many forecasts have been failures and have resulted in wrong policy decisions.[47] Not surprisingly, therefore, many countries have become sceptical about the value of the process.[48] Burton R. Clark has concluded that even centralised bureaucracies cannot effectively co-ordinate mass higher education, largely because they are not quick or flexible enough in their reactions: he quotes Thailand as a classic example.[49]

It has been suggested that the possible solution to some of the technical problems involved in manpower planning lies in continuing education. Under a traditional system of higher education, a three or four-year degree course would be expected to equip a graduate for forty years of working life, thus requiring the planner to adopt an impossibly long-term view. If, however, higher education were to consist of, say, a six-month course every five years, the planning horizon would become more realistic.[50] One other source of relief for the manpower planner lies in the fact of substitutability: there are comparatively few jobs for which the skills required are so specific as to exclude employing anyone except an individual trained for that job alone. For example, there are many different ways of staffing a hospital, let alone a factory or a shop.[51] Even in highly technical areas, a physics graduate may be able to perform as well as an electrical engineer.

Probably the first systematic attempt to relate the planning of higher education to the needs for professional personnel occurred in the Soviet Union in the 1920s. During the next two decades these methods were adopted by several other countries with centrally planned economies.[52] In the Soviet Union today, all institutions of higher education are centrally controlled and have their enrolments and specialisms calculated to meet the targets of Gosplan, the state economic planning agency. Planning is done on a five-to-seven-year base. The institutions are highly specialised – monotechnics, as it were, rather than polytechnics. The chain of command runs directly from the Central Committee of the Communist Party, through the USSR Ministries of Education and Higher Education, to the constituent Republics and so on down the line. Everything is prescribed, right down to the number of hours per week per subject and the specification of lectures or seminars in terms of teaching style.[53]

Another centrally planned economy is that of Romania. There, as in the USSR, the goals of higher education constitute an integral part of the national plan for the socio-economic development of the country. At the end of their course, new graduates are assigned to vacant posts according to the results they have obtained during their studies. Married couples are assigned according to the higher grade obtained by either the husband or wife, and both are sent to the same district. All graduates are required to remain in their first post for at least three years.[54] Thus to some extent the centrally planned economies avoid the graduate unemployment which sometimes occurs in the market economies. Nevertheless, the planned economies, such as the German Democratic Republic, Hungary and Poland, do temper their dedication to the needs of the economy by encouraging the participation of young people from workers' homes and from rural areas, even if they are not as well qualified as other students; they also allow some measure of individual choice of course.[55]

Clearly, manpower planning is more likely to be successful in planned economies than in market economies;[56] but it must not be assumed that the central governments of western European democracies are altogether powerless in this respect. To begin with, they usually provide much of the finance for higher education; they control emigration, military service, student grants, and a host of other relevant factors. Often they intervene directly to influence the numbers of teachers or doctors produced by the system.[57] That having been said, it has to be admitted that the record of manpower planning in western economies is not impressive. In the United Kingdom, for example, an inaccurate assessment of the rising birthrate in the 1950s led to an increase in teacher-training provision. In the 1960s, when the teachers entered the market, the expected demand had not materialised. Conversely, admission to British medical schools was deliberately limited in the late 1950s but by the early 1960s there was a shortage of doctors, and in 1968 the Todd Report recommended that admissions should be almost doubled compared with the 1961 level.[58]

The principal difference between the planned economies and the market economies is that provision of higher education in the former is determined by the expected needs of the economy, while in the latter it is largely determined by social demand. However, just as the planned economies make some allowance for social equality and personal choice, so the market economies intervene to influence the level of provision in expensive fields such as medicine. The result is that although the two political systems have very different theoretical approaches, the gap between the practice of the two groups of nations is not as wide as might be expected. A recent study has suggested that the gap is still closing.[59] For example, countries such as the United Kingdom, the Federal Republic of Germany, the Netherlands and Sweden are now beginning to emphasise the vocational element in courses; Poland and the German Democratic Republic are beginning to talk about education for innovation and creativity, while returning much of the vocational component to employers.[60] Thus the two systems are beginning to converge in their solutions to the problems they face. The main difference is that the planned economies make adjustments at the point of entry to higher education, while countries using social demand as the main criterion for the level of provision have problems of adjustment at the point where new graduates enter the labour force; at present, therefore, the market economies still place a greater emphasis on flexibility and the substitution of skills.[61]

Economists are divided into those who believe in manpower planning and those who do not; it is a highly controversial subject.[62] The main arguments in favour of manpower planning are that higher education makes heavy demands on a nation's resources and therefore ought to be as efficient and effective as possible; also, many of the students clearly believe that higher education has vocational implications for them. The main argument against manpower planning, desirable though it may be in theory, is that it appears to be impossible to assemble sufficiently accurate data to permit long-term forecasts to be made; a lesser argument is that the possibility of substitution between most categories of manpower makes planning unnecessary.[63]

Conclusions drawn from the study of organisation theory, investment, and manpower planning

The conclusions which I draw from this chapter are simply that organisation theory and the consideration of universities as an investment both enable us to see more clearly what universities are, what they could be, and the tasks which various stakeholder groups envisage for them. Such studies provide no simple answer to what the goals of a university should be, but they do provide a wider frame of reference within which to form judgements.

On the question of manpower planning it has to be said that the techniques do not work very well in practice, and in the United Kingdom manpower planning has never been adopted on any significant scale. The Robbins Report explicitly rejected the possibility of determining the number of places in higher education on the basis of manpower needs,[64] doing so for both moral and practical reasons.[65] Some twenty years later, in the Leverhulme seminar on higher education and the labour market, there was a general consensus against manpower forecasting of any kind.[66]

Nevertheless, the wisdom of this collective view must be questioned. Manpower-planning techniques may be imperfect, but allowing the system to be dominated by market forces is also unsatisfactory. All too frequently, students and institutions respond to an increase or a fall in demand for say, engineers, only to find that by the time their response takes effect the situation has changed yet again. These 'cycles of mismatch' have been well documented.[67] In the face of these problems, several nations have concluded that while there are considerable difficulties in making reliable forecasts of qualified manpower needs, it is increasingly desirable to attempt such calculations.[68] Even if the central planning authority is unable to forecast demand without error, it may well be able to forecast it more accurately than individual students or institutions. Furthermore, the personal choices of students are by definition not choices made in the national interest. Centralised control may therefore have rather more to offer than the British love of liberty allows us to admit. Judgements by British writers of the effectiveness of manpower-planning techniques are all too easily coloured by a dislike of the consequences for the individual; awareness of the benefits for society can be correspondingly muted.

Not surprisingly, perhaps, the British Government has historically sought to resolve the situation by compromise. Governments have usually sought to influence the supply of scientists or engineers on a 'broad-steer' basis,[69] and in March 1984 the Secretary of State for Education and Science indicated that this approach would continue.[70]

Notes

1 Fenske (1981), page 178.
2 Thomas and Taylor (1974), page 38. The statement is endorsed by Silverman (1970), page 8.
3 Silverman (1970), page 9, and Hoyle (1979), page 160.
4 Nosow and Clark (1976), page 7.
5 Ansoff's term: Ansoff (1979), page 9.
6 Ibid., page 10.
7 Perkins (1973), page xv.
8 Ibid., page xvi.
9 Fenske (1978), page 81.
10 Cohen and March (1974), page 2. Their conclusion was based on 218 interviews in 42 different institutions (page xxi).
11 For instance, Enderud (1980), page 235.
12 Clark (1979), page 1.
13 Cohen and March (1974), page 3.
14 Ibid., page 196.
15 Elton (1981), page 23.
16 Rice (1970), page 109.
17 Points made by Enderud (1980), page 237.
18 These arguments are advanced by Cohen and March (1974), page 200.
19 Jones (1967) distinguished eleven different kinds of systems.
20 Whole books were also written on the subject. See, for example, Immegart and Pilecki (1977), and Hamelman (1972).
21 Kraft and Latta (1972), page 5.
22 Ackoff (1981), page 30.
23 Ibid., page 33.
24 By Johnson. Quoted by Jones (1979), pages 513 and 514.
25 Parkes (1983), page 20.
26 Thomas (1980), page 73.
27 See, for example, *Management Today* (1984).
28 Robbins (1963), page 5.
29 Halsey (1981), page 11.
30 Teichler, Hartung and Nuthmann (1981).
31 Robbins (1980), page 10.
32 A view put forward by Edwards (1982). In 1984 the UGC argued that widespread higher education is a necessary but not a sufficient condition for economic growth. See University Grants Committee (1984).
33 Bowen (1979) page 4.

34 Bowen (1977a), pages 447 and 448.
35 Marris (1984), page 14.
36 Teichler, Hartung and Nuthmann (1981), however, express some doubt about the relationship between income and education.
37 Halsey (1981), page 186.
38 Marris (1984), page 15.
39 Bowen (1977a), page 447.
40 This definition is adapted from Horowitz (1978).
41 Morris, Woodhall and Westoby (1977), page 47.
42 Wolfle (1978), page 2709.
43 McVoy (1978), page 2713.
44 This brief account of the manpower-planning process is derived largely from Horowitz (1978) and Wolfle (1978).
45 Wolfle (1978), page 2709.
46 McVoy (1978).
47 Wolfle (1978), page 2710.
48 Ibid. Also Morris, Woodhall and Westoby (1977), page 47.
49 Eurich (1981), pages 57 and 58.
50 See Fulton, Gordon and Williams (1980), page 104.
51 Ibid., page 88.
52 McVoy (1978), page 2713.
53 Grant (1985).
54 Burloiu (1980).
55 Fulton, Gordon and Williams (1980), page 109.
56 Ibid., page 112.
57 Wolfle (1978), page 2709.
58 McVoy (1978), page 2727.
59 Fulton, Gordon and Williams (1980).
60 Ibid., page 84.
61 Ibid., page 93.
62 Morris, Woodhall and Westoby (1977), page 50.
63 Fulton, Gordon and Williams (1980), page 85.
64 Committee of Vice-Chancellors and Principals (1978), page 3.
65 Williams (1983), page 13.
66 Blaug (1982), page 170. See the final volume of the Leverhulme Report (*Excellence in diversity*), page 39.
67 Pearson (1985), page 194, for example.
68 Fulton, Gordon and Williams (1980), page 95.
69 Times Higher Education Supplement (1984a), page 1.
70 Ibid.

4

The Development of the British University System

I want to emphasise at the outset that this chapter is not intended to be a potted history of British universities.[1] The historical development of the university system is reviewed here for two reasons: first, to discover what goals were envisaged for British universities, both at the time of their foundation and subsequently; and secondly, to identify the major landmarks in the history of higher education in the United Kingdom. Landmarks in this context are defined as events which have influenced the goals of universities, either directly or indirectly. Consequently, when I mention such key documents as the 1987 White Paper on higher education, I do not attempt to give a full account of its contents; I merely mention those aspects which seem to me to have a bearing on the questions of goals. The survey is limited to events occurring before the end of 1987, and, as in other chapters, some conclusions will be outlined at the end.

The early universities

Oxford University was founded in 1214, Cambridge University in 1318; for five hundred years they were the only universities in England, though St Andrews, Glasgow, Aberdeen and Edinburgh were established north of the border.[2] These ancient universities were founded to promote the training of the clergy, doctors and lawyers.[3] In the process of training those professional classes, the universities came to emphasise the pursuit of truth and learning; thus was established an important and resilient tradition.[4]

In the post-mediaeval period the universities' position as centres of vocational training declined (except as far as the church was concerned).[5] Unfortunately it cannot be said that they made up for the decline by developing in other directions. Three great intellectual movements – the Renaissance, the scientific revolution, and the Enlightenment – all came about without much impetus from the universities.[6] Substantial contributions to experimental science and technology were made by men with no university background at all.[7]

The nineteenth century

It is fair to say that the growth of new universities in the nineteenth century was a result of the failure of Oxford and Cambridge to meet the nation's needs.[8] Early in the century, non-conformists, Jews and Roman Catholics were still refused admission to Oxford and Cambridge, a situation which in 1826 led to the foundation of University College, London, where there were no such bars to admission. In 1836, University College, together with King's College, was granted a charter as the University of London, an event which had beneficial and far-reaching effects both in Britain and overseas. From 1858 the University of London acted as a degree-giving body for students at other institutions. This meant that civic colleges such as Owens College, Manchester, could offer degree-level courses and qualifications.[9]

Pressures to reform the curriculum at the older universities were firmly resisted, and 'the most powerful argument for founding new colleges was the reluctance of the older universities to train the middle class in science applied to industry.'[10] The first physics classes in the Clarendon Laboratory at Oxford did not take place until 1870; the building of the Cavendish physics laboratory at Cambridge began in 1871.[11] Oxford and Cambridge remained what they had been for centuries, i.e. great centres of education for the Church of England; they also continued the academic study of law and medicine, but they played little part in the training for those professions.[12]

Society's needs were both national and local, and the older 'civic' universities, such as Durham, Manchester, and Birmingham, were originally intended to serve local needs;[13] those needs had often been created by the industrial revolution.[14] In almost all cases, however, the founders of the civic universities had a vision beyond immediate local utility,[15] a vision which encompassed both general cultural concerns and also national needs.[16]

National needs were brought into focus by the Great Exhibition of 1851. The public began to realise that to maintain Britain's position as the workshop of the world it would be necessary to strengthen education in science and technology.[17] The fear of industrial competition from the continent was a powerful stimulus. There was increasing awareness of the success of the German universities, which subordinated all other functions to the concept of *Wissenschaft* – the university as a centre for research.[18] The new civic universities absorbed *Wissenschaft* 'in their very foundation stones'.[19]

There were two other important elements in the German idea of a university: *Lernfreiheit* (the freedom of the student to learn what he wishes) and *Lehrfreiheit* (the freedom of the teacher to teach whatever he wishes).[20] *Lernfreiheit* caught on in America[21] but not in Britain; *Lehrfreiheit*, on the other hand, was accepted here.[22]

The institutions which were founded as a result of these stimuli did not begin life as fully fledged universities, and at first many of them struggled for survival.[23] The college at Manchester did not receive a penny from the city until it had been in existence for forty years.[24] It was therefore perhaps just as well that two eminent scientists, William Ramsay, FRS, and W. M. Hicks, FRS, persuaded the Government in 1889 to make a grant of £15,000; this was used to alleviate the financial problems faced by the eleven university colleges and was described by Ramsay, prophetically, as 'the thin end of the wedge'.[25]

Despite their origins, the new universities of the nineteenth century did not remain local in their curriculum and purpose for very long,[26] and they eventually became institutions offering a variety of courses and drawing students from all over the country.[27] However, the growth of British universities in the nineteenth century, and the growth of government investment in them, was comparatively slow. In 1902 Germany had 22 universities for a population of about 50 million; in the same year England had 7 universities for a population of 31 million. In 1897 the British Government gave £26,000 in grants to universities; the Germans gave nearly £500,000.[28]

The early twentieth century

The period prior to the depression of the 1930s witnessed an important expansion of British universities.[29] The universities of Birmingham, Liverpool, Leeds, Sheffield and Bristol were all founded in the first decade of the twentieth century.[30]

Other universities were conceived during this period even if they were not formally established: in 1920, for example, an appeal was launched to establish the Leicester, Leicestershire and Rutland University College.[31] The Committee responsible for the appeal pointed out that 'To procure a University education a young man of Leicester or its neighbourhood must go away for three years.' This was considered wrong. The young men of Leicester 'should live in Leicester and yet learn all that Leicester requires of them.' The appeal document went on to point out that Leicester was the centre of the boot and hosiery trades, and that the purpose of the University College would be to provide advanced education in 'those branches of Technology that are vital to Leicester'.[32] The perspective was not, however, entirely parochial: the Appeal Committee also noted the need for education 'in the pure Sciences, in Arts and Economics, and in the fine Arts'.[33] The appeal was successful, and the first classes began on 4 October 1921, when nine students assembled in a former lunatic asylum.[34] Sixty years later, the Vice-Chancellor of Leicester stated firmly that 'the principal role of the University will continue to be a national one. Few undergraduates, or graduates, will be drawn from the East Midlands and most of the University's research will be nationally funded and without local connection.'[35]

Another important development in the period before the First World War was the establishment of state support for academic research; this came about largely through the efforts of Richard Burdon Haldane. Just after the end of the First World War, Haldane, together with H. A. L. Fisher, persuaded the Vice-Chancellors of British universities to do two things: to begin offering research degrees, in particular the Ph.D., and to establish the Committee of Vice-Chancellors and Principals.[36]

Thus by 1939 most of the familiar strands of British university life – general education, vocational training, research, and scholarship – had become woven together.[37] However, one particular strand needs to be examined in some detail: the University Grants Committee (UGC).

The University Grants Committee

The Education Reform Bill of 1987 makes it clear that unless the Government suffers some unexpected reverse, the UGC will soon be abolished, to be replaced by a Universities Funding Council. For the moment, however, the UGC continues; and because it has for nearly seventy years played a major part in university affairs, its functions merit close examination. This chapter will describe UGC activities as they are currently carried out, and a note will be provided at the end about likely developments in the future.

As has been mentioned above, the first government grant to the university colleges was made in 1889. The grants gradually increased in size, and various committees were formed to advise on their allocation. Finally, in 1919, the UGC was established by a Treasury minute.[38]

The original terms of reference of the UGC were 'To enquire into the financial needs of university education in the United Kingdom and to advise the Government as to the application of any grants that may be made by Parliament towards meeting them.'[39] In the first instance, therefore, the Committee was not set up to decide what universities should be doing – it was merely to consider what financial resources they needed in order to achieve their goals.

In 1946 and 1952 the Committee's terms of reference were amended. The words 'Great Britain' were substituted for 'United Kingdom' in the original terms of reference, and the following sentences were added:

> To collect, examine and make available information on matters relating to university education throughout the United Kingdom; and to assist, in consultation with the universities and other bodies concerned, the preparation and execution of such plans for the development of the universities as may from time to time be required in order that they are fully adequate to national needs.[40]

The UGC's terms of reference thus imply that universities will have goals which are related to national needs, though presumably the universities may do other things as well; the terms of reference also make it clear that the UGC only 'assists' in making plans – it is not solely responsible.

The UGC has varied in size but it has usually consisted of about 20 members; they are all appointed by the Secretary of State for Education and Science. At the time of writing there are 16 members, of whom 10 hold academic posts in universities; there is also a full-time chairman. The existence of a majority of university members dates from 1943; a precisely opposite policy obtained prior to that date.[41] In addition to the main Committee there are a host of sub-committees, with 120 academic and 20 non-academic members, covering most of the subjects taught; the whole edifice is serviced by civil servants seconded from the Department of Education and Science.[42]

As noted above, the UGC was originally appointed by the Treasury, the reason being that in 1919 the Committee was to administer grants for the whole United Kingdom. The then Board of Education had power only over England and Wales, and hence the Treasury was made responsible, almost by default. That situation continued until 1963, when it was decided that responsibility for the universities should be located in the same place as responsibility for the rest of state-funded education, namely in the DES. Once it is understood why the Treasury was involved in the first place it is difficult to view the transfer to the DES as having the sinister implications which have sometimes been read into it.[43]

The terms of reference make it clear that the UGC has had two main functions: to advise the Government on the financial needs of the universities, and to advise on (effectively to determine) how the available grant is to be distributed to the individual institutions. These roles developed over the years. It seems clear that for several decades the Government accepted without question the UGC's estimate of the sum of money needed by the universities in each year. As late as 1939 the universities derived only a third of their income from the state, though now, of course, they are almost entirely funded by the taxpayer through one route or another. It was not until 1962 that the Chancellor of the Exchequer reduced the figure recommended by the UGC,[44] and on that occasion the Government naturally claimed that there never had been any rule, written or unwritten, that whatever the UGC asked for should automatically be made available.[45] Any lingering doubt on the matter has long been dispelled: in recent years the UGC has gratefully accepted whatever it can get.

Once a total grant has been allocated, the UGC then turns to its second task, which is to distribute the grant to the various universities. Here too there have been changes. Once it was a convention that the universities could, within reason, do whatever they thought fit with the grant they received. This was made clear by a Treasury spokesman in 1946 and was endorsed by Lord Attlee in 1957.[46] Those days have passed. Beginning in the 1960s the UGC has laid down firmer and firmer 'guidelines' on how the money should be spent.[47] Theoretically, of course, universities still do not have to follow the UGC's advice; the UGC cannot make them do so – but it can make them wish that they had.

The UGC does not have to explain the reasoning behind its division of the total grant,[48] and the Government, for its part, is happy to shelter behind the UGC. In 1962, for example, Mr Henry Brooke refused to answer questions about the size of the UGC's grant to Keele,[49] and in 1981 Mr William Waldegrave spoke of the Government's 'crucial policy decision not to try and interfere with the UGC'.[50] It is a cliché to say that the UGC is a buffer between the universities and state control, but for many years the cliché seems to have been true; in fact it has been argued by a former Chairman of the UGC that the UGC was forced to take up a more positive role in order to avoid direct control of the universities by the Government.[51] The present situation seems to be that the

Government listens to the UGC on the question of how much public money should be allocated to the universities; but it also takes other soundings, and there is no question of signing an open cheque. Secondly, the Government then allows the UGC to distribute the funds as it thinks fit; but the Government keeps a very close eye on what is done with its funds and it also drops increasingly heavy hints as to what should be done.[52] This again may be defended as nothing new: in the 1960s it was made clear that the identification of national needs in higher education was a job for the government machine and not for the UGC.[53]

This brief consideration of the historical role of the UGC shows us that the Committee was not intended to determine ends. But it can, if it chooses, offer advice on ends, as well as on means, both to the Government and to the institutions. In November 1983, the Chairman of the UGC, Sir Peter Swinnerton-Dyer, sent a questionnaire to all universities. The replies were considered during the course of 1984 and in September of that year the UGC presented its advice to the Government on a strategy for higher education into the 1990s. One of the questions in Sir Peter's letter (number 14) asked whether there is an essential difference in function between the universities and other institutions of higher education. This was, in a sense, an inquiry about goals, and one university at least (Bristol) declined to answer it. On the whole, however, the questionnaire did not venture into fundamental questions about the purpose of higher education, and Sir Peter declared himself wholly unrepentant when challenged on that issue. But in the course of preparing its strategy document the UGC did for the first time issue a statement about goals; that statement is the most important of its kind since the Robbins Report, and it will be considered in more detail in Chapter 7.

It is essential to record at this point that the UGC seems likely to be replaced by a new body, perhaps in 1989. In 1985 the Government appointed a Committee under the chairmanship of Lord Croham to review the role of the UGC. The Committee reported in February 1987 (the Croham Report), but the Committee's findings were soon overtaken by the Government's own White Paper on higher education, which was published in April 1987. The Education Reform Bill of November 1987 indicated the Government's intent to pass legislation incorporating much of what had been contained in the White Paper.

The Government's plan is for the UGC to be replaced by a Universities Funding Council (UFC). This will be a smaller body than the UGC, with about half its members drawn from outside the academic world and with a lay chairman; it is obviously intended to be more in touch with 'the real world'. The Government will provide planning guidelines for the university system as a whole; and the UFC will distribute funds under new contract arrangements, which have yet to be specified in any detail.

These proposals seem to embody many of the features of state control which British universities have hitherto avoided. For example, the new body will have no built-in duty or right to advise the Government, a feature which deeply disturbs the CVCP. Whether the UFC will in fact come into existence, and whether it will prove to be the monster that some university staff fear, remains to be seen. For the purposes of this book, however, the main point to note is that the Government seems determined that the money which it provides will be spent on purposes which it specifies.

Post-war developments prior to the Robbins Report

With the passing of the 1944 Education Act the Government became more committed to education and a process began which ultimately, in 1963, integrated the universities into the education system as a whole.[54] The route to integration was signposted by a series of Government inquiries.

In 1945 the report of the Special Committee on Higher Technological Education (the Percy Report) was published. This committee had been appointed to consider the provision of higher technical education in light of the needs of industry; it concluded that there were shortcomings in both the quality and quantity of technologists.

The year 1946 saw the publication of *Scientific manpower* (the Barlow Report); this was produced by a committee appointed by the Lord President of the Council. In effect this report determined post-war policy on university expansion. Its main recommendation was that universities should double their output of scientists, though not at the expense of the humanities. Other committees examined the manpower needs of education (the McNair Report), agriculture (the Loveday Report), medicine (the Goodenough Report), oriental languages (the Scarborough Report), and social studies (the Clapham Report). Successive Governments took heed: in 1938/39 there had been 50,000 students in universities, but by 1958/59 there were 100,000.

In 1951 a report on the future of higher technological education from the National Advisory Council on Education for Industry and Commerce was accepted by the Labour Government. Rather reluctantly, the Conservative Government which followed gradually became involved in industrial training, and in 1956 a White Paper on technical education proposed the establishment of Colleges of Advanced Technology, freed from local control; these later became universities.

The years 1945 to 1963 saw a considerable growth in the number of universities as well as in the number of students. In the 1940s and 1950s, charters were granted to former provincial university colleges at Nottingham, Southampton, Hull, Exeter, and Leicester. In the early 1960s, new universities were founded at East Anglia, York, Essex, Kent, and elsewhere.[55]

The pressures for expansion came from three main sources: from increased student demand; from the need to improve industrial and technological training; and from the recognition that much talent was being wasted.[56] The main motivation behind the increased demand was presumably the belief that a university degree would increase earning power; the need to double the output of scientists and engineers was argued by several reports, as stated above;[57] and the national waste of talent was highlighted by the Crowther Committee, which reported in 1959.[58]

Many of the universities founded in the post-war period retained their local and vocational inspirations. For instance, the 1948 Charter of the University of Nottingham states that the University should continue to pursue the objects of the University College: one of those was to provide students, 'especially those resident in the City of Nottingham and County of the said City', with 'such scientific technical and other instruction as may be of service in professional and commercial life'.[59] It has been argued, however, that the vocational emphasis in universities was at this stage half-hearted; certainly it was still possible in the late 1960s, and common in practice, for many professional qualifications to be obtained without study at a university.[60]

It is also worth noting that in the four-year period 1959–63 the total value of research grants allocated to universities increased some threefold.[61] This reflected, among other things, the panic caused by Russian successes in the exploration of space.

The Robbins Report

In 1961 the Prime Minister appointed a committee, under the chairmanship of Lord Robbins,[62] to consider the pattern of full-time higher education in Great Britain.[63] The Committee's origins lay firmly in 'the growing realisation of this country's economic dependence upon the education of its population'.[64] The Committee's Report was presented to Parliament in 1963, to be followed in 1964 by twelve volumes of evidence and statistical data; and in the view of the Emeritus Professor of Higher Education in the University of London (Professor W. R. Niblett), the Report still constitutes 'the most massive attempt by a single nation, through a governmentally appointed committee, to consider how its higher education should be patterned and should develop'.[65]

The Robbins Committee did something extremely rare in British higher education: it began by considering 'aims and objectives – what purposes, what general social ends should be served by higher education?'[66]

The Committee decided that in a properly balanced system there were four aims or objectives (the words were used interchangeably).[67] These may be summarised as follows:

1 Instruction in skills suitable to play a part in the general division of labour. This was placed first not because it was considered the most important, but because the Committee thought it was sometimes ignored or undervalued. Twenty-five years later, that risk seems remote.

2 Secondly, the Committee argued that 'what is taught should be taught in such a way as to promote the general powers of the mind. The aim should be to produce not mere specialists but rather cultivated men and women.'

3 'Thirdly, we must name the advancement of learning.' It is clear from the context that the advancement of learning, or the advancement of

knowledge, means research. 'The search for truth is an essential function of institutions of higher education.'

4 'Finally, there is a function that is more difficult to describe concisely, but that is none the less fundamental: the transmission of a common culture and common standards of citizenship. . . . Universities and colleges have an important role to play in the general cultural life of the communities in which they are situated.'

It is possible, indeed easy, to be critical of the terms in which these aims are expressed. For example, what precisely is meant by 'the general powers of the mind' or 'a common culture'? There is ample scope for debate about those phrases. But the critics are being decidedly ungrateful. Consideration of purpose is so rarely found in the literature of British higher education that the Robbins Report constitutes the most important statement of its kind until 1984.

The Report devoted considerable attention to the question of 'deep and broad courses',[68] and concluded forcefully that a much higher proportion of students should be receiving a broader education for their first degrees.[69] The large expansion of the universities which was recommended by the Committee would not have been proposed if the members had not been 'confident that it would be accompanied by a big increase in the number of students taking broader first degree courses'.[70] For better or for worse, that was not to be: the expansion took place, but the greater provision of broader courses did not. This means that, as Robbins himself pointed out nearly twenty years later, an essential condition of the Committee's major recommendation has not been fulfilled.[71]

The Robbins Report made 178 recommendations in all: most of them were not addressed to the Government but to universities and other educational institutions.[72] On a rough count, about 10 per cent of the recommendations were implemented, 10 per cent involved no change from the existing practice, and about 20 per cent have been partly implemented; the other 60 per cent have been forgotten.[73]

The most famous recommendation was the so-called 'Robbins principle': this was that 'courses of higher education should be available for all those who are qualified by ability and attainment to pursue them and who wish to do so.'[74] This was immediately accepted by the Government of the day and by the opposition parties,[75] and was adhered to by successive governments, at least until 1978.[76] Thus the Robbins Committee recommended, and for nearly twenty years British society accepted, that demand for higher education should govern supply, in an open-ended manner, with the cost of supply being largely met by the state. It is hard to think of any other field of activity in which this principle has been accepted by governments, on behalf of the taxpayers, and the situation therefore requires careful consideration – particularly as it must reveal a great deal about the assumed effects (and therefore, by implication, the goals) of higher education.

The Robbins Committee explicitly rejected the notion that the amount of higher education provision should be determined by estimates of the need for particular skills, i.e. by the techniques of manpower planning. The technical difficulties involved in making quantified projections of manpower needs were considered too great,[77] and estimates of demand were considered more reliable.[78] Secondly, student demand was accepted by the Committee as an appropriate means of determining provision because the Committee believed that modern societies could not achieve their aims of higher economic growth and higher cultural standards without making full use of the talents of their citizens.[79]

In accepting the Robbins principle, British governments, and the voters who elected them, must presumably have accepted these same arguments: in other words, they considered that the financial investment in universities was worthwhile in terms of its return, expressed both as increased wealth (national and personal), and as an increased level of 'culture', 'civilisation', and 'education'. Little thought seems to have been given at the time, or later, to the fact that the volume and emphasis of research would effectively be determined by the whims of those who decided to seek a degree: perhaps it was just assumed by all concerned that this too would be a sound investment. The Robbins Committee also wished to see a higher proportion of students on science and technology courses: but student demand has ensured that many of the extra places have been in the social sciences and the arts.[80]

The impact of the Robbins Report was great. Both the public and the politicians were convinced that an expansion of higher education was desirable,[81] and it duly took place. Nine Colleges of Advanced Technology were given university status.[82] It can be argued that the expansion in Britain would have occurred at that period even without a Robbins Report, as it did in most other European countries,[83] but I do not find the case convincing.

Perhaps the most important point of all, however, is that the Robbins Report proposed that higher education should be dominated by an enlarged university sector which was beyond the direct control of any minister or elected authority; and it has been alleged that the Department of Education and Science was appalled by this prospect.[84] Whatever the truth of the matter, it is certainly true that it was not long before central authority made an attempt to gain an increased measure of control over the management of higher education.

The binary policy

In August 1982 an editorial in *The Times Higher Education Supplement* stated that the binary policy is 'the nearest thing we have to an authoritative statement about the purposes of higher education'.[85] In October of the same year another editorial in the same journal stated that 'Far from being an administrative irrelevance, structure is a powerful metaphor about the public purposes of higher education.'[86] It will be as well, therefore, to examine carefully the binary policy, the structure which it involves and the purposes which it implies.

The Robbins Report of 1963 recommended a unitary system of higher education.[87] In 1965, however, the unitary concept was decisively rejected by the Secretary of State for Education, Mr Anthony Crosland. In a famous speech on 27 April 1965, at the Woolwich Polytechnic, Crosland announced the creation of what he first described as the dual system, and in a subsequent speech as the plural or binary system.[88]

The binary system involved the creation of a separate sector of higher education in addition to the universities. The new sector would be headed by the polytechnics, and would include the teacher-training colleges and various other technical colleges.[89] The universities would continue to be independent, autonomous bodies financed through the UGC and awarding their own degrees; the polytechnics would be financed through, and under the control of, the Local Education Authorities, and their degrees would be validated by the Council for National Academic Awards.[90] A few years later, when Mrs Margaret Thatcher became Secretary of State, she confirmed that the binary policy was bipartisan,[91] and it has continued to this day.

No one who reads Crosland's Woolwich speech can be left in any doubt about the two essential ideas behind the creation of the binary policy: governmental control and vocational education. Control was to be located close to the provision: Crosland claimed that it was a valuable feature of our democratic tradition that elected representatives and local authorities should have a stake in higher education.[92] Evidently the Government considered that greater control was necessary because British universities were exceptionally autonomous by comparison with those in other countries.[93] Control was to be achieved through the method of financing; this, according to one very experienced academic (Lord Annan), is in fact the only way in which the policy of a central government can be imposed in the field of higher education.[94]

The need for vocational, professional and industrially based courses was the other key factor mentioned by Crosland. He claimed that the demand for such courses could not be fully met by the universities, but it must be fully met 'if we are to progress as a nation in the modern technological world'.[95] The universities, it was implied, were not sufficiently responsive to national needs.

Now that the binary policy has been in effect for over twenty years, it is relevant to inquire whether there are in fact any major differences between the universities and the flagships of the binary system, the polytechnics. It has often been pointed out that the polytechnics' original terms of reference were ambiguous, nebulous or non-existent.[96] However, by 1970 the CVCP had decided that universities and polytechnics had essentially different purposes. Polytechnics were comprehensive institutions combining a certain number of first-degree courses with teaching at a variety of other, non-degree, levels on a full or part-time basis; they concentrated on vocational training. Teaching in universities, on the other hand, was concentrated almost entirely on degree-level courses and was spread over a much broader subject range; the teaching in universities was also enhanced by the deep involvement of academic staff in research.[97] Ashby, in 1976, declared that universities were concerned with education, polytechnics with instruction. Education involved skill with ideas; instruction involved skill with things.[98] By 1981 the DES had decided that the universities' distinctive characteristic was their contribution to wholly new knowledge through research; a polytechnic's key contribution lay 'in its provision of courses specifically designed to reflect the opportunities and requirements of the country's employment market'.[99]

Whether these distinctions are valid is a moot point. Lord Robbins pointed out with some perplexity that the universities are heavily involved in vocationally orientated courses.[100] Furthermore it is not obvious that the University of Bath has a less vocational teaching orientation than, say, Bristol Polytechnic. It is true that the polytechnics are not funded for research, but the Council for National Academic Awards expects them to do some anyway.[101] In the face of these facts, one former Vice-Chancellor has concluded that the only valid definition of the difference between universities and polytechnics 'relates to the constitution or legal status of the institution'.[102]

The 1960s and 1970s

It can be argued that the student unrest of the late 1960s had a vital bearing on the goals of British universities.[103] For a year or two the newspapers and television screens regularly provided pictures of students rioting, supporting extreme causes, and generally putting forward their views in a vigorous, not to say aggressive, manner; such disturbances occurred in most countries in the western world. Whatever the rights and wrongs of the issues, the fact is that the universities received a great deal of unfavourable publicity,[104] and they were not able to respond to it by putting forward a unanimous, reasoned case for continued public support.[105]

The 1960s and 1970s also saw the publication of some further important reports. In 1968 the Dainton Report appeared; this was the findings of a committee set up to examine the swing away from science in schools. The Report recommended less specialisation and more mathematics in sixth forms; it was quietly resisted in all quarters.[106]

In 1972 a committee under the chairmanship of Lord James reported on teacher education and training. The Committee's conclusion was that all teachers should be graduates, having undertaken a minimum four-year course.

The James Report was closely followed by the Government's 1972 White Paper, entitled *Education: a framework for expansion*. The White Paper proposed an impressive expansion of full-time higher and further education over the following ten years, albeit with a lower unit of resource from government sources. Expansion, however, was not to be confined to the universities: the intention was that the number of students in non-university institutions would ultimately equate with the number in the universities. The White Paper also prepared the way for the closure of many colleges of education and the conversion of many others into institutions of higher education offering degrees validated by other bodies.[107]

The cuts of 1981

In 1981 the Government announced that it intended to reduce substantially its expenditure on the universities,[108] and the UGC was faced with the problem of allocating a much reduced grant. After years of expansion, or at worst a period of standstill budgets, the effect of the cuts was traumatic. Universities protested bitterly but there were few sympathisers.

It has to be remembered that by 1981 public opinion had changed, and not only as a result of the student unrest. Higher education had been portrayed by the Robbins Report and by politicians of the 1960s as a solution to many social ills and needs: but by 1981 it could be argued that the system had failed to deliver, and the atmosphere was right for money to be saved.[109]

Sir Edward Parkes, who was Chairman of the UGC in 1981, has noted that the Government which was elected in 1979 'had no clearly developed philosophy with regard to higher education, but it did come in with a commitment to the reduction of public expenditure.'[110] A government spokesman declared that the impact of the world recession had been severe, and the sole reason for the 1981 cuts was to save money, not to punish the universities for having failed in some way.[111] There was a secondary aim or requirement, however: it was to adjust the university system 'in favour of science and engineering'.[112] Sir Keith Joseph assured the House of Commons that 'Few Members of Parliament would disagree with the modest move from the arts towards science, technology and engineering.'[113]

The actual implementation of the cuts was left to the UGC, which chose to apply them selectively. Towards the end of 1981 the UGC explained to the House of Commons Select Committee on Education, Science and Arts how it had made its cuts in July of that year.[114] It had considered various options, such as equal percentage cuts for all, and reducing the number of institutions receiving grants (which would effectively have closed the ones left without support); it had also considered setting up a tiered system, with some universities funded for research and others financed principally as teaching institutions. These options were all rejected in favour of making cuts of varying size in the light of certain criteria. Of these criteria the most important were probably the numbers of research students, research income, the quality of the student intake, and the relative cost of departments as an indicator of efficiency.[115] Less popular courses were rationalised so that they were available somewhere but not everywhere, and a fall of from 3 to 5 per cent in the number of students, over three years, was to be linked with an increase in the numbers reading mathematics, physics, business studies, medicine, engineering and technical subjects.[116]

Opposition to the cuts was at first loud, from those within universities, but was ultimately muted, even within the system. After the dust had settled, *The Times Higher Education Supplement* concluded that the absence of a really concerted opposition reflected 'a fundamental disagreement about values and priorities'.[117]

What were the effects of the cuts? First of all it is doubtful whether much money was actually saved, at least in the short term;[118] scientific research, it is claimed, was dealt a major blow in that the cuts damaged the universities' ability to provide basic facilities;[119] and a large number of academic staff took early retirement on generous terms. The Government's supporters could point to some allegedly beneficial outcomes. The admission of fewer students meant that those with marginally acceptable qualifications were turned away, and research priorities were tightened up in favour of relevance, i.e. relevance to immediate and practical needs.[120]

Whatever the balance of advantage and disadvantage, one thing is clear: it is that in 1981 the Robbins principle, that all those suitably qualified should have the right to higher education, was ignored if not abandoned. The principle had formed the basis of successive governments' 'policy' on higher education for twenty years. But as Lord Robbins himself pointed out in the autumn of 1981, 'the recent instructions of the University Grants Committee, in the past so admirable, are a complete reversal of this principle.'[121] In 1984 and 1985 attempts were made to reformulate a policy for access to higher education, and that debate will be considered in Chapter 10.

The Leverhulme Inquiry

The Leverhulme Inquiry into the future of higher education was organised by the Society for Research into Higher Education with the aid of a grant from the Leverhulme Trust.[122] The Inquiry began in 1981 and lasted two years; it took the form of eight seminars at which over seventy papers were presented and it generated ten monographs and a final report.[123]

Such a volume of print cannot be summarised in a few paragraphs, but four major strands of opinion can be detected in it.[124] The first is a belief that there is an urgent need to widen access to higher education, not only on the grounds of social justice but also in the interests of economic efficiency.

The second major theme is the need to reform the content and structure of courses. A system of two-year ordinary degrees was proposed, topped up with a variety of vocational diplomas and academic courses. It was argued that the domination of the system by specialised three-year honours degrees should be ended by the introduction of broader forms of undergraduate education; these would be more easily modified in the light of changing manpower needs.

The third Leverhulme theme is an endorsement of the broad intentions of the binary policy because they safeguard institutional diversity. The final report strongly emphasised the value of diversity. It did not favour a merger of the University Grants Committee and the National Advisory Body (which co-ordinates policy in local authority higher education); it did, however, advocate the establishment of an overarching advisory body and a higher education policy studies centre.

The fourth theme is the need for more professional management, as a part of which institutions were encouraged to draw up mission statements.

The Leverhulme Inquiry undoubtedly represents an important landmark in higher education. But the Inquiry was always concerned with means, rather than ends; it did not attempt to reformulate the Robbins Report's statement about aims, and the monographs contain comparatively little about values.[125] For the purposes of this book the Leverhulme study therefore provides few ideas which were not already available elsewhere. The final report also had the misfortune to be published thirteen days before a general election, which muted its initial impact. More recently, however, some of the proposals have re-surfaced. Leverhulme favoured wider access to higher education, on the grounds of both justice and economic efficiency: the Government has accepted the point, though evidently on the latter ground rather than the former. Leverhulme argued for a reduction in undue specialisation and a reform of the structure of courses: the 1985 Green Paper stated that broader courses have a significant part to play in higher education, and that the Government is prepared to consider two-year degree courses on an experimental basis. The Jarratt Report, also published in 1985, echoed and endorsed the Leverhulme Inquiry on a number of points of detail: greater lay involvement, annual appraisals for staff, and the establishment in each university of a strategic planning group with joint lay and academic membership. By 1987, annual appraisals for academic staff had been imposed on universities as part of a pay deal, and the body which is likely to replace the UGC may even have a majority of lay members. Like Leverhulme, Jarratt emphasised the need for a clear understanding of the aims of particular activities, both in teaching and research. The two publications were in complete agreement in arguing that institutions should provide a strategic plan and mission statements for each department; resources should be allocated accordingly. Both agreed also that present arrangements for national policy setting were unsatisfactory: Leverhulme argued for a higher education policy studies centre, Jarratt for a review of the UGC. Subsequently, in the 1985 Green Paper and the 1987 White Paper, the Government fully accepted its own responsibility for determining central policy; and the provisions of the 1987 Education Reform Bill make it very plain that the Government intends to impose that policy through tight control of funding. In short, the influence of the Leverhulme Inquiry has been greater than its reception at the time might have suggested.

The events of 1987

For the university world, 1987 was a highly eventful year. The Croham Report appeared in February, the White Paper on higher education in April, and the Education Reform Bill was published in November. In July the Advisory Board for the Research Councils (ABRC) produced a controversial paper entitled *A strategy for the science base*.

It is worth re-emphasising at this point that in referring to these documents I am not attempting even to summarise all their key points. I am merely drawing attention to what they tell us, in broad terms, about the kind of goals for universities which were envisaged by their authors.

The White Paper stated explicitly that institutions of higher education should serve the economy more effectively and should pursue basic scientific research and scholarship in the arts and humanities; they should have closer links with industry and commerce, and should promote enterprise. The country, it stated, needs highly qualified manpower and the Government will therefore plan for a substantial increase in student numbers, partly by admitting students without the traditional 'A' level qualifications. The Government will study the needs of the economy so as to achieve the right number and balance of graduates in the 1990s; and it will further develop continuing education. Steps will be taken (e.g. staff development and appraisal) to secure better teaching; research will be more selectively funded, and performance indicators will be applied. As stated in the section on the UGC, a UFC will be established, to fund universities through a system of contracts. The use of contracts is apparently intended to define what is expected of institutions more clearly, and to establish closer links between future funding and past performance.

To some, the statements in the White Paper seemed very shocking and indeed intolerable; they seemed to presage an unacceptable level of state control. To others the only surprising thing was not that the Government had decided to dictate how its money should be spent, but that it had taken so long to insist on the point.

Further waves on the surface of university life were caused in July 1987 by the ABRC publication *A strategy for the science base*. In short, this document argued that the shortage of resources and the need for large-scale effort in many areas of experimental science led to the conclusion that there should be a three-tier university system. The top tier, of perhaps fifteen universities, would be fully funded for research, and the bottom tier would consist of universities which would confine themselves to teaching only; the middle group would be funded for substantial research in a few fields rather than all. This concept of a three-tier structure was by no means a new idea: the UGC had considered it in connection with the 1981 cuts, and it had surfaced periodically in the press thereafter. But this time much alarm was caused among those who were convinced that high quality teaching can only be provided against a background of high quality research. The debate rumbles on as I write, and, like many other topics touched on in this section, it will be discussed in more detail in a later chapter.

Finally, in November 1987, the Education Reform Bill produced even greater consternation among university staff, although the Bill was almost entirely concerned with schools rather than with higher education. The Bill proved that the Government had been serious when it talked about the UFC; and that was considered bad enough by some. But the Bill also proposed to deprive academic staff of tenure without seeking to protect academic freedom in other ways. This proposal, of course, was consistent with the rest of the Government's thinking. There is clearly no intention to allow academic staff to remain a financial burden on the taxpayer if their services are no longer required; and the Government apparently feels little inclination to support *Lehrfreiheit* or research-*freiheit*, at any rate when financed with public funds. In more general terms, the Bill granted powers to the Secretary of State which prompted several

Vice-Chancellors to begin talking about parallels with South Africa and totalitarianism.

The position in the late 1980s

The present size and nature of British universities can be outlined with a few statistics. In 1957 there were only 24 institutions on the UGC list; by 1982 there were 53.[126] In 1957/58 there were 97,000 full-time students in British universities; ten years later there were 205,000,[127] and in 1986/87 there were 316,290. In 1984/85 there were about 573,000 full-time students in higher education as a whole.[128]

About half the students in universities are studying science-based subjects, and a substantial proportion of arts-based students are taking courses in such vocational subjects as accounting, law, business and management studies.[129] The professional institutes have a significant influence over the curriculum of many degree courses, perhaps one third of them.[130]

The universities stand at the peak of the British system of education and exercise a profound influence over the rest of it. The universities currently have a multi-purpose role: they provide general education; they undertake research; they train students for the professions; they assist industry, commerce and the public services; and they make a contribution to the arts.[131] Nearly two thirds of all graduates entering permanent employment in this country go directly into industry and commerce.[132]

In practice the Government exercises a powerful influence over the universities, and the provisions of the 1987 Education Reform Bill suggest that this influence is likely to increase substantially. In 1983 the editorial columns of the *The Times Higher Education Supplement* were already noting that when the Secretary of State addresses the Chairman of the UGC he does so in the tone of a master addressing his servant.[133] This situation arises chiefly from the fact that 60 per cent of universities' total income comes in the form of a block grant from the Government;[134] much of the universities' remaining income also comes from the taxpayer in one form or another.

Conclusions drawn from the review of the development of the British university system

This chapter has reviewed the goals which were envisaged for British universities both at the time of their foundation and subsequently. The evidence suggests that the principal conflict in the area of goals has been between the supporters of vocational and non-vocational higher education. This is not surprising in view of the two contrasting philosophies of higher education which were discerned in Chapter 2.

It has been suggested by a number of commentators that universities have usually succumbed to 'academic drift'; that is to say, they have started out as vocational institutions and have gradually lost interest in the real world.[135] Those who make this charge regard the tendency as a regrettable one. Universities have, however, been defended in this respect. Scott, for example, claims that technological subjects and the applied social sciences were not forced on universities by the state; the universities adopted them voluntarily. Similarly the enthusiasm for applied as opposed to pure research is not confined to industrialists;[136] many academics prefer to work in that field.

Whatever the truth of the matter, the tension between the vocational and the non-vocational is clearly apparent. The CVCP, in its response to the 1983 UGC questionnaire, took up the issue in no uncertain manner. Noting that the Secretary of State wished to see a shift towards 'vocationally relevant forms of study', the CVCP stated that this represented 'a view of society which we cannot share. There can be no doubt that the ultimate goal is to establish and maintain an economically successful society, but it is vital that that society is one of whose culture, in the widest sense, we can all be proud.'[137] This conflict of views between the Government and many academics seems to be sharpening as the 1980s progress.

A less pronounced conflict is apparent over the question of broad-based degree courses as opposed to specialised courses. Both the Robbins Report and the Leverhulme Inquiry called for broader forms of undergraduate education: the response appears to have been lukewarm at best. But there is a growing realisation that wider access, as proposed by the Government, will involve changes in teaching methods and, probably, broader-based courses.

Research is also becoming controversial: historically there has been a gradual acceptance of research as a university function, but in 1987 the ABRC suddenly focused attention on the possibility of concentrating all major research in about fifteen universities, and leaving some universities with no research function at all. Political preferences for applied rather than 'blue-sky' research have made that an issue for public discussion.

The determination to abolish tenure demonstrates that, insofar as it appreciates the problem, the Government sees no reason to give academics special protection if they choose to question received wisdom, either in their teaching or in their public pronouncements.

The only other points which need stressing in this summary are the massive growth in the numbers of students and institutions which has taken place, particularly since 1945, and the concomitant change in the universities' clientele. From the thirteenth century to the early sixteenth, the universities were primarily professional schools catering to the needs of the church.[138] In the early sixteenth century a change took place and the universities began to cater for laymen as well as clerics; but even so, entry to higher education was almost entirely confined to the sons of the land-owning aristocracy.[139]

In the seventeenth century, some philosophers, such as Comenius, began to argue in favour of education for all, regardless of birth or wealth,[140] but the impact on British society was minimal. Even in the nineteenth century Oxford and Cambridge were essentially finishing schools for the children of the governing classes, with a smug Anglican bias.[141]

After the 1914–18 war the picture began to change, and the impact of the war can scarcely be over-rated: it marked the end of the aristocratic tradition in England.[142] In 1920, state scholarships and county awards were instituted, and gradually boys from lower-middle and working-class homes began to enter the universities. Women, too, were admitted in greater numbers. The University of London had allowed women to take its degrees from 1878, but there had been much scorn and obstruction;[143] similarly it was not until 1947 that Girton and Newnham were accorded a status similar to that of the men's colleges at Cambridge, and at Oxford the change was delayed until the 1960s.[144]

In the 1950s the desire for equality of opportunity gathered strength, and the Robbins Report highlighted the gap between the proportion of children from professional families entering higher education and those from skilled manual families.[145] In fact, the working-class share of entry to the universities did not rise in the twenty-five years after the 1944 Education Act.[146] Nor has the situation changed much since: indeed the Leverhulme Inquiry drew attention to a marked decline in working-class students in universities.[147] The participants in the Leverhulme discussions argued that there are still vast reserves of underdeveloped talent amongst children from working-class homes: they drew up a strategy which was intended to encourage access from a rather broader social spectrum than is the case at present.[148] The 1987 White Paper is also much exercised by the question of wider access.

The overall growth in the numbers of students and institutions in the post-war period tells us that much was expected of higher education; the public acceptance of a reduction in university resources, and the indifference to other changes, tell us that many of those expectations have now been modified. Part 2 of this book will therefore examine in detail the views on universities which have recently been expressed by the interested parties.

Notes

1   Those who seek a potted history of British universities might consider Mountford (1966), supplemented by Robbins (1980). Ross (1976) provides a very readable account of the development of universities from an international perspective.
2   University of Wales (1964), page 151.
3   Robbins (1963), page 6; also Robbins (1980), page 4, and Dainton (1981), page 3.
4   Chaplin (1978), page 3208.
5   Caine (1969), page 26. Also Robbins (1980), page 4.
6   Scott (1981a), page 24.
7   Caine (1969), page 26. Also Ashby (1966), page 6.
8   Ashby (1966), page 29.
9   Sanderson (1975), page 80.
10 Ashby, quoted by Silver (1981), page 6.
11 Barnett (1979), page 123.
12 Caine (1969), page 27.
13 Robbins (1963), page 23.
14 Mountford (1966), page 21.

15 Ibid., page 22.
16 Halsey and Trow (1971), page 54.
17 Dainton (1981), page 3.
18 Beard, Healey and Holloway (1970), page 27, and Ashby (1966), page 18.
19 Ashby (1966), page 40.
20 Ashby (1974), page 5.
21 Chaplin (1978), page 3216.
22 Ashby (1974), page 5.
23 Mountford (1966), page 26.
24 Ibid., page 20.
25 Dainton (1981), page 5.
26 Silver (1981), page 63.
27 Robbins (1963), page 23.
28 Barnett (1979), page 124.
29 Halsey and Trow (1971), page 57. Also Entwistle, Percy and Nisbet (1971), page 21.
30 University of Wales (1964), page 151.
31 Leicester, Leicestershire and Rutland University College (1920).
32 Ibid.
33 Ibid.
34 University of Leicester (1981), foreword by the Vice-Chancellor.
35 Ibid.
36 Dainton (1981), pages 5 and 6.
37 Ibid., page 6.
38 Owen (1980), page 256.
39 Ibid., page 255.
40 Ibid., page 263.
41 Ibid., pages 261 and 262.
42 Committee of Vice-Chancellors and Principals (1978), paragraph 60.
43 Owen (1980), pages 258 and 259. Barnes (1973) regards the change as significant: see page 161.
44 Barnes (1973), page 161.
45 Owen (1980), page 273.
46 Barnes (1973), page 160.
47 Ibid., page 162. See also the UGC's Annual Report for 1968/69, quoted in Committee of Vice-Chancellors and Principals (1978), paragraph 128.
48 Owen (1980), page 273.
49 Ibid.
50 Footman (1982), page 4.
51 Sir John Wolfenden, quoted by Owen (1980), page 275.
52 Crequer and Jones (1982) describe a row about teacher-training quotas, 'the first illustration of the Government's new resolve to direct UGC policy'.
53 Owen (1980), page 269.
54 The summary of government inquiries etc. in this section is derived from MacLure (1973).
55 Halsey and Trow (1971), page 58.
56 Hall, Land, Parker and Webb (1975), page 233.
57 Ibid.
58 Ibid., page 234.
59 Letter from the Registrar of the University of Nottingham, to the author, 26 January 1982.

60 Caine (1969), pages 30 and 31.
61 Phillips (1986), page 820.
62 Robbins (1963), title page.
63 Ibid., page 4.
64 Ibid., page 5.
65 Niblett (1981), page 1.
66 Robbins (1963), page 6.
67 Ibid., pages 6 and 7.
68 Ibid., page 91.
69 Ibid., page 93.
70 Ibid., page 269.
71 Robbins (1980), page 23. He repeated the point in a comment on the 1981 cuts, reported in *The Times Higher Education Supplement*, 16 October 1981, page 13.
72 Carter (1983), page 11.
73 Williams (1972), page 18.
74 Robbins (1963), page 8.
75 Robbins (1980), page 23.
76 Department of Education and Science (1978), page 1.
77 Morris, Woodhall and Westoby (1977), page 48.
78 Strickland (1982), page 115.
79 Bevan (1983), page 443.
80 Scott (1983b), page 10.
81 Williams (1972), page 18.
82 Aston, Bath, Bradford, Brunel, Chelsea, City, Loughborough, Salford and Surrey. Halsey and Trow (1971), page 58.
83 See Elton (1983), page 125.
84 Annan (1983), page 11.
85 Scott (1982a), page 24.
86 Times Higher Education Supplement (1982a), page 32.
87 Robbins (1980), page 99.
88 Weaver (1983), page 14.
89 Robbins (1980), pages 99 and 100.
90 Lowe (1973), pages 116 and 117.
91 Weaver (1983), page 14.
92 Ibid.
93 Scott (1983c), page 32. This diagnosis is confirmed by Jadot (1981), page 57, and Clark (1979), page 30.
94 Annan (1983), page 14.
95 Crosland, quoted by Bevan (1983), page 444.
96 Silver (1981), page 50.
97 Committee of Vice-Chancellors and Principals (1970), page 6.
98 Ashby (1976), page 24.
99 Quoted by the Committee of Vice-Chancellors and Principals (1984), page 9.
100 Robbins (1980), pages 100 and 101.
101 Points made by Fowler (1982), pages 131 and 137.
102 Carter, quoted by Burgess (1981), page 190.
103 See Ross (1976), page 139.
104 The only thing most people can remember about the University of Stirling is that a student insulted the Queen by drinking from a wine bottle as she walked past him.
105 Ross argues that in the late 1960s 'determining the purpose of the university was a

major and serious problem for the English academic system.' Ross (1976), page 139.

106 MacLure (1973), page 327.

107 This account of the 1972 White Paper is derived from Evans (1978).

108 In his circular letter 10/81, sent to all universities on 1 July 1981, the Chairman of the UGC stated that the overall loss of recurrent resources between 1979/80 and 1983/84 would be between 11 and 15 per cent. In December 1981 the House of Commons was told that £200 million a year would be saved out of a total recurrent grant of about £1 billion. Hansard, 21 December 1981, page 766.

109 Buss (1975), page 431.

110 Parkes (1983), page 2. In its brief for the Expectations of Higher Education Project, the DES itself declared that the 1980s would mark a change from provision determined largely by student demand to provision which would be 'expenditure led'. See Kogan and Boys (1983), page 1.

111 Footman (1982), page 7.

112 Hansard, 18 November 1981, page 301.

113 Ibid., page 305.

114 The evidence is reported by Crequer (1981).

115 An assessment by Dr Bryan Taylor, Planning Officer at the University of Bath.

116 David (1981a).

117 Times Higher Education Supplement (1984c). Although public interest in the cuts soon died down, the universities themselves did not forget or forgive. In 1984 they took advantage of the Swinnerton-Dyer questionnaire to give vent to 'widespread and trenchant criticism of the UGC'.

118 Kogan (1983) argues that 'it is uncertain whether the policy saved money – and, if so, how much.'

119 Silcock (1984).

120 These 'benefits' are those claimed by the Times Higher Education Supplement (1984d) in an editorial.

121 Robbins (1981).

122 Times Higher Education Supplement (1983a).

123 Scott (1983d). The various publications are referred to collectively as the 'Leverhulme Report' and are listed under that heading in the references section.

124 Times Higher Education Supplement (1983b).

125 A point made by Scott (1983d).

126 Scott (1983a). The 1985 Green Paper (paragraph 4) states that there are 46 publicly funded universities, 29 polytechnics, 73 colleges engaged mainly in higher education, and 298 other colleges.

127 Ibid. Numbers rounded off to the nearest thousand.

128 Department of Education and Science (1986), page 3, is the source for the 1984/85 figures. The 1986/87 figure for the universities' population comes from the Universities Statistical Record (1987), page 11.

129 Committee of Vice-Chancellors and Principals (1981), page 4.

130 The influence of the professional bodies will be discussed in Chapter 7.

131 Association of University Teachers (1979), page 1.

132 Committee of Vice-Chancellors and Principals (1981), page 4.

133 Times Higher Education Supplement (1983c).

134 Beverton and Findlay (1982).

135 See, for example, Burgess (1979), Fowler (1982), and Pope (1979).

136 Scott (1983e).

137 Committee of Vice-Chancellors and Principals (1984), page 1.

138 Kearney (1973), page 2.
139 Ibid., page 3.
140 Chaplin (1978), page 3211.
141 Green (1969), page 101.
142 Kearney (1973), page 9.
143 Green (1969), page 120.
144 Ibid., page 127.
145 Ibid., page 126.
146 Leverhulme Report, final volume (*Excellence in diversity*), page 41.
147 Leverhulme Report, volume 2 (*Access to higher education*), page 2.
148 Leverhulme Report, final volume (*Excellence in diversity*), page 4.

Part 2

5

The American Approach to
University Goals

Introduction to Part 2

Part 1 of this book examined certain aspects of what might be termed educational theory and practice, to see what they could tell us about the range of possible goals for universities.

The main aims of Part 2 are to describe the extent to which the various stakeholder groups have formally considered what the goals of British universities should be, and to identify areas of actual or potential disagreement, both within and between groups.

This chapter describes the American approach to the issue of university goals; American attitudes and practices are then contrasted with the situation in the United Kingdom (Chapter 6). Chapter 7 records the views which have been expressed on goals by British universities themselves and by their principal stakeholder groups; and in the last two chapters in Part 2, a catalogue of potential goals for British universities is provided, and six issues which are currently controversial are discussed in detail.

American awareness of the need to establish goals

In the course of some earlier research into the resource-allocation procedures of British and American universities,[1] I became aware that, for at least two decades, many American universities have been required by law to state their goals and objectives.[2] The laws which various states have imposed were inspired by a belief that clear thinking about goals is advantageous. Once in existence, the laws created an atmosphere in which goal-setting became a matter of accepted good practice; and the practice has often persisted even in those cases where the legal requirement has lapsed.

In August 1965 President Lyndon B. Johnson ordered all the major civilian agencies of the federal government to install a 'very new and very revolutionary' Planning, Programming and Budgeting Systems (PPBS).[3] Many states, notably California, followed the federal example and imposed PPBS on all state agencies, including institutions of higher education. In 1969 the US Office of Education funded a major PPBS development programme in thirteen western states; this programme later developed into the National Center for Higher Education Management Systems.[4]

Despite President Johnson's statement to the press, PPBS was neither very new nor very revolutionary. It emerged from conceptual work undertaken by the Rand Corporation after the Second World War[5] and was first applied, with considerable success, in the US Department of Defense. There never was a standard version of PPBS, but the essential point to be noted is that the first stage of the procedure, in every instance, required the organisation to define its mission and objectives.[6]

After a few years it became obvious that although PPBS had numerous virtues, it also had defects. It was an excessively complex procedure which consumed huge amounts of staff and computer time.[7] It had been possible, within limits, to quantify the outputs of the Department of Defense (tanks and ships, for example), but the quantification of the outputs of education proved to be a much more difficult task.[8] In 1971 the federal government abandoned the requirement for budget submissions to be made in the PPBS form, though agencies could continue to use it if they so wished.[9] In 1973 the State of California followed suit, thus discarding seven years' development of PPBS at a cost of several million dollars.[10]

PPBS was, in a sense, succeeded by Management by Objectives (MBO), though fewer institutions of higher education adopted it.[11] MBO for higher education was developed by Dean George Odiorne at the University of Utah from principles expounded by Drucker.[12] Again, there was and is no standard system of MBO,[13] but all the variations involve not only the clarification of an organisation's goals, but also the setting of quantified objectives in the form of standards of performance, right down to the level of individual members of staff.[14] It is assumed in MBO that if a person has a clear, quantified description of what he or she is trying to achieve, the chances of success in achieving the stated objective are greatly increased.[15]

MBO was adopted at about the end of the 1960s by a number of American colleges and universities, notably the University of Utah and the University of Tennessee.[16] These institutions were at first enthusiastic,[17] but difficulties with the system emerged after a number of years' experience.[18] Davies argues that MBO may have come too close to 'the sensitivities of the academic'.[19] In any event, MBO did not prove to be the magic formula which some had hoped, and by the mid 1970s a new system was being talked about: zero-based budgeting. This third system required that the goals and objectives of an organisational unit should determine its budget – and not the converse.[20]

The point to be noted here is that for at least twenty years many American universities have been obliged both by law and by logic to consider their goals and objectives in detail.

American research into the measurement of opinions on goals

Once it became recognised in American universities that it was important to clarify goals, it was not long before attempts were made to establish whether members of particular groups held similar views, and if so whether those views differed from the opinions of other groups. The seminal work in this field was carried out by Gross and Grambsch and was reported in their book *University goals and academic power*, published in 1968.[21]

Gross and Grambsch surveyed samples of faculty and administrators at 68 universities, using an inventory containing 46 goal statements. The survey was carried out in 1964.[22] It distinguished between 'output goals', defined as those which involve a product of some kind, and 'support goals', which support a university's main activities. Each respondent was asked to indicate, on a five-point scale, how much emphasis he felt a given goal actually received at his institution, and how much it should ideally receive.[23] The questionnaire was expected to take a minimum of an hour and a half to complete; some respondents took three hours over it.[24]

The work of Gross and Grambsch is important in that it alerted researchers and others to the possibility of systematic, quantitative analysis of opinions on institutional goals.[25] The results of the survey cannot easily be summarised, and need not be, since they relate to American universities of twenty years ago: in essence, however, the survey provided 'no flattering picture of the ability of university faculties to agree on the aims and purposes of higher education'.[26]

In 1971 Gross and Grambsch repeated their 1964 study in order to determine what changes had taken place in the seven-year interval. In general, very few differences were observed. American universities remained fundamentally the same: that is to say they were still institutions orientated chiefly towards 'research and scholarly production, set up to provide comfortable homes for professors and administrators, and according students and their needs a distinctly secondary position'.[27]

In 1973 the Carnegie Commission on Higher Education published a three-part report on *The purposes and performance of higher education in the United States*.[28] This was a much fuller consideration of aims than that provided by the approximate British equivalent, the Robbins Report, and it gave further impetus to the academic study of goals.

At much the same time as the Carnegie Commission's publication was being prepared, a group of staff at the Educational Testing Service (ETS) in Princeton were preparing the Institutional Goals Inventory (IGI);[29] this is the most elaborate instrument for the measurement of opinion on the goals of higher education which has so far been devised. Its purpose is to measure the opinions of stakeholder groups on the questions of how important certain goals actually are within the institution, and how important respondents think the goals should be.

The ETS's original concern was with institutional evaluation; however, the researchers decided that if there was to be any systematic assessment of an institution's success, there first had to be a clarification of the organisation's goals.[30] (Those who are currently concerning themselves with performance indicators in a British context might do well to consider this point.) The planning of an institutional goals inventory began in 1969, and after a number of experiments an instrument was published in 1972 which has subsequently been widely used.

The basic version of the IGI consists of 90 statements of possible institutional goals. The statements cover 13 'outcome' goals and 7 'process' goals; completion of the questionnaire is expected to take about 45 minutes. Respondents are invited to state how important each goal actually is in their institution, and how important it ideally ought to be.[31] In 1979 and 1980, the IGI was adapted to produce the Community College Goals Inventory and the Small Colleges Goals Inventory.[32] A Canadian IGI is available in both French and English, and versions have also been prepared for use in Saudi Arabia and Thailand.[33]

By 1977 about 350 institutions had made use of the IGI.[34] In 1972, in one study alone, it was administered to 24,000 respondents in 116 colleges and universities in the State of California;[35] a volume of comparative data has been published.[36]

The IGI inspired a number of other researchers, and attempts were made to take the consideration of goals still further. Romney, for example, tried to assess the opinions held by various groups on the appropriate criteria for assessing progress towards given goals.[37] Butler tried to establish what use the institutions actually made of the IGI results, once they were available.[38]

Butler's work, in fact, reaches to the very heart of the matter. The statistics about the widespread use of the IGI are not in themselves important: the important question is, have the results been of value? Have all those diligent respondents, putting ticks in boxes for 45 minutes, been doing anything useful? In my judgement the answer is yes, but not without qualification.

My own view is that it is undoubtedly valuable for an institution's decision-makers to know the extent to which certain groups of stakeholders agree or disagree on what the goals of the institution are or should be. But the high level of agreement within a group or between groups does not necessarily mean that those goals are the 'right' goals, however 'right' may be defined; with several years' hindsight, it might well become clear that the goals which once commanded wide support were not 'right' at all. Similarly, the demonstration of a high level of disagreement does not suggest any means for resolving the differences, or even, necessarily, that they need to be resolved.

Fenske has suggested that goals studies are often seen as worthy but impractical; many of them repose undisturbed in filing cabinets. Fenske has also expressed concern about the difficulties of translating goals as described in the IGI into procedures which will actually improve efficiency; this is a process of converting abstract ideals into quantitative operational measures.[39]

Despite all the conceptual problems, it is clear that many American universities have spent much time and effort on considering their goals, either with or without the help of the IGI. Many of them have also succeeded in summarising a broad consensus of opinion in the form of a mission statement; and it is to these interesting and important documents that we now turn.

Mission statements of American universities

Some American universities have their mission defined for them, by state law.[40] Many other universities are obliged, or consider it prudent, to prepare a mission statement as part of their budget submission to state funding agencies.[41] Such statements frequently cover goals, and sometimes objectives, in addition to 'mission' as defined in Chapter 1.

Whatever the motivation, there is no doubt that many American universities devote great care to drawing up their mission statement. The Pennsylvania State University's 84-page document was the result of two years of intense study;[42] the State University of New York at Albany issues a booklet 52 pages long.[43]

It has to be said, however, that length and labour are no guarantee of value, and some of these mission statements are less than impressive.[44] An institution which tells us that it sets out to 'provide an educated citizenry', or 'to serve as a dynamic force in shaping society' does not tell us anything of significance; references to providing 'richer and more meaningful cultural and social experiences' border upon self-parody.[45] Similarly the booklet issued by Florida's public universities consists of 46 pages of vague and woolly statements accompanied by a large volume of data which does nothing to illuminate either mission or goals.[46] The unsatisfactory nature of some of these publications has not gone unremarked by commentators within the United States.[47]

The best American mission statements are, however, a different matter. They address difficult issues with clarity and vigour. For example, a Princeton University publication frankly acknowledges the elitist nature of the institution as follows: 'Broadly, our purpose is to advance the cause of the human race, to benefit mankind. We aim to accomplish this through the leverage of uncommon individuals and through the leverage of important ideas.'[48] Indiana University tackles head-on an issue which some would gloss over:

> Institutions of higher education have a responsibility to foster an honest and ethical academic atmosphere. As part of that effort, each discipline must arrange for its students to consider and ponder the moral questions of the field. Whether this will be done by integrating ethics into all courses or by the introduction of specific ethics courses remains to be seen and must be answered soon. Regardless, our graduates should develop during their time here a keen sense of professional responsibility in these complex and changing times.[49]

Likewise the University of Cincinnati:

> Finally, as a moral community the University is concerned with choices and values, behavior and actions, judgments and decisions as to what is equitable, worthy, and just.[50]

Having looked at a considerable number of mission statements it seems to me that the major American universities have four primary goals. They are:

1 A process variously described as the discovery, acquisition or creation of knowledge (in one word, research).
2 The transmission or dissemination of knowledge (teaching).
3 The application of knowledge to human problems in the interests of public service.
4 The preservation of knowledge in libraries, museums and archives.[51]

At this point many British readers may well be asking themselves what, precisely, is the point of drawing up a mission statement? What does it gain a university to commit the sometimes considerable time and effort needed to produce such a document?

There are a number of answers to such questions. One is that a good mission statement undoubtedly helps a university to obtain resources. Another is that to have conscious goals enables a university to evaluate its performance more effectively. Harvard University, for example, has investigated not only what alumni believe the University did for them, but what changes their years at the University actually brought about in students. Tests have been devised to measure the extent of the improvement, if any, in writing skills and critical thinking; this latter ability is one which is valued highly by British academics. Gains in moral reasoning ability in Harvard graduates have also been measured.[52]

Perhaps the best justification for drawing up a mission statement has been provided by the State University of New York at Albany. Noting that the University might 'be making more of the business of mission redefinition than some universities', the document goes on to say:

> The great discontinuities of our times – the financial exigencies which loom in such sharp contrast with the past – give us the choice of directing the affairs of the university in time with the new age, or of being shaped – perhaps misshaped – by the forces of blind fate. The first choice, we believe, is the strong choice.[53]

Conclusions on the American approach to university goals

This chapter has demonstrated that one nation at least has generally accepted the argument that if a university is to be effective it needs clearly formulated goals. Steps have been taken within the USA to measure the congruence of opinions on goals both within and between stakeholder groups. And many American universities, having clarified their goals, have issued public statements which describe what they are.

Notes

1 Allen (1979).
2 Balderston and Weathersby (1972), page (ii).
3 Ibid., page 3.
4 Ibid., page 4.
5 Fielden (1969), page 50; Balderston and Weathersby (1972), page 6.
6 The best description of PPBS is perhaps that provided by Balderston and Weathersby (1972). See also Fielden (1969), page 6, Kirst (1975), page 535, Fielden and Lockwood (1973), page 215, and Hartley (1968), page 158.
7 Kirst (1975), page 538. Fielden (1969), page 17.
8 Balderston and Weathersby (1972), page 8.
9 Ibid., page 94.
10 Kirst (1975), page 535.
11 Davies (1976), page 1.
12 Temple (1973), page 99.
13 Davies (1976), page 1, and Baron (1978), page 17.
14 Ibid.
15 Mullen (1974), page 53.
16 Temple (1973), page 99.
17 Ibid; also Winstead (1978).
18 Ashley, Tinsley, Lewis and Arnold (1981), page 10; Davies (1976), page 2; and Polczynski and Thompson (1980), page 256.
19 Davies (1976), page 21.
20 Fincher (1978), page 56.
21 Gross and Grambsch (1968).
22 Summary derived from Fenske (1978), page 34.
23 Gross and Grambsch (1968), page 107.
24 Ibid., page 21.
25 Fenske (1978), page 34.
26 Fincher (1972), page 755.
27 Quoted by Fenske (1981), page 187.
28 Carnegie Commission (1973).
29 Peterson and Uhl (1977), page 12. The ETS is, in my view, the world centre for research into the measurement of opinions on goals. One indication of the extent of British interest in this topic that, at least until 1986, I was the only member of staff of a British university who had ever visited the ETS to discuss their work on goals. British academics have, of course, visited the ETS for other purposes.
30 Fenske (1978), page 37.
31 Ibid., page 36.
32 Educational Testing Service (1981).
33 Fenske (1978), page 44.
34 Peterson and Uhl (1977), page viii.
35 Ibid., page 12.
36 Educational Testing Service (1979).
37 Romney (1978).
38 Butler (1980).
39 Fenske, in a letter to the author dated 14 April 1981. See also Fenske (1981), pages 194 to 197.
40 The University of Maryland is one such. See University of Maryland (1980), page 1.

41 See, for example, University of Kansas (1981).

42 Pennsylvania State University (1980), page 1.

43 State University of New York at Albany (1977).

44 Bok (1974), page 159, and Fenske (1981), page 178, both criticise American colleges and universities for not making enough effort to define their aims.

45 All three quotations are from Washington State University (1978), pages 3 and 7. The goal statements of California State University, Los Angeles, are little better. See California State University, Los Angeles (1981).

46 Florida State University (1979).

47 See, for example, Perkins (1973), page 156.

48 Quoted by Bowen (1977b), page 10.

49 Indiana University (1981), page 10.

50 University of Cincinnati (1977), page 1.

51 This summary is drawn from Colorado State University (1982), University of Kansas (1981), and University of Kentucky (1981). It may be that the primary source for all three was the Carnegie Commission: see Perkins (1973), page 58.

52 Bok (1978), pages 12, 13 and 14.

53 State University of New York at Albany (1977), page 1.

6

The British Approach to University Goals

The aim of this chapter is to compare British attitudes towards the clarification of university goals with the American practices which were outlined in the previous chapter.

Goal statements by British universities

In 1973 Fielden and Lockwood published a book entitled *Planning and management in universities*; the subtitle was *A study of British universities*. This book subsequently acquired a substantial reputation as the authoritative text on the management of British universities, but the reader who searches the index for any mention of aims, goals, mission or objectives, will search in vain. There is, however, an interesting passage beginning on page 33:

> Whether as a participant in university management or as a manager of his own activities, the individual needs to have a clearer view of the nature of the university, to be aware of the distinction between mission, roles, programmes and objectives. Statements of mission or goal normally summarise the varied purposes of the university into one general statement set out in the Charter. These normally take the form of a statement, such as, to advance knowledge through the pursuit of teaching and research. Specific roles spring from that mission, of which the main three normally distinguished are teaching, research and public service. These roles can in turn be divided into programmes (e.g. undergraduate teaching) and sub-programmes (e.g. undergraduate teaching in the Faculty of Arts). Objectives operate at each of these levels; at the level of mission and role, objectives tend to be generalised (e.g. orientate teaching towards inter-disciplinary or vocational studies; to concentrate research in particular fields) whereas at the programme and sub-programme levels they should become quite specific (e.g. to have one hundred Economics students graduating in 1975). We are not at this stage advocating that organisational structures should be geared to the above conceptions of activities. Neither are we commenting on the difficulty, perhaps impossibility, of reaching agreement within a university about role priorities and

specific objectives. We are simply stating that the above frame of reference represents a useful method of obtaining an understanding of the multiple and competitive purposes of a university.

This seems to be a sensible analysis of the position (although the terminology used differs from my own). It is certainly true that most British universities seem to regard their charter as a sufficient statement of their overall aims. In December 1981 I wrote to the Registrar of every British university asking for a copy of any document or publication which set out the mission or goals of their institution. All but three universities replied; however, none of the respondents could produce anything which compared with an American mission statement,[1] or which seemed to me to provide an adequate statement of purpose. The University of Cambridge, for example, could only refer me to a statute drafted (in Latin) in the reign of Edward VI, reading as follows:

Deum timeto: regem honorato: virtutem colito: disciplinis bonis operam dato.[2]

Oxford University could do little better, quoting a section of the Oxford and Cambridge Act of 1877, to the effect that in making the statutes of the University the Commissioners should consider 'the advancement of art, science, and other branches of learning'.[3]

Some Scottish universities – Edinburgh, St Andrews and Glasgow, for example – were unable to produce a written statement of any kind. In at least two cases this was because they do not have a charter, and the papal bulls or Acts of Parliament which legitimate the institutions do not, apparently, make any reference to purpose.[4] Aberdeen is slightly better off: according to Sir James Mountford, the bull of Pope Alexander VI which established the University of Aberdeen made it clear that the University's main aim was to be the study of law and 'the promoting of civilisation among the Highland clergy'.[5] The Secretary of Edinburgh University commented that 'we do not have a Charter, nor does there seem to have been any need to set down a statement of our aims and purposes!'[6] South of the border, Reading was another university which could produce no official pronouncement of any description.

The response of the majority of universities was to refer me to a clause or clauses in the appropriate charter. This proved to be marginally more illuminating, though in a number of instances it appears that one purpose of the university is to provide a university education.[7]

A large number of universities have a clause in their charter which states that 'The object of the University shall be to advance learning and knowledge by teaching and research.'[8] Usually a number of other ideas are added to the end of that statement. For example, clause 3 of the charter of the University of Salford reads as above and then concludes:

. . . especially into the basic and applied sciences, and to enable students to obtain the advantages of University education.

The University of Bath's charter, clause 2, reads:

> The objects of the University shall be to advance learning and knowledge by teaching and research, particularly in science and technology, and in close association with industry and commerce.

And, as a final example, clause 4 of the charter of the Queen's University of Belfast:

> The objects of the University shall be the advancement and dissemination of learning and knowledge by teaching and research, and through the practice and inculcation of professional and other skills appropriate to the provision of higher education, and by the example and influence of its corporate life.[9]

The similarity of wording often arises from the fact that modern universities normally obtain their charter through the Privy Council,[10] and in 1963 that body issued a model charter to guide the various institutions which were then seeking university status.[11] The variations in wording reflect the different aspirations of each newcomer.[12] It is interesting that two of the newer Scottish universities attempt to cover a very wide field by referring to teaching and research 'particularly into the basic and applied sciences' (Strathclyde) or in 'Science and Technology' (Heriot-Watt), and then adding a phrase about enabling students 'to obtain the advantages of liberal university education' (both institutions).[13] It is also worth noting that some of the older universities refer to the 'Diffusion and Extension of Arts' – Hull, Nottingham and Southampton, for example.[14]

Most of the former Colleges of Advanced Technology make a direct reference in their charters to working in conjunction with industry and commerce; Aston and Bath are typical examples.[15] In this respect they follow in the footsteps of some of the older institutions, such as the University of Manchester Institute of Science and Technology, and the University of Nottingham.[16] Another common clause in charters, both old and new, is one which legitimises the provision of research and advisory services for industry, commerce and public bodies.[17]

At the time of my survey (1981/82), comparatively few universities could offer any evidence, apart from their charters, to indicate that the goals of the institution had been consciously and formally considered in any depth. During the period 1968 to 1972, Bristol had a working party to consider the aims and methods of university education; the working party eventually concluded that an adequate examination of the issues presented to it could only be undertaken if the work was established as a properly funded project with appropriate staff. The working party also concluded that 'the University was not in a position to finance projects in this field'.[18]

My survey established that two other universities had examined their role in some detail, though not recently. The Academic Planning Board of the University of Stirling, set up in 1964, concluded that the 'four objectives underlying the work of a university' should be those which were set out in the Robbins Report, though the Board did not acknowledge its source.[19] In 1972 the

University of Birmingham was the subject of a review by a body chaired by the Rt Hon. J. Grimond; this body also considered that the role of a university had been adequately described by Lord Robbins and his colleagues, but in this case the source was acknowledged. Interestingly, the review body placed considerable emphasis on fostering a capacity for critical analysis and on the ability to assume responsibility for moral choice.[20]

Aston University, in 1981, produced a revision of its academic plan. This began by noting that the University's charter 'gives little clue to what a technological university is', and went on to argue forcefully against liberal education and in favour of vocational education.[21] Ironically, Aston University, having articulated its aims more clearly than most, was among the hardest hit in the UGC's 1981 round of cuts.[22]

The responses to my letter of inquiry suggest that up to 1981/82 there had been little formal or high-level discussion of goals in British universities, and I was given no reason to suppose that my respondents believed that goals should be discussed. The attitude of most British universities was summed up by the Registrar of one of them when he said: 'I think that one takes the aims of a university very much as read.'[23] It is possible to attribute this situation to a sinister conspiracy: not having overt goals means that an institution cannot publicly be seen to fail; purpose can be redefined, retrospectively, to match performance.[24] It seems more likely, however, that without any external or internal stimulus, fundamental questions of purpose have been pushed aside by the day-to-day pressure of events.[25] PPBS and MBO were seldom discussed in British universities, and were certainly never implemented. Tradition, as amended (reluctantly) by the continuing political process, has been considered a sufficient guide to action.

This situation is easy to understand, but it is less easy to justify. One of my respondents, perhaps feeling embarrassed that his university had only the briefest of references to purpose in its charter, and could offer no other documents, remarked that 'to draw up any other statement would probably occupy a working party for two or three years!'[26] His exclamation mark suggests that such an idea would be unthinkable. But it would surely be good public relations, if nothing else, for a university which consumes perhaps £30 million of public money each year to be able to give a convincing explanation of what it is trying to do. Lord Robbins and his colleagues, as usual, can be depended upon for a balanced view:

> The absence of a plan for everything is not necessarily an indication of chaos. But higher education is so obviously and rightly of great public concern, and so large a proportion of its finance is provided in one way or another from the public purse, that it is difficult to defend the continued absence of co-ordinating principles and of a general conception of objectives.[27]

Unfortunately, some twenty years after Robbins, the Jarratt Committee was still making the same complaint. (See paragraphs 3.30(a), 3.33 and 3.42 of the Committee's report.)

Goal statements by polytechnics

In order to find out whether the position with regard to goal statements was significantly different in polytechnics, I wrote early in 1982 to a random sample of one third of the polytechnics' chief administrative officers; seven replies were received.

The replies revealed that four polytechnics had never drawn up or issued any agreed statement of the goals of the institution.[28] One respondent was able to provide a brief and woolly statement ('the importance of research ... is recognised'),[29] and the remaining two institutions had published longer and more thoughtful documents which were obviously the result of much work. Teesside Polytechnic's paper on its size and educational character is succinct (about 1,000 words) but makes it clear that the polytechnic is strongly vocational in character and that it pays close attention to the needs of industry and commerce in the region; it also seems to be a cultural centre.[30] Manchester Polytechnic's booklet entitled *Policy for development*[31] includes a summary of aims which is disappointing – the statement that the polytechnic seeks 'to provide an educational experience which enables people to live fulfilled lives' begs a number of questions – but the rest of the booklet is well written and interesting. It includes a plea which is possibly unique: that courtesy should prevail in all areas of activity. Unfortunately the publication has not been revised since 1974, but it is a credit to the institution which produced it.

This limited survey of the polytechnics suggests that they have devoted more effort to clarifying their goals than have the universities. This is borne out by a consideration of the limited amount of research which has been carried out in this country into the opinions of various groups on the goals of higher education; that research is described in the next section.

British research into opinions on goals

According to Professor Eggleston, 'Research into higher education in England is spasmodic, uneven and unco-ordinated.'[32] There is a Society for Research into Higher Education, which has produced a number of valuable publications, notably the eleven volumes generated by the Leverhulme Inquiry. But, so far as I can discover, at present only one British university (Surrey) has a Professor of Higher Education, and the chair at the University of London Institute of Higher Education has remained vacant since the retirement of Professor Niblett. It is not surprising, therefore, to find that comparatively little research has been carried out into the extent to which opinions differ on what the goals of universities (or polytechnics) should be. This section describes the principal studies which have been reported in the literature; the next chapter, which considers the views held by the various stakeholder groups, will refer to specific research findings, where appropriate.

In the 1960s and early 1970s, Entwistle and Percy conducted a number of studies under the aegis of the Joseph Rowntree Higher Education Project at the

University of Lancaster.[33] At an early stage in their inquiries they carried out a review of the aims and objectives which have been ascribed to different types of institution at different times. Here they soon found that they were 'operating in a research vacuum'; consequently they described their activities in this field as a pioneer effort.[34] Their principal conclusion was that there were 'great and irreconcilable differences between the objectives and the priorities of objectives claimed for the university'.[35] They decided that there was no general 'idea of a university' which all could accept and admire,[36] but they did note the strength of the belief in the university as a 'guardian of the spiritual, non-material, permanent values of the "life of the mind"'.[37]

Entwistle and Percy also persuaded a small number of lecturers (forty) to complete an attitude scale consisting of six sets of six statements; this was designed to shed light on the lecturers' opinions on the extent to which universities were or should be responsive to society's contemporary needs, and similar issues.[38] The sample was small, and was drawn from one university, one polytechnic and two colleges of education. The findings are therefore far from representative of all academic opinion, even at the time of the survey. A later study carried out by Brennan and Percy, into the predominant goals and aspirations of British students, was based on much larger samples of both students and staff and therefore provides a more reliable picture.[39] Both surveys will be referred to in the next chapter when appropriate.

By the mid 1970s an awareness of the extensive American research on goals had begun to filter through to a few British academics, and the IGI question-naire was used as the basis for two small-scale inquiries in the United Kingdom. Norris prepared a modified version of the IGI questionnaire and carried out a pilot test with the co-operation of 13 respondents at the University of Leeds. He then sought permission to carry out a larger-scale survey within the University, but the Leeds Senate was unimpressed and refused.[40] Norris's results came from too limited a sample to be of any value.

The IGI questionnaire was also used as the basis for an inquiry into the views of academic staff at the North East London Polytechnic; this study was carried out by Laycock.[41] The starting point for this particular project was the belief that the Polytechnic's goals should receive the closest scrutiny, so that the institution could eventually assess its performance. The major findings were that staff believed that courses should have real practical value, and that provision of an education which would develop the 'self' was considered to have a low priority;[42] this is in accordance with what is already known from other sources about the ethos of polytechnics. In the end, however, Laycock con-cluded that it might not be possible to assess the goals of the Polytechnic to any meaningful extent, and that this was a 'high-risk area' of research. Laycock was also brought face to face with a problem mentioned by Fenske, namely what to do with the results of the survey once he had them. His conclusion was that they should be regarded as 'a preparative word-picture to delineate the groundwork for future effort'. The groundwork may have borne fruit, because the Polytechnic later produced a formal mission statement which is now being used in forward planning.[43] In general terms, however, the work of Norris and

Laycock suggests that the IGI, even in modified form, is not appropriate for use in a British context.

The final project which must be mentioned in this survey of British research is the inquiry into the Expectations of Higher Education. This project was funded by the DES in 1980 at a cost of some £111,000;[44] it was under the direction of Professor Maurice Kogan of Brunel University, and took three years to complete its work. An interesting and valuable publication emerged from the project quite quickly: this was entitled *Expectations of higher education: some historical pointers*, and it was written by Harold Silver.[45] Various references to this book will be made in the next chapter. A useful short summary of the rest of the project's work has also been published.[46]

The Expectations of Higher Education project was intended to analyse the expectations which different groups had of higher education, particularly in relation to the employment of graduates. The principal groups considered were students, employers, and providers in educational institutions. It was hoped that the findings would offer information and generate ideas which would contribute to the formulation of higher education policy.[47] The project placed a heavy emphasis on interviews with members of the various groups drawn from a large number of institutions and industrial and commercial concerns. Student opinion was tested through a survey of 6,000 final-year students in 36 different institutions.[48] All in all, the Expectations of Higher Education project constitutes the single most extensive inquiry into the purposes of higher education which has ever been carried out in the United Kingdom. Further reference to the findings will be made in the next chapter.

Despite the importance of the Expectations of Higher Education inquiry, the overall picture of British research into university goals is one which in my view fully confirms Professor Eggleston's description, quoted at the beginning of this section. Researchers in the field have been few in number and, with the exception of Professor Kogan and his team, have operated on a limited scale – sometimes on a microscopic scale. To some extent the paucity of research arises from the fact that, as academic staff have sometimes remarked to me, this is a difficult area; ideally the researcher should have a wider view of universities than is common in an era of increasing specialisation. But the research record also reflects the degree of interest in goals which has been demonstrated by the British university system as a whole: that is to say, negligible.

Perhaps I should also mention in this context my own research project which sought to measure and to compare opinions on a number of issues related to university goals;[49] the results will be summarised in Chapter 9.

Conclusions on the British approach to university goals

The material contained in this chapter leads me to the conclusion that the Editor of the *The Times Higher Education Supplement* was not exaggerating when he stated that, in the United Kingdom, fundamental questions about the purpose of universities are 'habitually avoided'.[50] Within departments there is, of course, almost continuous discussion about course content, and it would be wrong to underestimate the extent or the seriousness of such debates.[51] But goals may easily be implied rather than openly acknowledged in decisions on the curriculum, and, judging by the evidence which universities can produce when asked, consideration of goals at Senate and Council level is extremely rare; the contrast between British and American universities in this respect is dramatic. Many senior academics seem to regard American practices, if they know about them at all, as politically naive. The prevailing attitude seems to be: 'We all know what a university is, so we don't need to discuss its aims. And in any case we're much too busy.'

The situation is slowly changing. In 1980 the House of Commons Committee on education recommended that universities should be obliged to produce mission statements, to be agreed with the UGC,[52] and their view was endorsed by the Leverhulme Report.[53] In 1985 Lockwood and Davies published a book entitled *Universities: the management challenge*. This contained much more discussion of mission and goals than had the earlier book, *Planning and management in universities*, which it was designed to replace. Lockwood and Davies conclude that the design of mission statements is 'a critical field of managerial endeavour for the future'[54] and I for one wholeheartedly agree.

Notes

1 Subsequently, in March 1984, the University of Ulster did in fact publish a mission statement. The statement was no doubt considered necessary following the merger of the New University of Ulster with Ulster Polytechnic. As mission statements go, however, Ulster's is not an impressive document. It deals primarily with means rather than ends, and like many public documents it tries to be all things to all men; on research, for example, it states that the 'implied orientation towards the applied will not be pursued to the exclusion of good pure research.' (Paragraph 7.)

2 Letter from the Registrary of the University of Cambridge, to the author, 5 January 1982.

3 Universities of Oxford and Cambridge Act, 1877, section 16. Quoted by Mr W. L. Bell, of the University of Oxford, in a letter to the author, dated 7 January 1982.

4 Letters to the author from Officers of the Universities of Edinburgh, St Andrews and Glasgow.

5 Mountford (1966), page 11.

6 Letter to the author, dated 5 January 1982, from the Secretary of the University of Edinburgh. The exclamation mark is his.

7 The charters of the following universities all include references to that effect, in one form of words or another: Aston, Essex, Heriot-Watt, London, Salford, Strathclyde, Sussex, the University of Manchester Institute of Science and Technology, Warwick, York, and the Open University. Sources: letters from Officers of the universities named.

8 See, for example, clause III of the Supplemental Charter of the University of Manchester. Quoted by the Registrar in a letter to the author, dated 5 January 1982.

9 All three clauses cited in this paragraph were quoted in letters to the author from the Registrars of the universities named.

10 Moodie and Eustace (1974), page 21.

11 Ibid., page 34.

12 Further variations upon the same clause can be found in the charters of the following universities: Aston, Brunel, Essex, Heriot-Watt, Kent, Lancaster, Sussex, Strathclyde, Warwick, York, and the Open University. Sources: letters to the author from Officers of the universities named.

13 Extracts from the charters of Heriot-Watt and Strathclyde universities were quoted in letters to the author by Officers of the universities named.

14 Sources: letters to the author from Officers of the universities named.

15 Also Bradford and Surrey. Sources: letters to the author from Officers of the universities named.

16 Sources: letters to the author from Officers of the universities named.

17 See, for example, the charters of the following universities: Aston, Bristol, Essex, Hull. Sources: letters to the author from Officers of the universities named.

18 Letter to the author, and enclosures, from the Registrar of the University of Bristol, dated 6 January 1982.

19 First report of the Academic Planning Board of the University of Stirling, page 3. Quoted in a letter to the author, dated 12 January 1982, from the Secretary of the University of Stirling.

20 Letter to the author, and enclosures, from the Registrar of the University of Birmingham, dated 11 January 1982.

21 Letter to the author, and enclosures, from the Registrar of the University of Aston, dated 4 February 1982.

22 UGC circular letter 10/81, dated 1 July 1981. See Parkes (1981).

23 Letter to the author, dated 14 January 1982.

24 See Weathersby (1979), page 6, for a discussion of this point.

25 Campbell argues that this has also happened in Canada. See Campbell (1975), page 53.

26 Letter to the author, dated 7 January 1982.

27 Robbins (1963), page 5.

28 They were: City of London, Leicester, Oxford, and South Bank. Sources: letters to the author from Officers of the polytechnics named.

29 Preston Polytechnic, quoted in a letter to the author, dated 25 January 1982, from the Chief Administrative Officer.

30 Letter to the author, and enclosures, from the Clerk to the Governors of Teesside Polytechnic, dated 25 January 1982.

31 Manchester Polytechnic (1974).

32 Eggleston (1983), page 66.

33 Entwistle and Percy (1973), page 1.

34 Entwistle and Percy (1970), page 2.

35 Entwistle, Percy and Nisbet (1971), page 19.

36 Ibid.

37 Ibid., page 20.

38 Ibid., page 25.

39 See Brennan and Percy (1975).

40 Norris (1978), pages 28, 29, and 37.

41 Laycock (1979).

42 Ibid., page 1.

43 See Toyne (1985).

44 Department of Education and Science (1980), page 1.

45 See Silver (1981).

46 Kogan and Boys (1983). Roizen and Jepson (1985) elaborate on the views of employers as revealed by the Expectations of Higher Education project.

47 Kogan and Boys (1983), page 1.

48 Ibid., page 2.

49 Allen (1986).

50 Times Higher Education Supplement (1984b).

51 For a particularly interesting account of the development of a new curriculum which *did* begin with a consideration of goals, see Bolton (1986).

52 House of Commons (1980).

53 Leverhulme Report, volume 9 (*The structure and governance of higher education*), pages 200 and 201.

54 Lockwood and Davies (1985), page 62.

7

The Views of the Stakeholders on the Goals of British Universities

If the universities themselves have not formalised their views on goals, what have other sections of society to say on the matter? In Chapter 3 I pointed out that a number of groups can usefully be regarded as stakeholders in the British university system. This chapter describes the views of the principal stakeholder groups as to what the goals of universities should be.

The information contained in this chapter is derived from a number of sources. I reviewed the available literature; I wrote to the appropriate national or professional bodies; and at least one member of every stakeholder group was interviewed. In some cases the stakeholders have expressed opinions on higher education through their official publications; in other cases views have been put forward by individuals who may be regarded as spokesmen authorised to speak on behalf of the group. However, some groups have not made formal statements of any kind on this question, and in those instances I have tried to assess their attitude either through the findings of surveys of opinion or through the comments of members of the group who are not official spokesmen. Analysing the views of the stakeholder groups has therefore called for the use of judgement. On the whole, I have given more weight to the findings of large-scale surveys than to statements made by individuals, but there may be exceptions: for example, the views of an 'elder statesman' may be more valuable than the findings of a research project with a low response rate. It also has to be borne in mind that those who are satisfied with the status quo do not often feel obliged to say so in public. Consequently the majority of published statements on any issue, and certainly the most provocative statements, will tend to be critical of the subject under discussion. Due allowance has to be made for this tendency.

The general public

A previous group of researchers found it 'a surprise to discover that there is little empirical knowledge of the public's views on the major functions of universities.'[1] The situation has not changed much since that was written, in 1971.

At the time of my inquiry, the Gallup Poll organisation had no information on the public's opinion of universities,[2] but its findings on education as a whole suggest that dissatisfaction is increasing. In 1984, 69 per cent of a nationally representative quota sample considered that Britain was not giving enough attention to education; in 1959 the figure was only 34 per cent. Similarly the proportion considering that their children were getting a better education than their own generation had received had fallen from 71 per cent in 1959 to 45 per cent in 1984.[3]

The Royal Society of Arts is a large and broadly based group which is heavily involved in education and training at all levels. The Society is unhappy with the state of affairs in both the schools and higher education, and its 'Education for capability' scheme reflects this concern. Traditionally, says the Society's spokesman, an 'educated person' has been 'thought of as a scholarly, leisured individual who has not been prepared to exercise useful skills; who is able to understand but not to act. This imbalance is harmful to individuals and to society.' Capability, as seen by the Society, is not just the ability to tackle a problem: it is the ability to feel rationally as well as to think rationally; this involves the cultivation of sensitivity, something which has lost ground in recent years to the pursuit of specialised knowledge.[4] Over the past few years the Society has given a platform to a succession of lecturers who have outlined what they consider to be the shortcomings of both the schools and the universities.[5] The need is said to be for more relevant curricula so that students can develop their specialised competencies and cope with both themselves and their environment.[6] In 1982 the Society produced a report on *The future of technological higher education in Britain*.[7] This report argued that in order to compete successfully in open international trade, Britain must develop a stronger base of higher technological education; this would require stronger links with industry and commerce, new methods of funding, and the creation of new institutions.

The Association of University Teachers (AUT) has obviously been conscious of public criticism in recent years. In 1982 the AUT thought it appropriate to counter a number of 'public myths'. One was: 'universities do not teach anything useful to students. They are ivory towers and are not concerned with and know nothing about the real world.' Another 'myth' was: 'much of university research is not relevant.'[8]

It can be argued that the general public demonstrates its faith in universities by applying for admission; but the admissions process involves only a small minority of the population at large. It seems more likely that Minogue was nearer the mark when he stated that 'universities have been almost constantly in a state of conflict with much of the society around them. They have been, so far as public reputation is concerned, almost permanently unsatisfactory institutions. Public discussion has been about little else but reforming them.'[9]

It appears from the evidence available that the general public is unenthusiastic about universities, at best. The public, however, has only a marginal and spasmodic contact with universities. It will therefore be useful to consider next the views of a group of people who are directly concerned with the products of universities: the employers.

The employers

Individual employers, chiefly in industry, have historically been very ready to speak their minds about the universities: what they have said has seldom been complimentary. The importance of employers' views has also been widely recognised by the universities and by the press, and the result is that the opinions of this particular group of stakeholders have been thoroughly documented.

The complaint that universities are insufficiently responsive to the needs of industry is not a new one: in 1903 a conference was held at Cambridge to discuss the failure of that University to provide an education suited to the needs of men who would shortly be engaged in business.[10] Since then there has been a constant stream of accusations levelled against the universities that they have failed to meet the needs of industry and of employers in general.[11] Universities have been criticised for producing men who are 'timid and irresolute, antagonistic to industry and commerce, and lacking in awareness of the profit motive'.[12] A long series of quotations would be wearisome but a few are necessary to give the flavour of the consensus view.

In 1981 *The Times Higher Education Supplement* featured the head of Unilever Research complaining about 'the ivory tower attitude of academics';[13] on the same page the President of the Confederation of British Industry (CBI) argued the need for the whole of education to be made more responsive to the needs of the economy.[14] In 1982 an editorial in the *Financial Times* stated that British universities have always set their faces firmly against vocational training and suggested that most of what was now taught was as useless as the ability to construe Greek verse.[15] In 1984 there were even proposals for a technological university funded by industry.[16]

Some of these comments can rightly be ignored as ill-informed generalisation, but the strength, volume and persistence of the criticism cannot easily be dismissed. Indeed the CVCP felt impelled, in 1981, to produce a booklet defending the universities' record.[17] It seems clear that many employers believe that a close connection between the universities and 'industry' (to use a general word for all forms of employment) is highly desirable. Most of them also sense a considerable resistance on the part of universities to providing what industry wants. The pressure from employers for a more responsive attitude on the part of universities seems to be increasing.

Within the last few years a number of research projects have described the employers' attitudes in some detail. In 1979 a survey was carried out by Bacon, Benton and Gruneberg.[18] Only 49 questionnaires were returned by employers of university graduates (a 56 per cent response rate), but the results indicated that the most sought-after qualities in university students were drive, motivation, leadership potential and adaptability. Interestingly, vocational training was ranked 13th out of 14 in the list. The survey also suggested that employers generally considered that the experience of being at a university did serve to enhance the qualities which were considered important; however, only 7 per cent of employers judged that the qualities which they sought were found in more than half the students they interviewed.

A very much larger inquiry into employers' attitudes was undertaken as part of the Leverhulme programme of study into the future of higher education.[19] This confirmed that the higher education sector was seen by employers as having failed to meet their needs.[20] It also established that the behavioural traits inculcated by higher education were more valued by employers than was cognitive knowledge. The general conclusion was that the higher education system and the labour market worked fairly well together in the sense that most surpluses or shortages of skills tended to be quickly eradicated.[21]

The CBI contribution to the Leverhulme discussion was particularly interesting in that it argued for a thorough investigation of the purpose and structure of higher education. The Government was requested to give the system a set of clear, long-term objectives, a policy 'firmly grounded on agreed educational goals'.[22] Developing such a strategy, it was stated, would involve consideration of the balance between vocational and more general courses, 'academic' or applied research, and the exercise of 'a certain leadership function' through influence on the public examination system.[23] Without such an overall policy, the CBI argued, the task of providing a rational and coherent pattern of provision would prove extremely difficult.[24] The CBI deserves respect for having devoted more thought to these issues than many other stakeholders.

Dissatisfaction with the relevance of university courses to industrial needs is not confined to employers. Beuret and Webb's research[25] shows that many young engineers are badly shaken when they discover the importance of non-technical abilities in their jobs. The importance to employers of non-academic characteristics was also highlighted by the Expectations of Higher Education project, funded by the DES;[26] and over a period of one year, 39 per cent of advertised vacancies for graduates were open to graduates of any discipline.[27]

It is necessary to make due allowance for the possible existence of a large number of employers who are well pleased with their graduate recruits and who do not make angry speeches or write to the newspapers. Having made such allowance, it is clear that many employers are critical of the universities on a number of counts. The Expectations of Higher Education project showed that a minority of employers do not accept that experience of higher education enhances the value of an employee at all.[28] In general, employers regard a degree as an indicator of basic ability – an ability which they can, with time, mould to their needs. The degree need not be a good one, and high academic ability may indicate an unsuitable case for treatment. The Chairman of the Manpower Services Commission recently asked: 'Can anyone think of somebody with a double First or a very good degree who has really succeeded as a captain of industry?'[29]

At this point the universities might be forgiven for making a complaint of their own, namely that employers criticise the product, but when pressed do not seem to be able to define what they want: 'the needs of industry' have simply not been stated in a coherent form.[30] Sir Monty Finniston asked employers what they would do to correct the situation which they all agreed was unsatisfactory, and found that they regarded that as a job for educationalists.[31] Even when courses have been redesigned, with the specific needs of employers in mind, there have been further criticisms.[32]

Nevertheless, despite the difficulty of substantiating complaints and clarifying needs, it remains a fact that employers as a group feel that the universities (and, for that matter, the polytechnics) are not providing graduates who meet their requirements. The relationship between employers and universities is for the most part distant,[33] and the fault is not all on the university side: it is questionable to what extent employers wish to become involved in course design and planning.[34] It is also undoubtedly true that this gap between employers and universities is important, if only because employers are a powerful and influential group. However, even if it were possible to design all courses to satisfy employers, it must not be forgotten that such courses might then be incompatible with the needs and demands of other stakeholder groups.

The professional institutions

Most laymen are familiar with the fact that British professional bodies exercise a powerful influence over their members: our daily newspapers frequently report cases where doctors or lawyers have been banned from continuing to practise their profession because of offences of one kind or another. What is not quite so well known is that many professional bodies also have a powerful influence over universities.

Universities were in many instances slow to react to demands for courses which were relevant to the professions:[35] in the early part of the twentieth century, medicine and engineering, for example, were well catered for, but it was often considered beneath a university's dignity to teach subjects such as accountancy or librarianship.[36] Eventually, however, pressure from the professional bodies, coupled with the universities' self-interest, saw to it that the needs of most professions were recognised by universities, albeit reluctantly. But the relationship between the two sides remains a sensitive one, with the professions often claiming the right to determine standards and curricula, and the universities insisting on academic autonomy.[37]

The present position exhibits considerable variation. The influence of some professional bodies is marginal and largely benign. There are, for example, six 'first-tier' accountancy bodies in Great Britain, each with its own pattern of examinations and its own criteria for recognising relevant degrees.[38] These bodies operate a joint Board of Accreditation which visits universities from time to time (if invited) and it is prudent for a university to keep the requirements of the various bodies in mind when designing or redesigning a degree course. However, the 'credit' given by the accountancy bodies for a 'relevant' degree is not very great at best, so if a particular degree is not regarded as relevant it is not a disaster for the would-be accountant: he simply has to take a few more examinations set by the professional body, in addition to his degree.[39]

By contrast, the power of the Pharmaceutical Society of Great Britain is much greater. The maintenance of a satisfactory system of training is a major objective of the Society, and it has developed elaborate means to secure this end. There are seventeen schools of pharmacy within British universities, and each is visited every five years by a group of the Society's delegates. These 'visitations' are in fact inspections, and if the Society is not satisfied with what it finds it can withdraw recognition of the degree as acceptable for the purpose of statutory registration. A university which could not show that its course was acceptable for registration would certainly not be able to attract pharmacy students. Thus the Society has, in effect, a stranglehold.[40]

To summarise, it is clear that the influence of the professional associations upon the universities is extensive and is increasing: in general, their major concern is to ensure that universities produce competent members of their profession. To that extent, they can be said to have thought about the goals of universities in some detail, and to have considerable influence in determining the implied goals of certain courses. With the passing of time, the senior officers of each association will tend to become those who entered the profession through the university route rather than through the old extra-university route: their interest in universities, and their ability to influence them, will probably be greater than at present. The growing interest in refresher courses and continuing education will also ensure a larger measure of involvement on the part of the professions.

It is worth noting that the relationship between the universities and the professional associations is by no means over-researched, despite its importance: this may be an indication of its extreme sensitivity. The Leverhulme Inquiry concluded that 'The relationship between the . . . professional bodies and . . . higher education institutions needs special study which we were not able to undertake.'[41]

The political parties

Education as a whole is evidently not a subject of great interest to politicians: Mr Callaghan is the only Prime Minister to have devoted an entire speech to it.[42] Not surprisingly, therefore, the major political parties have comparatively little to say about the goals of universities.

The Social Democratic Party

In 1982 the Social Democratic Party (SDP) produced a policy statement on education which indicated that the party considered that higher education was in urgent need of review.[43] An SDP statement published in October 1982 went on to recommend a shift from 'fundamental research to strategic and applied research'.[44]

As the general election of 1983 approached, the SDP issued a 'white paper' on education and training. This contained the only reference to the purpose of higher education made by any political party in its 1983 election material, albeit a brief and relatively innocuous statement. The purposes of higher education were said to be 'to develop the individual intellect and to serve the needs of society'; a third purpose was the advancement of scholarship.[45] The 'white paper' also argued in favour of a shift from single subject to broadly based degrees, and from Honours to General degrees, with a larger element of applied or job-based study.

Press reports of the SDP's 1986 conference indicated that the party was broadly in favour of two-year general degree courses (a Leverhulme idea), higher participation rates, and more science and technology. Greater investment in higher education was seen as justified in the interests of economic growth.

The Liberal Party

The Liberal Party published a report on higher education in 1977.[46] This was essentially a discussion document rather than a statement of agreed policy, but it gives some indication of the Party's views.

The report argued that education is a process which should benefit both the individual and society; there should be greater access to higher education;[47] closer links should be formed between institutions of higher education and their local communities; more attention should be paid to manpower-planning requirements; and universities should be free to criticise society as well as to serve it.[48]

In 1984 the Liberals criticised some of Sir Keith Joseph's recent statements, and argued that it was highly desirable to release the untapped demand for higher education which was present among women, ethnic minorities, the working class and potential mature students.[49]

The Labour Party

In response to an inquiry in connection with this book, a Labour Party Information Officer admitted that 'relatively little work has been done [by the Party] questioning the whole purpose of universities and colleges.'[50]

Perhaps the most elaborate consideration of higher education by the Labour Party dates back to 1973. In that year an 'Opposition green paper' was published.[51] Buried within it was a statement that 'post-school education should be a synthesis of liberal and vocational education.' This was scarcely an original idea, but at least it showed that the study group which prepared the report was aware of the need to say something about purpose.

In 1978 the Labour Party again came to grips with higher education policy in its discussion document *Higher education into the 1990s*. Here, however, the arguments were almost entirely about demography and cost rather than about what form of higher education was wanted, for whom, and for what purpose.[52]

The Labour Party's response to the 1981 cuts was to oppose them vigorously on the grounds that the 'national interest' required wider and more generous provision of further and higher education. The Party's policy was to secure expansion and change in higher education, though how much expansion and precisely what changes were not specified.[53]

In January 1983 the Labour Party issued a further discussion document on education after the age of 18.[54] This argued that investment in education was a major force for innovation and change, bringing greater control over their environment and destiny to a variety of disadvantaged groups. It was recommended that admission requirements for higher education should be reviewed in order to provide more open access, and that a more general sixth-form curriculum should be introduced. The document concluded with the thought that it was important that the universities should be given clear objectives by a future Labour government, together with the time and resources necessary to achieve those objectives.

Early in 1986 the Labour Party published *Education throughout life – a statement on continuing and higher education.* Among the chief recommendations were calls for broader-based 'A' level and first-degree courses, for research which is directed more towards industrial and social needs, and for teaching which aims at meeting the needs of industry without being narrowly vocational. The provision of higher education and continuing education, it was argued, should be co-ordinated through a national council chaired by the Secretary of State.

The Conservative Party

In 1981, when Professor Alan Walters was appointed as the Prime Minister's economic adviser, he asked to see the Government's policy papers: there were none.[55] In 1983, when a journalist asked for the Conservative Party's views on higher education, he was referred to the Party's manifesto and was told that there was no detailed policy on the universities as such.[56] That situation continued until the publication of the Green Paper on higher education in 1985; the Green Paper set out the Government's views on higher education, and it will be fully discussed in Chapter 10. In the meantime, it is worth recording what the Conservative Government has actually done while in office.

The Conservative Government of 1979 did not have any clearly defined philosophy of higher education, but it did have a firm commitment to reduce public expenditure;[57] hence the cuts of 1981. So far as can be ascertained from statements made at the time, the 1981 cuts were not imposed because of a belief that the universities had failed; they were made necessary by the world recession.[58] At the same time as the cuts were imposed, the Government was anxious to protect research and to encourage a shift towards the 'harder' sciences such as medicine and engineering.[59] The Government did not attempt to tell the UGC how to effect the desired policy, but it did give the UGC a clear indication of its wishes.[60]

By 1982, Mr Waldegrave, the Minister then responsible for Higher and Further Education, had decided that a genuine policy for higher education as a whole could now be formulated for the first time; this statement was apparently prompted by the advent of the National Advisory Body (NAB), which (at the time of writing) co-ordinates policy in local authority higher education.[61] Mr Waldegrave also noted that there was a need for reform, but that the Government's role in bringing about change should be limited.[62]

In 1983, the Education Secretary, Sir Keith Joseph, urged universities to become more cost-effective; he also reiterated the need to shift the balance of the system towards engineering and technology.[63] This represented a considerable shift of opinion for Sir Keith himself, who in 1974 had criticised the quest for 'relevance'. In an important and controversial article in *The Times Higher Education Supplement* Sir Keith had argued that vocational subjects were the business of the polytechnics; universities should be concerned with 'the pursuit of knowledge for its own sake'.[64]

In 1983 and 1984 there were further pointers to the Government's views. There was continued pressure for more emphasis on technology, science and engineering. Research was promised increased resources, if possible.[65] The Government expressed the wish that universities should be less dependent on public funds, partly to relieve the taxpayer and partly to concentrate the minds of academics more firmly on meeting the real needs of industry.[66] Mrs Thatcher herself said that universities must not only generate ideas but must see that they were taken up, 'whether in the arts or in the sciences, to the great advantage of all our people'.[67] And in case anyone should fear that all this emphasis on science and technology was unhealthy, Sir Keith Joseph acknowledged publicly that there was a need to teach culturally important subjects as well as economically important ones.[68]

Several commentators concluded that, judging by its actions, the Government had abandoned the Robbins principle that all those who are suitably qualified should have access to higher education if they wish to take advantage of it; that principle had formed virtually the sole basis of successive governments' 'policy' on higher education for some twenty years.[69]

The Government-inspired events of 1987 were highly significant for universities and have already been briefly outlined in Chapter 4; some of their further implications will be considered in Chapter 10.

Summary of the views of political parties

The evidence suggests that politicians are relatively uninterested in discussions of the fundamental purposes of higher education. However, all parties seem to acknowledge that higher education is beneficial, even if they consider it to be imperfectly administered at present.

It seems appropriate to conclude this section with a note on the views of the House of Commons Committee on Education, Science and Arts. In its fifth report, published in 1980, the Committee declared that it had been 'impressed by the need to define institutional objectives much more clearly, both to provide a more secure basis for future planning . . . and to serve as a discouragement to academic drift'.[70] As mentioned in Chapter 6, the Committee recommended that all colleges, polytechnics and universities should be asked to prepare statements of their purposes and objectives, for approval by the UGC or other bodies as appropriate. It was proposed that once the UGC (or other body) had approved the statement, it should be published; thereafter institutions would be left relatively free to run their own affairs with a minimum of national or local control; the Committee noted how successful this approach had been in the United States.[71] This recommendation was later echoed by the Leverhulme Inquiry and by the Jarratt Report, which is discussed in Chapter 10; it has not been given the force of law.

The Department of Education and Science

The DES has surprisingly little to say about the goals of universities or of higher education in general. A senior officer of the DES told me that 'You will not find a set of goals inscribed anywhere on tablets of stone.'[72] He went on to suggest that this was 'not quite so naive as it might appear' once the conflicting views of numerous authorities and bodies were taken into account. It appears, therefore, that rather than try to promulgate a policy on goals of its own, the DES prefers to let a working compromise emerge from the continual discussion about what universities should or should not be doing.

It seems to be formally accepted by the Government that the UGC has more expert knowledge of the universities than has the DES. In 1982 Mr Waldegrave praised the UGC's judgement in determining how the 1981 cuts would fall, noting that 'it was their decision based on the very much greater knowledge and skill that they have than the DES could ever have.'[73]

Only occasionally has the DES ventured into print about the purpose of higher education. One such instance occurred in 1970, when the DES declared that the overall aim of the teaching function was 'To provide higher education for those who could benefit from it, and to meet the requirements of society for qualified manpower.'[74] This reference to manpower tends to confirm the analysis of Slater and Tapper, who argue that the general educational ideology of the DES has an economic orientation.[75] The DES, according to this interpretation, is simply falling in line with the policy of successive governments, which is to give priority to the nation's industrial needs.

In the maintained sector of education, the DES is understandably very powerful.[76] However, as far as the universities are concerned, there appears to be no great steamroller of continuing policy which would crush all but the strongest ministers.

The University Grants Committee

It can be argued that every pronouncement from the UGC is of necessity based upon a conscious or unconscious assessment of what the goals of universities should be; the problem for the observer has been that until recently the UGC had never issued any formal statement of its views on basic goals.[77] In 1984, however, that omission was rectified, albeit at the instigation of another party.

In September 1984 the UGC and the National Advisory Body both submitted advice to the Government. The two bodies included in their reports a common chapter on the goals of higher education.[78] The chapter was first drafted by the NAB and was later adopted by the UGC; thus the NAB produced in three years a statement which the UGC had failed to produce in sixty-five.

The two bodies begin their joint statement by confirming that the four aims of higher education which were first described in the Robbins Report are still broadly valid. (What an impressive mileage has been obtained from those four brief aims.) They noted, however, that specific knowledge quickly becomes outdated and that initial higher education should therefore emphasise underlying principles and should develop basic skills: among the skills mentioned are the capacity to analyse complex issues, and the ability to communicate clearly, both orally and in writing. The conclusion is that higher education must be made broader, and to this end the universities must give a positive lead towards change in the sixth-form curriculum. The UGC advice emphasises that school-leavers should have followed courses in both arts and sciences throughout their secondary schooling.[79]

The third aim described in the Robbins Report, the advancement of learning (research), is also endorsed, as is the fourth, the transmission of a common culture. The joint statement notes, however, that there are now many diverse cultures within our society, and so this aim must in future be interpreted as referring to truly basic values, such as free speech and the examination of cases on their merits.

Finally, the UGC and NAB describe a new aim, which is the provision of continuing education in order to facilitate change and to meet individual needs. The statement concludes by restating the famous Robbins principle as follows: courses of higher education should be available for all those who are able to benefit from them and who wish to do so.[80] The new emphasis is on ability to benefit rather than on qualifications.

Apart from the 1984 joint statement with the NAB, other clues to the UGC's views on goals may be found elsewhere. The UGC's statement to the House of Commons select committee, following the 1981 cuts, reveals that among the criteria which the UGC took into account in 1981 were student demand and employment prospects.[81] Thus the UGC appears to believe that the teaching function of universities should be tailored (at least in part) to meet the needs of students and employers; the judgement of academic staff as to what is right and proper to be taught is not to be the sole, or even the most important, criterion. The events of 1981 also indicate that the UGC accepted the Government's contention that there should be an increase in the number of graduates in science and technology.

The academic staff

According to Burton R. Clark, British academic staff have a greater degree of control over the universities they work in than have the academics in France,

Japan, Sweden or the United States.[82] Whether Clark's view holds true in light of the 1987 Education Reform Bill is a moot point, but the views of academic staff on university goals are nevertheless particularly important.

Unfortunately, academic staff as a national group appear to have devoted little thought to the issue. When asked for a copy of any paper on university goals issued by the Association of University Teachers, the Assistant General Secretary wrote: 'It is with some embarrassment that I confess that despite the mounds of documents we have put out in the last few years I cannot recall the issue of such a statement.'[83]

In order to obtain an overview of the attitudes of academic staff we therefore have to go elsewhere; in particular we have to consult surveys of opinion. It will also be convenient to examine academics' attitudes in relation to the two major activities of universities: research and teaching.

Research

There is a considerable weight of evidence to suggest that most academic staff believe that their role should involve both teaching and research; this was suggested by Halsey and Trow in 1971[84] and has been confirmed since.

Halsey and Trow's large-scale survey showed that one third of academics regarded research as their first duty, with teaching very much in second place.[85] Of those who were interested in both teaching and research, a greater number leaned towards research rather than towards teaching.[86] Halsey and Trow's survey was based on a 51 per cent response rate, and must therefore be interpreted with some caution.[87]

More recently than Halsey and Trow's study, the fourth Leverhulme seminar demonstrated that many academics regard research as central to the university's mission.[88] The joint working party on research which was chaired by Sir Alec Merrison, and which reported in 1982, also stated that it could not emphasise too strongly its concern for the health of university research; the working party's report advocated that universities should channel funds into research 'notwithstanding adverse effects elsewhere'.[89]

Most of the arguments put forward in support of the research function emphasise its importance in terms of the nation's economic welfare, but it is perhaps worth noting that Startup established in 1979 that academics' main reason for undertaking research was not the nation's best interests, but the fact that they enjoyed it.[90]

Academics, and others, are often concerned with the question of whether research should be pure or applied. However, it would be wrong to assume that the growth of applied research has resulted solely from pressure by Lord Rothschild[91] and other external forces of the same persuasion; much of it has been undertaken voluntarily.[92] The CVCP seeks to resolve the argument by suggesting that basic, fundamental research is ultimately more useful for industry than the solution of short-term problems.[93] This kind of argument, which seeks to have the best of both worlds, is one which, as has been demonstrated in earlier chapters, is frequently used by those involved in the political process.

Finally there is the issue of whether teaching and research must necessarily be undertaken by the same individual. For some senior academics the answer is that if teachers were not also researchers 'we would not really have a *university* at all. . . . It is of the essence that the *same* people do both jobs.'[94] However, an entirely opposite view has been expressed by Sir Peter Swinnerton-Dyer, the present Chairman of the UGC; and, at the fourth Leverhulme seminar, the idea that good undergraduate teaching did not require a teacher to be simultaneously a good researcher was one which received wide assent.[95] Whatever the views about the involvement of individual members of staff, the published evidence suggests that virtually all academics agree that in this country an institution which did not undertake research could not reasonably be called a university.[96]

(General arguments for and against research as a university activity – as opposed to academics' views – will be discussed in Chapter 9.)

Teaching

The fear has often been expressed that teaching comes a poor second to research on the British academic's list of priorities.[97] However, Halsey and Trow established that teaching was of great importance to many academics; indeed the most common orientation among respondents to their survey was that of 'elitist teacher'.[98] It is also an undeniable fact that a great deal of teaching goes on in universities; and as Newman pointed out, whether or not the correct purpose of a university is 'to make its students "gentlemen"', still to make them something or other *is* its great object.'[99]

What then do academics consider to be the 'great object' of teaching? Taking a view over the past hundred years or so, Silver argues that the main emphasis has been on liberal education. Technology and vocational subjects have tended to be 'liberalised';[100] the same point about the great tradition of 'personal' education is made with approval by Dancy.[101] Halsey and Trow noted that part of the essence of the 'English idea of a university' is that it offers 'education' and not merely 'training'.[102] They also established that many academics considered that universities overemphasised the single-subject honours degree, and that there was too much emphasis on the training of experts and too little on the education of widely cultivated men.[103]

In the same year that Halsey and Trow's study appeared (1971), Entwistle, Percy and Nisbet published the results of a much smaller survey which provided similar conclusions. The major teaching objective of university academics was found to be to promote 'critical thinking', although the teachers were not always very effective in bringing about the desired result.[104]

As the 1970s passed, there were signs that changes were taking place. In his follow-up survey of 1976, Halsey found that two thirds of university teachers opposed the idea that universities should leave the newer and more vocational subjects to the polytechnics.[105] And by 1981, when the Government's emphasis on the vocational, scientific and technological aspects of education was fully apparent, many of those who believed in the value of the humanities and liberal studies felt that it was time to speak out strongly and to form alliances: a spate of articles and letters to *The Times* followed.[106]

The debate continues. It has been aptly described by Lord Ashby:

> Round every Senate table sit men for whom the word university stands for something unique and precious in European society: a leisurely and urbane attitude to scholarship, exemption from the obligation to use knowledge for practical ends, a sense of perspective which accompanies the broad horizon and the distant view, an opportunity to give undivided loyalty to the kingdom of the mind. At the same Senate table sit men for whom the university is an institution with urgent and essential obligations to modern society; a place to which society entrusts its most intelligent young people and from which it expects to receive its most highly trained citizens; a place which society regards as the pace-maker for scientific research and technological progress. And so universities find themselves searching for a compromise.[107]

The Committee of Vice-Chancellors and Principals

When united, the Committee of Vice-Chancellors and Principals (CVCP) can speak with authority on behalf of British universities. The problem is that the universities themselves differ markedly in many ways, and their variety and autonomy must sometimes – perhaps often – make it difficult to form a common view. However, when there is a fair measure of agreement, and when mutual interests require it, the CVCP makes its views known, sometimes in the form of a booklet, such as those on research and on the links with industry.[108] It is perhaps significant that there is no booklet on goals.[109]

In its 1984 submission to the UGC, in response to the Swinnerton-Dyer questionnaire, the CVCP contented itself by saying that the nature, range and purpose of university activities 'do not require elaboration'.[110] The paper went on to stress that it is the universities' contribution to fundamental research which chiefly distinguishes them from other institutions of higher education. The CVCP also endorsed the DES's statement that 'Non-university education's key contribution lies in its provision of courses specifically designed to reflect the opportunities and requirements of the country's employment market.' Universities, by implication, have other goals. Reference has already been made, in Chapter 4, to the CVCP's rejection, in the same document, of the Government's emphasis on vocationally relevant forms of study.

In 1986 the CVCP published a booklet entitled *The future of the universities*;[111] this was a response to the Government's 1985 Green Paper on higher education, and contained a number of statements which implied support for certain goals. The CVCP declared itself in favour of the following: a broader sixth-form curriculum (paragraph 2.13); balanced and objective teaching (3.19); fundamental research and scholarship (4.3). Graduates, it was argued, should be able to work alone or in groups, to think systematically, and to assemble and examine evidence objectively (paragraph 3.6); more should be done in the teaching process to develop personal skills such as effective oral presentation (3.10).

The students

The Robbins Report quotes Confucius to the effect that it is not easy to find a man who has studied for three years without aiming at pay. There are good reasons for supposing that students' attitudes have not changed much since Confucius's day.[112]

A considerable volume of research has been carried out into what students are looking for when they enter a university. In 1977 Percy and Brennan published the results of a survey based on returns from 2,595 students from 21 institutions.[113] This established that many students had drifted into higher education without clearly formed goals, and that their aspirations tended to be formed as a result of their experiences while at a university.[114] Most students also had multiple goals, giving rise, for example, to a demand for both vocational courses and for extra-curricular activities.[115]

Startup's study of *The university teacher and his world*, published in 1979, presented information about student attitudes based on questionnaires completed by 321 students in one university.[116] One interesting fact to emerge from Startup's work is that the students in his sample rated research very low in importance as one of the duties of academic staff (placing it 11th in a list of 24); activities relating to undergraduate teaching were rated much higher.[117] If this were true of many students it would seem to leave plenty of scope for friction between them and their teachers.

In chapter 4 of his book *Expectations of higher education: some historical pointers*, Harold Silver reviews a number of other surveys of student attitudes, and concludes that a large majority of students see the university's task as preparing them for a definite vocation or occupation.[118] Many staff, on the other hand, are committed to the 'intellectual' purposes of the institution, a situation which provides further ground for potential conflict.[119] Silver also concludes, as did Percy and Brennan, that students' expectations and goals frequently change as a result of their experience of higher education.[120]

As the title of his book indicates, Silver's study was part of the larger Expectations of Higher Education project, the research for which was carried out over the years 1980 to 1983.[121] The project included a survey of students' attitudes based on questionnaires sent to 6,000 students in their final year in 36 institutions (including polytechnics and colleges as well as universities). The survey demonstrated that in most disciplines a high proportion of university undergraduates embarked on their course mainly in order to learn more about a subject which they found particularly interesting; however, an equally high proportion expected a degree to help them to find a job and to increase their earning power.[122] Roughly a quarter of non-sandwich course students would have preferred their course to have been sandwich based,[123] but students generally believed that course content was less important to employers than other factors such as motivation and leadership potential.[124] Finally, a large proportion of students in all kinds of institutions were satisfied with their courses and felt that higher education had fulfilled their expectations.[125]

The National Union of Students is not quite so sanguine. The Union argues in a pamphlet on *The future of the universities* that universities are usually established to meet essentially local educational needs, but over time they become subject to 'academic drift' and lose touch with their origins.[126] What is needed, says the Union, is more inter-disciplinary courses and greater emphasis on teaching, which 'has never been of primary importance in universities.'[127]

Conclusions about the views of stakeholders

This chapter has summarised the available evidence on the views of stakeholder groups as to what the goals of universities should be. The chapter has demonstrated that few groups can claim to have given systematic consideration to the question. The employers have perhaps the most creditable record; the Conservative Party has filled a notable vacuum with the publication of the 1985 Green Paper, the 1987 White Paper, and the Education Reform Bill; but from such bodies as the DES and the CVCP there is mostly silence, at least on the subject of goals. A multiplicity of opinions have been voiced by individuals, most of them critical of the universities' performance, and most critics have urged the universities towards a greater awareness of the needs of industry. These criticisms have occasionally been met with a staunch defence from those who believe that the purpose of a university is not primarily to produce engineers and accountants but to ensure that graduates are civilised, rational individuals.

After I had completed my review of the range of views expressed by the stakeholders, I came to the conclusion that it would be useful to categorise the various possible goals of a university under appropriate headings. Such an analysis would facilitate the kind of discussion about goals, within stakeholder groups, which at present is notably absent. An attempt to provide a catalogue of goals for universities therefore forms the subject matter of the next chapter.

Notes

1 Child, Cooper, Hussell and Webb (1971), page 484.
2 Information provided by Mr Norman Webb, of the Gallup Poll organisation, 7 September 1983.
3 Gallup Poll figures quoted in the Daily Telegraph (1984).
4 See Weaver (1982), pages 68 and 69.
5 See, for instance, Barnett (1979), Handy (1979) and Ashworth (1982).
6 Weaver (1982), page 70.

7 Royal Society of Arts (1982).

8 Association of University Teachers (1982), page 3.

9 Minogue (1973), page 4.

10 Barnett (1979), page 123.

11 For a full account see Silver (1981), chapter 2.

12 Ibid., page 14.

13 McKie (1981).

14 O'Leary (1981).

15 Financial Times (1982).

16 Several reports in *The Times*, e.g. Johnstone (1984).

17 Committee of Vice-Chancellors and Principals (1981).

18 Bacon, Benton and Gruneberg (1979).

19 See Leverhulme Report, volume 1 (*Higher education and the labour market*).

20 Maynard (1983), page 94.

21 Blaug (1982), page 170.

22 Confederation of British Industry (1982), page 27.

23 Ibid., pages 27 and 28.

24 Ibid., page 28.

25 Turney (1983).

26 Kogan and Boys (1983), pages 4 and 7.

27 Calculation based on data in the *Statistical Quarterly*, August 1982 to May 1983, published by the Central Services Unit for university and polytechnic careers and appointments services.

28 Kogan and Boys (1983), page 7.

29 Young (1984), page 456.

30 Thomas (1978), page 7. Kogan and Boys (1983) point out, on page 3 of their report, that it is sometimes difficult to identify who is the spokesman for a particular firm. An editorial in *The Times*, 15 August 1984, also called upon employers to declare, for the first time, whether they wanted 'education' or 'merely technical training'.

31 Finniston (1983), page 369.

32 Standing Conference of Employers of Graduates (1982), page 2.

33 Times Higher Education Supplement (1983d).

34 Kogan and Boys (1983), page 12.

35 Cook (1973), page 9.

36 In 1984 it was argued within the University of Bath that social work and horticulture were subjects more appropriate for a polytechnic. The argument was, however, rejected.

37 Turner and Rushton (1976), page vii.

38 University of Kent (1983), page 7.

39 Ibid., page 8. Further information in this paragraph was supplied by Dr D. B. P. Sims, of the University of Bath.

40 In 1984 the UGC decided not to continue funding the pharmacy department at Heriot-Watt University. The Principal of Heriot-Watt called a meeting of three bodies: the UGC, the University, and the Pharmaceutical Society; presumably he viewed these as equal partners in the enterprise. See Wojtas (1984). Additional information for this paragraph was supplied by Mr J. I. Harris of the University of Bath.

41 Leverhulme Report, final volume (*Excellence in diversity*), page 14. A search of the British Education Index over the last five years revealed an increase in publications on professional education, but nothing at all on the influence of the professional associations.

42 In 1976. Source: Mr R. Wake, a member of Her Majesty's Inspectorate.

43 Flather (1982a).

44 Social Democratic Party (1982).

45 Social Democratic Party (1983).

46 Liberal Party (1977).

47 Ibid., page 3.

48 Ibid., pages 4 and 5.

49 Liberal Party (1984).

50 In a letter to the author, dated 29 January 1982. The Officer added: 'In fact it is a very long time since we can recall that this has been discussed even within educational circles.'

51 Labour Party (1973).

52 Geddes (1981).

53 Foot, Kinnock and Whitehead (1981).

54 Labour Party (1983).

55 Hogg (1982).

56 Jobbins (1983).

57 Parkes (1983), page 2.

58 See Footman (1982), page 7, for a statement to this effect by Mr William Waldegrave, Minister of State responsible for Higher and Further Education. See also Hansard, 21 December 1981, page 763.

59 See Footman (1982), pages 6 and 7. Also Hansard, 18 November 1981, pages 301 and 307.

60 Hansard, 21 December 1981, page 763.

61 O'Leary (1982).

62 Department of Education and Science (1983b).

63 Joseph (1983).

64 Quoted by David (1981b).

65 Joseph (1983).

66 Bradley (1983), page 4.

67 Jobbins (1984).

68 Flather (1984a).

69 Geddes (1981).

70 House of Commons (1980), page xxxv.

71 Ibid.

72 Letter to the author, dated 4 March 1982, from Dr V. J. Delany.

73 Quoted by Footman (1982), page 4.

74 Quoted by Birch and Calvert (1977), page 16.

75 See Collier (1983), page 100, for a summary of Slater and Tapper's views.

76 It forms a triumvirate with the Local Education Authorities and the teachers' unions. Collier (1983), page 99.

77 Information provided by two officers of the UGC, Mr Callaghan, 1982, and Mr Dickerson, 1984.

78 University Grants Committee (1984). See also Times Higher Education Supplement (1984h); the advice offered by the two bodies is fully described in a four-page supplement.

79 Times Higher Education Supplement (1984h), page iv.

80 Ibid., page i.

81 Crequer (1981).

82 Clark (1979), page 31.

83 In a letter to the author, dated 9 February 1984.

84 Halsey and Trow (1971), page 276.
85 Ibid.
86 Ibid., pages 278 and 280.
87 Ibid., page 509.
88 Scott (1982b).
89 The joint working party was set up by the UGC and the Advisory Board for the Research Councils. See Flather (1982b).
90 See Silver (1981), chapter 3.
91 Lord Rothschild produced a report in 1971 which argued that much civil research should be directed towards a specific end. See Cane (1971).
92 Scott (1983e).
93 Committee of Vice-Chancellors and Principals (1981), page 13.
94 The Vice-Chancellor of the University of Oxford, writing in Committee of Vice-Chancellors and Principals (1980), page 9.
95 See Swinnerton-Dyer (1984), page 5, and Flather (1982c).
96 Swinnerton-Dyer (1984), page 5.
97 Scott (1983d).
98 Brennan and Percy (1975), page 115.
99 Quoted by Beard, Healey and Holloway (1970), page 29.
100 Silver (1981), page 24.
101 Dancy (1981).
102 Halsey and Trow (1971), page 67.
103 Ibid., page 488.
104 Entwistle, Percy and Nisbet (1971), page 23.
105 Halsey (1979).
106 See, for example, the following: O'Hea (1981); Dancy (1981); Niblett (1981); Wiseman (1981); and even Ashworth (1982).
107 Ashby (1966), pages 69 and 70.
108 Committee of Vice-Chancellors and Principals (1980) and (1981).
109 In 1972 the CVCP did publish a report of a joint AUT/CVCP conference on *The function of the university – teaching and research*, but that report deals with functions and not with goals; that is to say it deals with means rather than with ends.
110 Committee of Vice-Chancellors and Principals (1984), page 9.
111 Committee of Vice-Chancellors and Principals (1986).
112 The suggestion in Robbins (1963), page 6, is echoed by the findings of the Expectations of Higher Education project; see Kogan and Boys (1983).
113 Percy and Brennan (1977).
114 Ibid., page 2.
115 Ibid., page 4.
116 Startup (1979), page 131.
117 Ibid., page 133.
118 Silver (1981), pages 31, 58 and 60.
119 Ibid., page 33.
120 Ibid., page 70.
121 Kogan and Boys (1983).
122 Ibid., page 5.
123 Ibid., page 6.
124 Ibid., pages 8 and 9.
125 Ibid., page 9.
126 National Union of Students (1981), page 3.
127 Ibid., pages 8 and 9.

8

A Catalogue of Goals for British Universities

Soon after I became interested in the subject of university goals it occurred to me that it would be very useful to have a classified list of potential or actual goals, something like Bloom's taxonomy of educational objectives but with specific reference to higher education. It seemed to me that such a list would be valuable for several reasons. It would make it easier to analyse the operative goals of an institution, and it would also encourage more direct discussion of this issue: with the aid of a catalogue, individuals or groups can familiarise themselves with the range of possibilities and can select the goals which they believe should be given the greatest emphasis.

Having decided that a catalogue of goals would be useful, I began to prepare a list of items to be included: every time I came across a statement of opinion as to what universities should be doing, or were actually doing, I jotted it down.[1] I soon had a list of several hundred statements, even after the obvious duplicates had been discarded. The next stage would have been to arrange the statements in groups, but fortunately I was spared that task. I came across a catalogue of goals which had been assembled, in an American context, by Howard R. Bowen and his associates.[2] In his book *Investment in learning*, Bowen describes how he and his collaborators combed through an extensive range of material on higher education; as a result of this search they assembled a list of 1,500 goal statements which formed the basis of their analysis. I myself found about 450 statements, so the catalogue which follows is now based on an even broader cross-section of opinion than before. I would not wish to claim that I have 'improved' Bowen's catalogue; what I have done is augmented it, altered it and clarified it wherever I considered such changes necessary. I am grateful to Professor Bowen for allowing me to make use of his work in this book. American readers may wish to consult the original version also.

1 The abilities and attitudes of individual students

This section takes the form of a list of abilities and attitudes; in recent years various authorities have declared these to be desirable attributes of students emerging from universities. If the authorities do not say so directly, they strongly imply that the goals of universities should be to instil the desired attitudes and to ensure that students acquire the desired skills. However, it is not suggested by any one authority that all students should invariably possess all these characteristics.

1.1 Cognitive learning

1.1.1 Verbal skills

Ability to comprehend through listening, reading and doing.
Ability to speak and write clearly, correctly, fluently, gracefully.
Ability to organise ideas and to present them in writing and in discussion; ability to argue a case.
Knowledge of more than one language.

1.1.2 Quantitative skills

Ability to understand statistical data and statistical reasoning.
Ability to use computers.

1.1.3 Substantive knowledge

1.1.3.1 A broad acquaintance with the cultural heritage of the west and of the student's own nation in particular, together with some knowledge of, and respect for, other traditions.

1.1.3.2 Broad awareness of the history and contemporary features of the worlds of philosophy, natural science, technology, art, literature and the social sciences.

1.1.3.3 A deep and detailed knowledge of one or more specific subjects, particularly in connection with training for the professions.

1.1.4 Rationality

Recognition of the importance of thinking logically; the ability so to do.
Ability and disposition to weigh evidence, to evaluate facts and ideas critically, and to think independently; ability to form prudent judgements and to make decisions; ability to decide whether strong emotional reactions are justified by facts or events.
Ability to analyse and synthesise; ability and disposition to solve problems; ability to plan ahead.

1.1.5 Intellectual perspective

Willingness to question orthodoxy and to consider new ideas.
Intellectual curiosity.
Appreciation of cultural diversity.
Ability to view events and developments in a historical and cosmopolitan perspective.
Understanding of the limitations of science and philosophy.

1.1.6   Aesthetic sensibility

Note: aesthetic sensibility is often classified under emotional development rather than cognitive learning, but since large elements of aesthetic awareness can be taught, it is included in the cognitive section of this analysis.

Knowledge of, interest in, and responsiveness to, literature, the arts, and natural beauty.

Appreciation of style; development of taste.

Participation in the arts.

1.1.7   Creativity

Imagination and originality in formulating new hypotheses and ideas, and in producing works of art.

1.1.8   Intellectual integrity

Disposition to seek and speak the truth.

Conscientiousness of inquiry and accuracy in reporting the outcomes of inquiries.

1.1.9   Lifelong learning

Awareness of the value of scholarship, research, and education.

Ability to undertake self-directed learning; ability to locate information when needed; capacity to benefit from in-service training and continuing education.

1.2   Emotional and moral development

1.2.1   Self-awareness

Knowledge of one's own talents, interests, aspirations and weaknesses.

1.2.2   Psychological well-being

Sensitivity to deep feelings and emotions and ability to cope with them: emotional stability and resilience.

Ability to express emotions constructively.

Self-confidence; spontaneity.

Ability to enjoy life despite its vicissitudes.

1.2.3   Human understanding

Capacity for empathy, thoughtfulness, compassion, respect, and tolerance – towards all others regardless of background.

Ability to co-operate.

1.2.4   Values and morals

Awareness of moral issues.

Awareness of traditional moral values.

A personal set of values and moral principles; capacity to make moral decisions.

Sense of social responsibility.
Conscientiousness; honesty.

1.2.5   Religion
An awareness of, and respect for, the varieties of religious thought.
The foundations of a personal world-view.

1.3   Practical competence

1.3.1   Traits of value in practical affairs generally
Ability to apply knowledge in order to solve practical problems.
Motivation towards accomplishment.
Initiative, energy, persistence, self-discipline.
Ability to cope with change; resourcefulness in coping with crises.
Capacity to learn from experience.
Ability to negotiate and willingness to compromise.

1.3.2   Leadership
Capacity to win the confidence of others.
Willingness to assume responsibility.
Readiness to seek advice.

1.3.3   Citizenship
Understanding of and commitment to democracy.
Knowledge of the major political philosophies.
Knowledge of governmental institutions and procedures.
Awareness of social issues and knowledge of current affairs.
Respect for, and knowledge of, the law.
Commitment to justice and peace.

1.3.4   Work and careers
An awareness of the needs of industry and commerce (through direct experi-
    ence).
Ability to make sound career decisions.
Knowledge and skills directly relevant to first employment.
Adaptability.

1.3.5   Family life
Personal qualities relevant to the maintenance of a satisfying family life.

1.3.6   Leisure
Capacity to maintain an appropriate balance between work, leisure, and other
    activities.
Resourcefulness in finding rewarding uses of leisure time.

1.3.7 Health
Understanding of the basic principles of physical and mental health.
Participation in sport and physical recreation.

2 The needs of society

This section lists in broad outline a series of goals relating to the needs of society and the world in general; as before, the sources consulted have suggested that these needs should be met by the universities.

2.1 Knowledge

2.1.1　To preserve all the knowledge which has so far been accumulated, through scholarship, publications, libraries, museums, and other means.
2.1.2　To disseminate such knowledge as is required to achieve the goals listed in section 1 of this catalogue.
2.1.3　To discover new knowledge through research, both pure and applied.
2.1.4　To apply knowledge, both old and new, to the solution of practical problems in industry and commerce and in society at large. To do so both by invitation, as in contract research, and spontaneously, through individual members of the university acting as social critics.

2.2 The arts

To act as a centre of the arts for the benefit of both students and the surrounding community, through the provision of lectures, concerts, plays, exhibitions, and other means.

2.3 The discovery and development of talent

2.3.1　To identify those individuals with particular skills which are needed and valued by society; to develop those skills; and to certify the level of skill which has been achieved by each student.
2.3.2　To provide the skilled manpower which is necessary for the maintenance and growth of national productivity.
2.3.3　To offer opportunities for study to all those who seek a university education (including those from overseas), whether possessing formal qualifications or not, whether rich or poor, on either a part-time or full-time basis.
2.3.4　To provide continuing education courses, both vocational and non-vocational.

2.4 The university experience

To provide direct satisfaction and enjoyment for employees, students and other participants in university life.

There are a number of comments to be made about the catalogue given above. The first is that it does not include all imaginable goals. For example, it would be perfectly possible to propose that a university should teach students how to kill enemies of the state; but in fact I have never seen such a suggestion in print and it is therefore not in the catalogue.

A second point is that the catalogue concentrates on ends, not means. For example, it may be argued that in order to develop human understanding (section 1.2.3) it is desirable to arrange for students to live in halls of residence rather than at home or scattered throughout the community. But in Gross and Grambsch's terms the goal of setting up halls of residence is a process goal, rather than a primary goal, and it is therefore not listed here. The same point could be made about fund-raising and many other important university activities.

Perhaps I should also emphasise, lest there be any doubt, that not all the goals are applicable to every university or to every student: no university, however conscientious or prestigious, could achieve the miracle of transforming every graduate into a creature possessing all the attributes listed in section 1. Some of the goals are in any case controversial.

The list appears to place heavy emphasis on students, while research occupies only one line (section 2.1.3). This illustrates the point that the space devoted to the various goals is not intended to be proportionate to their importance.

Anyone who reads the catalogue thoughtfully will notice that it interlocks and overlaps: for example, many of the cognitive abilities are useful or even essential in achieving the goals relating to emotional and moral development. There is also no compelling reason why the catalogue should begin with the abilities and attitudes of students and proceed to the needs of society: the order could easily be reversed.

The catalogue is very much of its time and place; a similar list, prepared a hundred years ago, would have been very different. The present list is surprisingly short: Bowen comments on the frequency with which the same ideas recur in the work of those who write on the subject.[3] It is also overwhelmingly 'civilised', in the sense that it is suffused with western/Christian/democratic values; this is not surprising, considering that the ideas are drawn from British and American sources, or from writers who have been influential within those two nations. The emphasis is on peace, culture and tolerance, not on war, conflict and dogmatism. The perspective is international, with scarcely a hint of patriotism. Religion, which was once central to the early universities, now occupies a much less important position, and there is no suggestion that students must hold a particular set of religious beliefs.

The catalogue can be used as it stands, but it is capable of further development. For example, a computer program could be written which would enable sixth-formers to choose the goals which they considered most important. The program could then give them guidance on the courses, universities or extra-curricular activities which would best enable them to achieve their goals.

At first glance it may appear that there is little in the catalogue which could reasonably be rejected as a goal; but in fact, buried within some apparently innocuous phrases, there are a number of historically controversial issues. Six of those issues will be considered in detail in the next chapter.

Notes

1 All the books and papers listed in the reference section were included in this process. In addition, a considerable number of books, papers, etc. which are not referred to directly in the text were also surveyed. Statements made during the course of interviews were also included.
2 Bowen (1977a), pages 53 to 59.
3 Bowen (1977a), page 53.

9

Six Controversial Issues in Relation to University Goals

In previous chapters, notably those on the philosophy of higher education, the history of British universities, and the views of the stakeholders, I have provided ample evidence to show that there have always been differences of opinion as to what the goals of a university should be. The aim of this chapter is to identify six areas of controversy which I consider to be particularly important in the late 1980s and to examine them in more detail.

The six issues which I have selected are closely related to the principal functions of universities, which are usually described as teaching, research and public service. The issues have been chosen (1) because differences of opinion on each of them reflect differences of opinion on the underlying goals, (2) because arguments about them have persisted over many decades, and (3) because in a time of shrinking resources the debate about them is likely to become particularly acute.

The six issues are summarised below; each is then considered separately.

Teaching: (1) whether courses should be liberal or vocational; and (2) whether they should be broad-based or specialised.

Research: (1) whether research is an essential function of a university or not; and (2) whether it should be pure or applied.

The role of academic staff: (1) whether a lecturer should argue a particular point of view or should allow students to form their own conclusions; and (2) in relation to society, whether a lecturer should adopt a passive 'civil servant' role, or be an active critic and an instigator of change.

Courses: liberal or vocational?

In earlier chapters I have described briefly what constitutes a liberal (or a liberal arts) education but it will be useful as this stage to examine the concept more closely.

A lecturer at Oxford in 1914 has been quoted as follows:

Nothing that you will learn in the course of your studies will be the slightest possible use to you in after life – save only this – that if you work hard and intelligently you should be able to detect *when a man is talking rot*, and that, in my view, is the main, if not the sole purpose of education.[1]

That is the liberal philosophy in an extreme form. Likewise John Stuart Mill:

Universities are not intended to teach knowledge required to fit men for some special mode of making their livelihood. Their object is not to make skilful lawyers, or physicians, or engineers, but capable and cultivated human beings.[2]

The aim of liberal courses is thus to make students familiar with the 'heritage of Western civilisation'[3] and to create a community of wise and tolerant individuals. With reference to the catalogue given in Chapter 8, liberal courses may be said to emphasise the goals listed in the following paragraphs: 1.1.3.1 and 1.1.3.2 (substantive knowledge), 1.1.4 (rationality), 1.1.5 (intellectual perspective) and 1.1.9 (lifelong learning). Many courses will also seek to develop aesthetic sensibility (1.1.6), creativity (1.1.7), intellectual integrity (1.1.8) and some of the goals listed in the section on emotional and moral development (1.2). Most supporters of the liberal philosophy would also maintain that the experience of taking a course based on these principles will develop leadership, citizenship, and the skills needed for the use of leisure and a satisfactory family life. Thus the goals of liberal courses are multiple: it is the shotgun approach as compared with the rifle.

The distinction between liberal and vocational courses is definitely not a distinction between courses in the humanities and in the sciences, though there has been a tendency to think so.[4] A vocational course might best be described as one which equips a student for employment (usually first employment) and thus contributes to successful economic performance. In extreme cases the course is the only route to certification of the right to practise as a member of a given profession (for instance pharmacy); for this reason it is sometimes argued that the more appropriate term is professional education.[5]

A vocational course will often require a student to absorb a large amount of factual information. More sophisticated vocational courses will also be designed to develop the behavioural traits (or transferable skills) which are known to be essential to satisfy the demands of employers: leadership, adaptability, negotiating ability, initiative, etc. The emphasis, however, will be on practice rather than theory. Referring to the catalogue given in Chapter 8, vocational courses will tend to emphasise the goals listed in paragraphs 1.1.3.3 (knowledge of specific subjects), 1.3.1 (traits of value in practical affairs generally), 1.3.2 (leadership), and 1.3.4 (work and careers).

Some implications of the two contrasting philosophies are worth noting. The first is that support for the vocational type of course involves an acknowledgement of the right of employers, professional bodies and the state to have a measure of control over the institutions providing the courses: academic autonomy is weakened, but the case for state funding is strengthened. The converse applies to the liberal philosophy: academics who take advantage of their autonomy to design a course which pays no heed to the requirements of

employers, professional associations or the state can, of course, please themselves as to what they include in it; but it may be harder to persuade the taxpayer
to foot the bill.

It can be argued that the distinction between liberal and vocational courses is
unreal, in that those students who undergo a liberal education can successfully
tackle anything. Thus Dr John Kemeny, President of Dartmouth College in the
USA, claims that he was able to make a contribution to computer science not
because he had ever been trained in the use of computers (there were none in his
youth), but because of 'the breadth of a liberal arts education I was fortunate
enough to acquire, because of learning to think in a certain way, and having
been prepared to react to totally unexpected challenges.'[6] Another American,
Sterling McMurrin, argues that a 'liberal education as now conceived is not
useless and impractical, as many still insist. On the contrary, it is eminently
practical, as it is essential to the pursuit not only of numerous vocations but of
the full, satisfying life as well.'[7] It can also be argued that the best vocational
courses must of necessity cover a good deal of liberal territory, because a
good general education is an asset in many professions; some employers
are not interested in a graduate's subject but only in his overall intellectual
skills.

There is some truth in both these arguments, and, clearly, liberal and
vocational courses do overlap to some extent. However, I can only say that in
my view they are fundamentally as different as chalk and cheese. After all,
lumps of chalk and cheese have some characteristics in common: they both
contain calcium and carbon; they may both be yellow (or white); they may both
weigh a pound; but if you take a bite out of each you will surely be convinced that
they are different.

Courses: broad-based or specialised?

Historically, there has been a link between liberal arts education and the broad
course. Defenders of the liberal philosophy often argue that degree courses
should not be too specialised but should provide an understanding of several
different fields of knowledge.[8]

There is no corresponding tradition that vocational courses must necessarily
be specialised. In practice many of them evidently are, and the calls from some
sections of industry to include larger amounts of practical knowledge may
increase the tendency. However, it is now well understood that much of the
practical information which is being taught in universities will become obsolete
within a decade; even for vocational purposes it may be preferable to reduce the
amount of hard fact which the student is expected to absorb and to concentrate
on developing skills, such as the ability to undertake self-directed learning. One
vocation for which the single-subject honours degree is still eminently suitable
is, of course, the academic profession.

The Robbins Committee was very much in favour of an increase in the
number of students taking broad-based degrees, and the call for greater breadth

was echoed by the Leverhulme Inquiry.[9] The Leverhulme solution was for less specialisation in the sixth-form and in the early years of higher education;[10] the universities obviously have a massive influence on the schools in that schools will try to equip pupils for university entry. The Leverhulme proposal for a modification of the sixth-form curriculum was generally welcomed by the universities,[11] but in the responses to the Swinnerton-Dyer questionnaire of 1983 not one university favoured the Leverhulme concept of two-year broad-based degree courses. Many considered that an opening-out of sixth-form studies could only be achieved by extending degree courses to four years.[12] The CVCP has supported this view,[13] but it seems highly unlikely that financial support for such a development will be forthcoming.

Once again, it can be argued that the distinction between broad-based and specialised courses is a false one, in that both can constitute a route to the same goal, whether it be liberal or vocational. This is perhaps marginally more convincing than the argument that liberal courses will equip students for the world of work and that vocational courses can provide a good general education. Nevertheless it is clearly the case that a student who has taken a broad-based degree course will have a very different frame of reference from a student who has specialised in perhaps one area of one discipline. It is also the case that different goals can be achieved much more easily by the different types of course. For example, an ability to view events in a historical and cosmopolitan perspective (paragraph 1.1.5 in the catalogue of goals in Chapter 8) is more likely to be developed by a broad-based history course than by a highly specialised one. Consequently I myself take the view that the decision to offer (or to take) a broad-based as opposed to a specialised degree course is one which is ultimately based on a conscious or unconscious choice between different sets of goals.

Research: for or against?

Should research be carried out in universities or not? That is the question which this section addresses, and as we have seen it has been a matter of some debate historically. In 1987 the discussion became quite heated following publication of the ABRC report, *A strategy for the science base*, which advocated a three-tier university system; if that proposal were implemented, only about fifteen universities would be fully funded for research.

Society demonstrably has a certain need for research, as described in paragraphs 2.1.3 and 2.1.4 in the catalogue of goals in Chapter 8. The USA and the USSR are agreed on the importance of science and technology to economic and social development, if on nothing else. But before considering the arguments for and against research being undertaken within universities, it may be useful to recall the distinction between research and scholarship. Broadly speaking, scholarship means keeping up with the latest developments in a subject, while research means developing new knowledge.[14] There is some overlap between the two activities, and it is easier to make the distinction in the natural sciences than in the arts,[15] but in principle they are clearly different.[16] University charters and other publications often refer to 'the advancement of learning' and the 'advancement of knowledge'; it would be helpful if the former term were always used as a synonym for scholarship and the latter for research, but it seems unlikely that this has been the case in the past.

Various different kinds of research can readily be identified: pure (or fundamental) and applied research, for example; more will be said about these two categories in the next section. It can also be argued that strategic research deals with policy questions while tactical research deals with short-term problem-solving.[17] Charles Carter has described ten different kinds of research, including theory construction, observing and chronicling, experimenting, and others.[18]

The evidence suggests that, on average, academics in British universities currently spend about one third of their time on research;[19] the AUT puts the figure at one third to a half.[20] This research is funded from two main sources in a 'dual-support' system: the basic funding is provided by the UGC in its recurrent grant to universities, and additional funds are provided, for selected projects, by the Research Councils.[21]

The volume of research undertaken in universities has increased markedly since 1945, and its place in universities is well established. Indeed, in view of the current emphasis on research within the university community, it would be easy to assume that the bulk of the nation's research is carried out there, and that nothing of consequence is done elsewhere. The CVCP claims that universities provide 'most of the fundamental and a very considerable amount of the applied research undertaken in the United Kingdom, and are responsible for the initial research training of virtually all research workers.'[22] The situation can, however, be viewed from a very different perspective. In a paper presented to one of the Leverhulme seminars, Dr Stuart Blume, of the London School of Economics, pointed out that research in higher education amounts to only 10 per cent of the national research effort.[23] In 1982 a government minister informed a House of Lords Select Committee that the universities' contribution to research amounted to only 5 per cent of the total;[24] this estimate was recently confirmed by a Vice-Chairman of the UGC.[25]

The point to be considered here, however, is not the precise volume of research undertaken within universities, but whether *any* research should be undertaken in that context; after all, in some nations, notably Russia, research is carried on in institutes which have no connection with universities.[26] The main argument in favour of maintaining research in universities is that it improves the quality of teaching; it is claimed that the academic who is at the cutting-edge of his subject is the one best qualified to teach.[27] To believe otherwise is often considered heretical, but the Leverhulme study was agnostic on the issue of whether research and good undergraduate teaching are indivisible.[28] Sir Peter Swinnerton-Dyer and Charles Carter are two eminent academics who also doubt whether there is any necessary connection between teaching and research;[29] and as Christopher Ball has pointed out, it is difficult to maintain that proper teaching can only be carried out against a background of research when at least 50 per cent of British students obtain their degrees from poly-technics and colleges which are funded for teaching only.

From a practical point of view it is often alleged, and widely believed, that academic staff have a contractual obligation to do research.[30] Interestingly enough, the present Chairman of the UGC (Sir Peter Swinnerton-Dyer) has stated publicly that while every university teacher has a duty to pursue scholarship, none has a duty to do research.[31] In summary then, it seems possible that what once appeared to be a united academic front on the issue of research as a function of universities may now be beginning to crack. It remains to be seen what developments will result from the UGC's new policy of funding research on a selective basis and from the ABRC report. It seems likely that before long some departments, if not whole universities, will be funded for teaching only.[32] However, to remove the function of research from all univer-sities seems most unlikely to be recommended by anyone in the near future, and would be very difficult to achieve in practice.

Research: pure or applied?

Pure research (sometimes called basic or fundamental research) is concerned with exploring the unknown, mainly for the sheer satisfaction of doing so: the researcher follows up lines of inquiry which interest him and leaves to others the areas which do not interest him. Applied research, by contrast, is directed at solving problems which have arisen in everyday life, often in an industrial or commercial context. Pure researchers have to apply to Research Councils and persuade them to part with funds. Applied researchers are mainly approached by outside bodies and are offered money in return for seeking a solution to a specific problem. In a famous report published in 1971, Lord Rothschild argued that applied research should by definition have a customer.[33]

The CVCP claims that 'most of' the fundamental research which is under-taken in the United Kingdom is carried out in the universities; the Merrison report estimates that the proportion is two thirds, and the UGC settles for 'over half'.[34] Blume claims that the total amount of fundamental research undertaken in this country is comparatively small,[35] and it is sometimes suggested that Lord Rothschild's influence is to blame.[36]

Historically, pure research was often undertaken by wealthy gentlemen at their own expense, and politicians are sometimes reluctant to spend the taxpayers' money on it today. However, the CVCP argues that there are three major grounds for the support of pure research: (1) its essential role in providing the basic understanding of man's natural and social environment; (2) its function of generating and testing creative ideas which may turn out to have important applications; and (3) the part played in the stimulation and edu-cation of students.[37] Examples of pure research projects which turned out to have important practical applications are the splitting of the atom and the discovery of DNA.[38] It is also noteworthy that if Gregor Mendel had had to apply for a research grant for his work on genetics it might well have been entitled 'How to segregate round from wrinkled peas'. This would scarcely be an obvious candidate for support, and yet the practical value of his work has been enormous.[39]

The case for applied research needs little elaboration, but just as pure research can have practical results, so the applied variety can yield fundamental insights and new knowledge. Irving Langmuir's Nobel-Prize-winning work on surface chemistry began as an effort to improve light bulbs; Louis Pasteur's work on microbiology began as a consultancy for the French beer industry; and Arno Penzias and Robert Wilson were able to learn more about the origins of the universe by using a radio antenna designed for satellite communications.[40]

These arguments that pure research can yield practical results and that applied research can generate fundamental knowledge are reminiscent of the arguments that liberal and vocational courses can lead to the same ends, and to me they are equally unconvincing. The facts are that most pure research is significantly different in purpose from most applied research. Pure research is individualistic: its guiding principle is the interest and satisfaction of the researcher. Applied research is collectivist in the sense that it has the interests of society at heart; it could perfectly well be undertaken by a disciplined researcher who cordially disliked the activity but who regarded it as a job to be done. Pure research takes a long view; applied research concentrates on the problems close at hand. In recent years, opinion outside the universities appears to have favoured the applied variety.

Lecturers: expository or didactic style?

The fifth controversial issue relates to the teaching role of lecturers.

There are some facts about which there is virtually no dispute. For example, we can identify two chemicals which, if mixed together at a certain temperature, will explode. When teaching students about these two chemicals, a lecturer will tell 'the truth': that is to say, he will inform the students that under certain specified conditions, mixing these two chemicals together will cause an explosion with the accompanying risk of injury or death.

In many cases, however, a lecturer will find himself teaching students about subjects which are open to dispute. In history, for example, there may be conflicting accounts of events; in medicine there may be opposing views about the best way to treat a patient's illness; and in management studies we come across contrasting styles of leadership for business enterprises. What is the lecturer to do then? Is he to explain the issues as fully as possible, and allow students to make up their own minds? Or is he to persuade students to accept the view which he himself considers to be the right or best one? In other words, should a lecturer adopt what we might call an expository style, or a didactic style?

There is a long-standing tradition in British academic life that, whenever controversial material is being dealt with, the lecturer has a moral responsibility to present both sides of the issue objectively.[41] Despite the argument that security of tenure is provided for academic staff so that they should not be inhibited from expressing unpopular views, there seems to be great resistance to the idea that freedom of expression extends to a right to convert students to a particular point of view. A recent survey of the general public showed that one in two of those questioned believed that homosexuals, 'revolutionaries' and 'racist extremists' should be barred from teaching in higher education.[42] There seems to be a widespread reluctance, on the part of both the teachers and the taught, to get involved in discussions of values.

In practice, presenting a neutral point of view may not be easy. Dr Paul Hirst, of the University of London Institute of Education, has described how some of his students criticise him for not 'coming clean at the outset'. He suggests that a lecturer's best plan may be 'to explore ideological issues as widely as possible, state his own position, and assess students' responses as neutrally as possible.'[43]

The acuteness of the lecturer's dilemma varies from subject to subject, but politics, religion, medicine and social studies all provide difficult situations. The lecturer may believe passionately that a particular view is the right one; but he has to make a second judgement, of a moral nature. Should he seek to persuade or convert his students, or should he content himself with placing the facts before them? As has been the case in all the other issues discussed in this chapter, the lecturer's decision will ultimately reflect a conscious or unconscious judgement about the goals of university education.

Lecturers: passive or active role?

The last of the six controversial issues I wish to consider in this chapter concerns the relationship between academic staff and society as a whole.

The view has often been advanced in recent years that one of the services which universities can render is to provide serious and direct criticism of the society of which they are a part.[44] Indeed, by virtue of the fact that they produce new knowledge, universities can be said to be almost inevitably subversive, in that they alter the status quo; and as noted above, one of the functions of tenure has been to make academics immune from penalty or pressure when expressing unpopular views.[45] If the 1987 Education Reform Bill becomes law, and tenure is abolished without some compensatory legislation on academic freedom, the whole context in which criticism takes place may change.

The Carnegie Commission explored this issue in some depth,[46] and concluded that the so-called 'critical function' of universities involves three activities: (1) developing in students a capacity to think critically; (2) allowing individual members of the university to act as social critics; and (3) the taking of direct action against society by the university itself (which the Commission opposed).[47]

The idea that academic staff might adopt the role of active critic and instigator of change is a comparatively recent one. The earliest universities were monastic in origin; the teachers in them remained unmarried and uninvolved in public or civil life.[48] Today, however, a member of academic staff has a choice of roles. If he has a high reputation in his field he may be approached by government bodies or commercial organisations for information and advice. He may choose to sit passively and wait for such approaches, and when they arrive he may adopt an expository stance: that is to say, he may provide information, set out both sides of the issue, and generally act as a British civil servant is traditionally supposed to act, leaving the policy decision to others. However, it is equally possible for an academic to adopt a much more positive stance; furthermore, he need not limit himself to the areas of his professional expertise. This active role would involve not just the presentation of neutral facts but the arguing of a forceful case with all the tools available for that purpose. In some cases it could involve direct political action, such as standing for office, participating in demonstrations, or even breaking a law which was considered unjust. In the past, many important social changes have resulted from just such activities: gains in women's rights and improved conditions for workers are obvious examples.

Universities vary in their attitude to the academic as social critic. Some try to maintain a policy of 'civic celibacy' by restricting participation in extra-mural activities; others expect their academic staff to take their civic responsibilities seriously.[49] In an editorial published in 1984, *The Times Higher Education Supplement* urged that the critical role of universities should be reaffirmed, claiming that 'higher education can fairly be described as a system of institutionalised subversion.'[50]

Academic staff themselves vary in the extent to which they are prepared to become involved in 'social action': as a result of their training, scientists tend to be particularly reluctant to express an opinion unless they are absolutely sure of their facts. In a paper based on Australian experience, Martin argues that most social activists are not academics but students and ex-students, with a sprinkling of junior staff.[51] This is in a sense surprising, because, as Martin points out, academics are well placed to identify social problems and to take effective steps towards finding solutions. Martin suggests that one reason for academic reluctance to become involved is that those who do are passed over for promotion or are penalised in other ways. Nevertheless, he suggests that academic staff are on average more active in this respect than some other groups, such as company executives.

An academic is a citizen, and he is therefore just as entitled as anyone else to play a part in the discussion of social issues. But the academic is also an expert in a particular field of study, and as such he has the potential to make a more significant contribution than most citizens. What the academic will always have to decide is whether, in relation to society, he will adopt a passive or an active role.

General conclusions about the six controversial issues

This chapter has described six controversial issues in relation to university goals. In drawing conclusions from the above sections I am not going to suggest that there is any 'right' view about any of the six issues; powerful arguments can be put forward on either side. However, I am convinced by the arguments that organisations which are united around an agreed set of goals are likely to be more efficient and more effective than organisations which are continually at war with themselves and with their environment: I believe that this is as true of universities as of any other organisation. In my view it would create severe difficulties for a university if the attitudes of the various groups within it, towards any of the six issues described in this chapter, were markedly different. It would create even more difficulties if the attitudes of those within the university differed significantly from the views of the politicians and the taxpayers who (in the United Kingdom at any rate) provide the bulk of the funds.

It may be argued that, in practice, severe differences of opinion between such groups do not occur. Students who seek a vocational education do not go to a university with a 'liberal' ethos; teachers who do not wish to undertake research are prevented from joining the staff of a university in the first place. The essence of these arguments is that the continuing political process ensures that the views of the stakeholders in any particular university are in a state of equilibrium; any differences of opinion which do occur will be marginal and will merely serve to make minor adjustments to what is basically an agreed set of goals.

There is much sense in these arguments: universities often do develop an individual character which is readily recognisable. But the earlier chapters of this book show that there was a large post-war growth in universities. That growth was followed by a gradual loss of faith in higher education on the part of society as whole; in recent years the public's attitude has been made manifest in a serious reduction in university funding. Ample evidence has also been provided to show that there are not only differences of opinion between those who work in universities and those outside it, but also within universities. Consequently, any group which has views on university goals which it wishes to see implemented would be well advised to find out what the views of other influential groups are, and to monitor changes in opinion as they develop. Those who do not take this precaution are likely to receive some unpleasant shocks, as was the case in those universities which were hardest hit by the 1981 cuts.

There are a number of ways in which interested parties can obtain information about the views of stakeholder groups. One way is to review the official statements of such groups, and to interview some of their members; I myself took a number of such steps in the course of writing this book, and the results have been described in earlier chapters. One other significant means of obtaining information is to sample opinion through the use of a questionnaire, a technique which I have also used. It may be useful, therefore, to summarise the results of that research.[52]

Research into attitudes towards the six issues

In 1984 I devised a questionnaire which was intended to measure the attitudes of certain stakeholder groups towards the six issues which have been described in this chapter. The primary aim was to establish the extent to which the views of the various groups differed from each other.

I decided that it would be interesting, and perhaps useful, to test the views of certain groups within the University of Bath (where I am currently employed). As a contrast to those opinions I also decided to test the same groups within a university which was as different as possible from my home university.

The University of Bath was founded in 1966 and was formerly a College of Advanced Technology. Not surprisingly, it retains a heavy bias towards science and technology, with Engineering being one of the largest Schools. Only one third of the students study arts subjects, and the arts courses which are on offer are notably limited in scope: it is not possible to take a degree in History or English, for example. About 60 per cent of the students are taking sandwich courses, and the University's Charter calls upon it to work in close association with industry and commerce; few of the University's graduates experience any difficulty in finding employment. In summary, the courses offered by the University of Bath may be said to be largely vocational. Academic staff are strongly encouraged to undertake research; given the terms of the Charter, applied research is just as acceptable as pure.

The Comparator University (which wishes to remain anonymous) is about the same age and size as the University of Bath, but it is situated in the east of England. Two thirds of its students are taking 'arts' subjects, and no sandwich courses are offered. English, law and history are the major disciplines, and the first year of study is broad-based, enabling students to delay the choice of their final specialisations. There are no courses in technological subjects, and graduates of this University find it harder to get jobs than do Bath students. In its response to the 1983 UGC questionnaire, the Comparator University placed great emphasis on inter-disciplinary study, on the pursuit of truth and sound learning, and on the development of critical judgement. The University stated that 'the main task of a university is not to provide a vocational training but rather to teach students to think with a rigour which will stand them in good stead later in life.'

These two universities were *not* selected, I must emphasise, because they were considered to be representative of the system as a whole; the results of the survey do not give a guide to what similar groups at other universities may or may not have been thinking.

In the spring of 1984 my questionnaire was administered to samples of the following eight groups:

Academic staff in the University of Bath and the Comparator University.
First-year students in the University of Bath and the Comparator University.
Conservative and Labour Members of Parliament (MPs).
Employers who recruit from the University of Bath and the Comparator University.

Those who filled in the questionnaire were asked to indicate what they thought a university *should be* doing, rather than what any particular university actually was doing at the time. Response rates were gratifyingly high, averaging

85 per cent for all groups except the MPs. The response rates for Conservative and Labour MPs were 40 and 48 per cent respectively, which is theoretically on the low side; however, given the severe difficulty of persuading MPs to fill in forms of any kind, these returns must be counted a success. Replies were received from a number of leading politicians on both sides of the House, including a former Secretary of State for Education and Science.

The results of the research project can be summarised as follows.

Courses: liberal or vocational?

All groups tended to favour liberal rather than vocational courses, with Labour MPs being the most liberal and Conservative MPs very close to preferring vocational. Sixty per cent of all respondents agreed that the main aim of university degree courses should be to produce well rounded human beings; similarly just over half the respondents disagreed with the statement that a university degree course should prepare a student for a specific career. Among Labour MPs (the most 'liberal' of all the groups), only one respondent (out of 36) had a mean score indicating that he favoured vocational courses. Both groups of employers were clearly unenthusiastic about what might be called a crudely vocational approach.

Courses: broad-based or specialised?

All groups except Conservative MPs showed a slight preference for broad-based courses. Labour MPs were more in favour of broad-based courses than was any other group, only two of them (out of 36) favouring specialised courses. Conservative MPs' views fell just within the 'specialised' range.

Research: for or against?

All eight sample groups were in favour of universities undertaking research, some of them heavily in favour: this was particularly true of the two sets of academic staff and the Comparator employers. Out of 440 respondents, only three agreed with the statement that 'Universities should not be concerned with research'.

While there was overwhelming support for research as an activity to be undertaken within universities, there was less agreement about the extent to which each individual lecturer needs to be involved. The statement that 'A university lecturer can be very good at his job without discovering any new facts about his subject at all' produced a very varied response; there were 176 respondents on the 'disagree' side, 199 on the 'agree' side, and 62 respondents with mixed feelings.

Research: pure or applied?

All but one of the eight sample groups considered that research should preferably be of the applied variety: only the academic staff at the Comparator University preferred 'pure' research. Both sets of students were more 'applied' than their teachers. Eighty-four per cent of all respondents agreed that scientists in universities should be concerned with the practical problems of industry. The Conservative MPs were the most 'applied' group of all.

Lecturers: expository or didactic style?

The questionnaire statements about the lecturer's relationship with students clearly touched on a sensitive subject. All the sample groups were very much in favour of an 'expository' style for academic staff: that is to say, they preferred lecturers to explain both sides of controversial issues without attempting to persuade students to support one side rather than the other. Ninety-two per cent of all respondents agreed that a lecturer should allow students to form their own conclusions.

Lecturers: passive or active role?

All groups except Conservative MPs preferred an active to a passive role for academic staff in relation to society: that is to say, in broad terms, they preferred lecturers to be prepared to become involved in public controversy. However, there was greater disagreement on this point, both within the sample groups and between the groups, than on any other issue. The gap between Conservative MPs and Labour MPs was the largest found on any of the issues, and within some groups, such as the Bath employers, there was a wide spread of opinion.

The one thing that was absolutely clear was that the Conservative MPs who completed the questionnaire certainly did not want any smart-alec academics telling them what to do.

Comments

I must repeat that the results summarised above provide no guide to what academic staff, or students or employers, were thinking across the nation as a whole. Nevertheless, the implications of the research findings are really rather interesting; I have explored them in detail elsewhere[53] but it is worth making a few comments here.

The survey results on the issue of whether research is an essential activity for a university or not represent an unqualified triumph for the research lobby. First-year students and employers might well have been expected to be relatively unconcerned and uninformed about research; in fact, like everyone else, they were in favour of it. Both sets of MPs were also surprisingly convinced that research is an appropriate function for universities.

The results on the choice of an expository or didactic style for lecturers illustrate a potential source of danger for all universities. The level of agreement on this issue is so high, and opinion is centred at a point so far towards the end of the scale, that the few exceptions to the general rule are likely to stand out all the more clearly and may well prove of interest to the news media. The most obvious risk is that a dedicated and stubborn Marxist will attract the attention of those who fear political indoctrination of that particular variety. A report submitted to the Secretary of State for Education and Science in 1985 suggested that a body should be set up which would recommend the withdrawal of state funding from institutions which engage in 'blatant indoctrination'.[54]

Finally, it seems to me that the issue of the academic's role in relation to society is particularly important, because in the past certain universities have been damaged by bad publicity to an extent which was out of all proportion to the original incident: Stirling and Essex are two cases which come to mind. Thus the senior officers of all universities might well be concerned about the activities of outspoken staff who are determined to effect change. Academics have no special right to make public pronouncements, but they are often in a position to have detailed knowledge of controversial issues, and some of them will continue to have tenure, which is designed to protect them while expressing unpopular views. This combination of circumstances is designed to benefit society, and does so, but it is also a recipe for a public-relations disaster in particular instances. Just as a university can benefit from the presence on campus of a Nobel Prize-winner, so it can be harmed by eccentrics, or even by ordinary men and women with strong views on controversial issues. Universities which are conscious of this danger must try to create among their staff an awareness of the delicacy of the situation while at the same time not appearing to impose censorship or to stifle free speech.

American research into attitudes towards university goals has shown that the results tend to be consigned fairly quickly to filing cabinets, where they lie undisturbed until eventually shredded. I would not claim that my own contribution produced any startling consequences; however, it certainly made me and a number of colleagues more aware of the attitudes of members of the University of Bath, and to that extent at least it was useful.

Notes

1 Quoted by Middlemas (1977), page 99.
2 Quoted by Bowen (1977a), page 40.
3 This is the theme of the famous Harvard University report on general education. See Ashby (1974), pages 11 and 12.
4 For a discussion of this point see Beard, Healey and Holloway (1970), page 33.
5 See University of Aston (1981), page 2.4. The reference to successful economic performance is derived from *Competence and competition*; see Institute of Manpower Studies (1984), introduction.

6 Quoted by Bowen (1977b), page 12.
7 McMurrin (1976), page 9.
8 See Bok (1974), page 4.
9 Times Higher Education Supplement (1983b).
10 Swinnerton-Dyer (1983), question 26. See also Leverhulme Report, final volume (*Excellence in diversity*), page 4.
11 Swinnerton-Dyer (1983), question 27.
12 Times Higher Education Supplement (1984f).
13 Committee of Vice-Chancellors and Principals (1984), page 7.
14 Caine (1969), page 36; Dainton (1981), page 15; Swinnerton-Dyer (1983), question 17.
15 Swinnerton-Dyer (1983), question 17. Also Swinnerton-Dyer (1984), page 10.
16 Caine (1969), page 36.
17 A distinction made during the Leverhulme discussions. See Flather (1982c).
18 See Carter (1980), chapter 8.
19 This figure is based on the CVCP's 'diary' research project of 1969; see Committee of Vice-Chancellors and Principals (1972a). The figure is accepted by Moore (1984), page 611. Beverton and Findlay (1982) suggest that the true figure may be lower.
20 Association of University Teachers (1983), page 10.
21 See Committee of Vice-Chancellors and Principals (1980), page 49, for a fuller discussion.
22 Committee of Vice-Chancellors and Principals (1984), page 9.
23 Blume (1982).
24 Turney (1982). The figure of 5 per cent (or less) was endorsed by the Leverhulme Inquiry. See Leverhulme Report, final volume (*Excellence in diversity*), page 52.
25 Moore (1984), page 610.
26 Robbins (1980), page 6.
27 See, for example, Committee of Vice-Chancellors and Principals (1980), page 9, and Times Higher Education Supplement (1984g).
28 Leverhulme Report, final volume (*Excellence in diversity*), page 15.
29 See Swinnerton-Dyer (1984), page 11, and Fowler (1982), page 138. Professor Niblett also accepted this point. Other academics who have questioned the necessary connection include Professor Elton (see Moore (1984), page 616), and Caine (1969), page 36.
30 See, for example, Association of University Teachers (1983), page 10.
31 Reported by Crequer (1983).
32 Swinnerton-Dyer (1984), page 12. The 1985 Green Paper says that there is no evidence that all academic staff must engage in research (paragraph 5.4).
33 Booth (1983). Swinnerton-Dyer (1984), page 13, makes the same distinction.
34 See Committee of Vice-Chancellors and Principals (1980), page 5, Flather (1982b), and University Grants Committee (1984), page 15.
35 Blume (1982).
36 See Times Higher Education Supplement (1982b).
37 Committee of Vice-Chancellors and Principals (1980), page 5.
38 Times Higher Education Supplement (1982b).
39 Bowen (1979), page 7.
40 Ibid.
41 See Passmore (1984a).
42 Flather (1984b).
43 Hirst (1983).

44 Burgess (1979), page 146.
45 Martin (1984), page 19.
46 Carnegie Commission (1973), chapter 7.
47 Ibid., page 43.
48 Passmore (1984b).
49 Ibid.
50 Times Higher Education Supplement (1984b).
51 Martin (1984), page 17.
52 The results have been written up in much greater detail in my Ph.D. thesis: see Allen (1986).
53 Ibid., chapter 13.
54 Scruton, Ellis-Jones and O'Keeffe (1985).

Part 3

10

The Universities' Environment in the Late 1980s – Factors Affecting Goals

Introduction to Part 3

The aims of Part 3, as of the rest of the book, are to clarify issues relating to university goals, to encourage discussion of topics which are often avoided, and to provide practical assistance to those who wish to determine what the goals of universities actually are, what they could be and what they should be.

This part of the book perhaps contains rather more of my own opinions and conclusions than Parts 1 and 2, but I hope that I have managed to distinguish, where necessary, between what is my personal view and what is established fact. Part 1 largely dealt with the past; Part 2 surveyed the present; and Part 3 looks to the future.

Chapter 10 deals with the environment of British universities in the late 1980s. I have tried to identify the major factors which are affecting, or are intended to affect, the universities' choice of goals. A number of relevant bodies have recently expressed strong views on the ways in which universities should respond to the needs of the environment; these views have been recorded in such documents as the Jarratt Report, the Government's 1987 White Paper on higher education, etc. The implications of all these documents are examined.

Chapter 11 summarises a number of ways in which the goals of universities can be clarified or selected by organisations. Some suggestions are made for improving the British system of university planning.

Chapter 12 moves from the consideration of goals by organisations to the consideration of goals by individuals. Organisations are simply groups of individuals, and if organisations are to make rational decisions about goals it follows that as many members of the organisation as possible must be in a position to make informed judgements. Chapter 12 therefore provides individual readers with a method of inquiry by means of which they can investigate (1) the goals preferred by the environment of British universities, and (2) the explicit and implicit goals within any particular university, at any given time. Armed with the results of this inquiry, readers will be in a position to decide whether or not they are satisfied with the goals which are being pursued either by the university system as a whole or by one university in particular. The procedure which is described has been designed to be applied in a British context, but it could easily be used elsewhere.

Chapter 13 provides an example of a mission statement; and the final chapter, Chapter 14, records the conclusions and recommendations which I have drawn from the book as a whole.

The environment

Previous chapters (notably Chapter 4) have demonstrated that outside influences (the environment) have frequently had a profound effect on British universities: for example, external forces have largely determined the number of universities, their size and their wealth. Traditionally, however, once a university has been established, the environment has played little direct part in shaping its goals: universities have been regarded as autonomous bodies, well placed to determine for themselves how best to serve society, albeit while taking account of external views. That situation is changing. During the 1970s and 1980s there have been unmistakable signs that public confidence in the universities' wisdom, and in their power to respond quickly and appropriately to changing needs, is dwindling: evidence of that change has been provided in Chapters 4 and 7. It appears increasingly likely that in the remainder of the twentieth century the environment will wish to determine universities' goals more directly than in the past. This chapter will therefore describe the universities' environment as it exists in the late 1980s: it will do so chiefly by examining the implications of several important publications: the Jarratt Report;[1] a letter from the UGC (circular letter 12/85);[2] the 1985 Green Paper on higher education;[3] the 1987 White Paper on higher education;[4] the ABRC publication, *A strategy for the science base*;[5] and the 1987 Education Reform Bill.[6] Most of these publications have been mentioned earlier in the text but their key points will be summarised here in order to assess the changes which the environment is likely to force on universities over the next few years. There is, of course, no substitute for reading the original documents themselves, and the parts of them which are highlighted here are only those parts which have a direct bearing on the choice of university goals – not the parts which relate to other aspects of higher education or education in the schools.

The Jarratt Report

In April 1984 the CVCP appointed a committee under the chairmanship of Sir Alex Jarratt to report on the efficiency of universities. The Committee's Report was published in March 1985.

The Committee judged that its task was (in its own words) 'to examine whether the management structures and systems of universities were effective in ensuring that decisions are fully informed, that optimum value is obtained from the use of resources, that policy objectives are clear, and that accountabilities are clear and monitored.' (Paragraph 1.2.) The phraseology is inelegant, but I suppose the meaning is reasonably clear.

The Committee was evidently not impressed with the management processes of universities, though it did not find evidence of waste on a large scale. 'Even if the universities have a clear idea of what they want to do,' says the Report (thus implying that, at present, universities have *no* clear idea of what they are trying to achieve), 'they will not be able to achieve their aims unless they have the necessary structure.' (Paragraph 2.13.)

Broadly speaking, the Committee recommended that a number of standard (almost elementary) management techniques should be applied to the university system, at all levels. It was proposed that the Government should provide broad policy guidelines within which the UGC and individual universities could undertake strategic and long-term planning; it was also recommended that the Government should review the role of the UGC. The Report commented that, as far as was known, the Government still accepted the objectives of higher education as stated by the Robbins Committee. Within universities, Councils should assert their responsibilities in governing their institutions, notably by bringing planning, resource allocation and accountability together into one process. (Councils, it should be remembered, normally have lay majorities.) Conflict between Councils and Senates was viewed as creative and beneficial. Vice-Chancellors should act as chief executives; Heads of Departments should have clear duties and responsibilities; and arrangements should be made for staff development and appraisal. Thus the Jarratt Report called for goals to be considered at a national level as well as within institutions.

The Report considered the planning processes of six universities in detail and concluded that university aims and objectives were defined only in very broad terms. No evidence was found of a thorough examination of options and the means of achieving objectives; the lack of performance indicators was viewed as a major omission. To rectify these errors in planning, the Report recommended that each university should be required to prepare a forward plan, every two or three years, with clear statements of its aims. Many universities, it was argued, needed to make more positive efforts to define what they were trying to achieve in broadly measurable terms.

It is in many ways pathetic that in 1985 the universities should have had to be urged to take these steps, and the fact that it was necessary is revealing of the ways in which universities had previously operated. Some opponents of Jarratt have argued that the 'industry' model of 'top-down' management is not appropriate to universities, and that in any case the record of British industry provides no recommendation for the adoption of its management methods.[7] But these arguments are not really a fair summary of what the Report was saying, and in my view the Jarratt Report was long overdue.

UGC circular letter 12/85

On 9 May 1985 the Chairman of the UGC wrote to all Vice-Chancellors about planning for the late 1980s. The Chairman warned universities that they should prepare for a decline in the UGC's recurrent grant of at least 2 per cent per annum in real terms over the next few years. The Government's wish to see a higher proportion of students studying subjects of 'vocational relevance' was noted, together with the Secretary of State's expectation that there would be the greatest possible shift to science and technology within existing resources.

The letter then provided details of the UGC's intention to be more selective in its support for research. Notice was given of the Committee's intention to change the method of distribution of its funding for research in such a way as to support areas of special strength or promise. In addition to giving some universities larger grants than others, the UGC would encourage more selective distribution within institutions.

In order to enable the UGC to make these decisions on resource allocation, circular letter 12/85 called for large volumes of information. Perhaps the most interesting item, from the point of view of the study of goals, was a request for a short statement of each university's overall objectives for the planning period. The word 'objectives' in this context seems to mean the university's intentions in terms of subject balance and research priorities. It was suggested that universities should consider the rationalisation of departments, both individually and in co-operation with other institutions. The letter stated that the UGC might be willing to make grants to help to implement arrangements between universities, and that the UGC might have to take the initiative itself in order to protect or to provide for the national need. Finally the letter warned universities that it would be necessary to develop and to use indicators of performance for teaching, research and the provision of academic services.

Circular letter 12/85 was therefore (among other things) a half-hearted attempt to require universities to clarify their goals, particularly in respect of research. It gave warning that the external pressures for the evaluation of performance were now so great that they could no longer be ignored.

The Green Paper of 1985

In May 1985 the Government published a Green Paper entitled *The development of higher education into the 1990s*. The paper was intended to convey the Government's thinking on higher education, and comments on the issues raised in the paper were invited.

The first section of the paper identified the Government's main concerns. Economic performance of the United Kingdom since 1945 was described as disappointing; higher education, it was argued, must therefore contribute more effectively to the economy, in particular by producing more scientists, engineers and technologists. Institutions must avoid 'anti-business snobbery', must foster positive attitudes to work, and must develop their links with industry and commerce; they must be more flexible in responding quickly to new needs for qualified manpower. The provision of cultural and recreational facilities for the local community was also considered valuable.

The Green Paper stressed the need to protect free speech; it endorsed the introduction of a more selective research policy. A decline in student numbers of about 14 per cent was anticipated in the 1990s and it was considered 'not improbable that some institutions of higher education will need to be closed or merged at some point during the next ten years.' (Paragraph 1.13.) It was reported that the Government had asked the advisory bodies to consider the optimum distribution of students between the binary sectors in the medium and longer terms.

The Jarratt Report's assumption that the Government accepted the aims of higher education as defined by Robbins was confirmed in paragraph 2.1. (This acceptance can either be construed as a tribute to the powers of analysis of Robbins and his colleagues or as an indication of the lack of any serious attention being given to the matter in the intervening years.) The Government's wish to maintain a distinct emphasis on technological and directly vocational courses was also confirmed, with a passing note that the arts were important too; the proportion of arts places in higher education was, however, expected to shrink. It was suggested that the UGC and the NAB should co-operate to achieve a closer balance between supply and demand in such areas as architecture and pharmacy.

The joint UGC and NAB reformulation of the Robbins formula on access, to the effect that 'courses of higher education should be available to all those who can benefit from them and who wish to do so', was accepted with caveats. It was argued that so long as taxpayers substantially finance higher education, the benefits provided by the system have to justify its cost. (Paragraph 3.2.)

The Green Paper included a section on education throughout life. Continuing education was accepted as one of the principal parts of higher education's work, though the arguments for taxpayer support were not considered as strong as in the case of initial higher education; employers and students were expected to bear the costs in most instances.

On research, the Government's aim was for higher education to continue its contribution to the nation's research on about the present scale, with the universities retaining their chief role for basic or fundamental research. However, the view that all academic staff must engage in research was rejected, and it was stated that there would definitely be greater concentration and selectivity: some departments or even whole universities might lose research funding. Links with industry and commerce on the research side were strongly encouraged; the Government was anxious to translate academic expertise into products.

The Green Paper noted that within universities the broadening of the undergraduate curriculum which had been recommended by the Robbins Committee had been constrained in practice by the rapid growth in knowledge in many subjects. The paper gave encouragement to the broadening process, but only in terms which appear lukewarm.

Like the Jarratt Report, the Green Paper considered the management process in higher education. It recommended that specific objectives should be established, both for whole institutions and for the separate faculties and departments. Stress was placed not only on the efficient use of resources but on the effectiveness of the results achieved. The need for reliable measures of perform-ance was highlighted yet again and the topic was discussed in detail in an annex. The annex stated that higher education has three main outputs: highly qualified manpower, research, and other social benefits; it claimed that significant progress in developing performance measures had been limited to the first of these, and several tables were supplied showing recurrent costs per student by discipline, non-completion rates, 'A' level scores, employment rates, etc.

The Green Paper stated that 'as far as possible' the changes which the Government wished to see brought about would be left to the responsible institutions. The Government also undertook to initiate a review of the role, structure and staffing of the UGC, as recommended by Jarratt. (This led to the Croham Committee, referred to in Chapter 4.) The Government saw no practical scope for a national planning body for higher education which would 'overarch' the UGC, the NAB and the associated bodies for Northern Ireland, Wales and Scotland; such a body had been recommended by the Leverhulme Inquiry. Instead, the Government accepted its own responsibilities for central policy.

The White Paper of 1987

In April 1987 the Government issued a White Paper on higher education with the subtitle 'meeting the challenge'. In appearance it was most unusual for a white paper, featuring glossy colour photography, bar charts, and diagrams, all of which made it look rather like the annual report of a public company. The content also showed some changes from the past: for one thing, the White Paper began with a section on aims and purposes – and this, as we have seen, is a very infrequent practice in British higher education.

The opening section confirmed (as the Green Paper had) the Government's support for the Robbins Committee's analysis of the aims and purposes of higher education. It declared that higher education should serve the economy more effectively, and should pursue basic scientific research and scholarship in the arts and humanities. Closer links with industry and commerce were called for (again), and there was support for the promotion of 'enterprise'.

The question of access to higher education was a major concern of the White Paper. It was anticipated that student numbers would rise in the next few years, then fall back to present levels in the mid 1990s (because of the demographic decline), and finally begin to grow again. The Government undertook to study the needs of the economy so as to achieve the right number and balance of graduates in the 1990s, and it planned to increase participation rates, particu-larly among young women and mature entrants. There would be further development of continuing education, particularly professional updating. The Government confirmed its Green Paper commitment to the modified Robbins principle, namely that places should be available for all who have the necessary intellectual competence, motivation and maturity to benefit from higher education and who wish to do so. The universities were urged to move towards admitting more students holding qualifications other than 'A' levels.

The third section of the White Paper dealt with quality and efficiency. Quality, it was stated, would be enhanced by improvements in the design and content of courses; by better teaching (resulting from training and appraisal); and by more selectively funded research. The prospects for commercial exploitation would be a factor in research funding. Quality was to be judged partly by the extent to which courses meet the needs of employers, but mainly by reference to students' achievements when set alongside their entry standards (paragraph 3.15). This paragraph alone surely represents a revolution in thinking, particularly with its insistence that the essential data on the performance of each institution should be published. I find it hard to believe that ten years ago any politician would have felt strongly enough to suggest that the actual effects of university education should be measured! And if anyone had had the effrontery to suggest it, the universities would surely have brushed the idea aside instantly.

The White Paper stated that greater efficiency was to be achieved by improvements in institutional management, by changes in the management of the system, and by the development of performance indicators. The intention to end the practice of offering tenured contracts of employment was clearly indicated.

The section on research stated that higher education 'provides the knowledge base for industry and commerce to build upon' (paragraph 3.17). There is not much evidence in that statement of a concern for the pursuit of truth for its own sake.

Perhaps the most vital aspect of the White Paper, from the universities' point of view, was the announcement of the intention to replace the University Grants Committee with a Universities Funding Council, membership of which could contain a strong element of people from outside the university world. The Government, it was stated, would provide planning guidelines for the university system as a whole, and the UFC would be responsible for the distribution of funds among universities under new contract arrangements.

The White Paper also announced far-reaching changes in the status and funding of polytechnics, but those proposals lie outside the scope of this book.

A strategy for the science base

In July 1987 the Advisory Board for the Research Councils published a report entitled *A strategy for the science base*. The Chairman of the ABRC, Sir David Phillips, acted as the Board's spokesman in publicising the ideas contained in the document. In essence, the argument was that there was insufficient money to finance full-scale research in all universities; furthermore, it was maintained that in some areas of experimental science there were in any case sound reasons for forming large teams of researchers. This situation led the Board to propose that in future there should be three types of university, as follows:

Type R: offering (and funded for) undergraduate and postgraduate teaching, with substantial research activity across virtually the full range of academic disciplines;

Type X: offering (and funded for) teaching across a broad range of fields but with substantial research activity in particular fields only, in some cases in collaboration with other institutions; and

Type T: offering (and funded for) undergraduate and master's level teaching only, with associated scholarship and research but without any advanced research facilities.

The Board also argued that potential utility should play a greater part in the allocation of funds for basic research (paragraphs 2.5 and 2.8); industry should help to decide priorities. There was a strong emphasis on the exploitation of research to reduce the gap between science and business.

Despite the fact that the universities already had much to think about, Sir David Phillips soon found himself under fierce attack, as desperate lecturers saw their chances of obtaining research grants dwindling to nil – not to mention their chances of promotion and a successful academic career. In all the uproar it was sometimes overlooked that the ABRC report was concerned only with disciplines which require laboratories. In that respect it seems likely that Sir David Phillips was right, in the sense that the nation will not be able to equip every university to undertake all the most expensive forms of research in, say, chemistry. There probably will have to be some universities with 'well found' laboratories, some with 'not-too-badly found' laboratories, and some with rather basic facilities. But there seems to be no sensible reason why the limitations imposed by the high cost of scientific laboratories should condemn whole universities to be teaching-only institutions, especially if they happen to have excellent departments of history or English literature.

The Education Reform Bill of 1987

The Education Reform Bill of 1987, which is still being debated as this book goes to press, is almost entirely concerned with schools rather than with higher education. The Bill as a whole contains 147 clauses and 11 schedules, but less than 10 per cent of the clauses and only two of the schedules are relevant to universities.

The Bill outlines major changes for the universities in two areas: funding, and tenure. (Perhaps the Government regards tenure as related to funding.) The Government's intention to set up a Universities Funding Council, to replace the UGC, is confirmed. The Council will have fifteen members, to be appointed by the Secretary of State; of these, between six and nine will come from higher education and the rest from other backgrounds. The Council will administer funds provided by the Secretary of State. The Secretary of State may attach terms and conditions to the award of funds, as may the UFC when it distributes them to individual universities; and indeed the Secretary of State may call for the repayment of sums paid by the UFC, with interest, if the conditions are not complied with! (It is worth noting, however, that the Bill itself does not mention contracts at all.)

The second major area in which the Bill announces changes is in academic tenure. Staff whose appointments are made or who enter into contracts after 20 November 1987 (the date of the Bill's publication) are not to be protected from dismissal on grounds of redundancy or financial exigency; and provision will be made for dismissal for inefficiency in future.

Soon after the Bill's publication, great concern at the proposals began to be expressed in official university circles, though the occasional call for academics to take to the streets in protest was met with overwhelming apathy. To be specific the CVCP instituted a Parliamentary lobbying campaign on three major points: the Vice-Chancellors were worried that the UFC was provided with no statutory right to advise the Government about the needs of universities; they were concerned at the massive powers being allocated to the Secretary of State (and were not placated by the informal statements that of course he would never use them); and they wanted some form of words enacted in the eventual statute which would protect academic freedom even if it allowed lecturers to be dismissed when redundant.

The Bill also contains highly significant proposals for the polytechnics and other main colleges of higher education, which are to be freed from local authority control and will receive their funding through a Council similar to the UFC.

By the time this book is published the Bill will presumably have become an Act, with or without amendment.

A summary of the trends affecting British universities in the late 1980s

The publications discussed in this chapter surely make it plain that there are a number of trends developing which will have massive consequences for British universities over the next few years. Some commentators have described what is happening as a revolution, and in a sense it is, if only because many academic staff do not seem to have realised what is afoot. The major trends, as I see them, are as follows.

First, the age of university autonomy appears to be over (although it is symptomatic of the general confusion that the Government denies it). Once upon a time the universities were genuinely free to spend their block grant as they thought best; no longer. From now on, the Government will probably not make grants at all; it will buy services. Furthermore, in the worst-case scenario, universities which fail to deliver what the Government has ordered may find themselves having to repay the funds they were given, with interest, after they have been spent.

The present Government has repeatedly stated its intention of laying down policy for the universities centrally, and it will control student numbers in the interests of the economy. This not only marks the end of academic autonomy, but it also means the abandonment of the old Robbins idea that courses should be made available to meet student demand.

There is clearly pressure from the environment for more vocational courses, for more science and technology, and for closer links with industry and commerce. Servicing the needs of the economy is seen to be a primary function of both teaching and research – perhaps *the* primary function.

Since the economy requires more manpower, the universities and higher education generally will be called upon to admit a larger proportion of the population. That will inevitably mean that teaching methods will have to be altered, and course content will have to be changed – probably broadened. There will also be a greater emphasis on continuing education, particularly professional updating.

Research is going to be much more selectively funded. It seems inevitable that, in the expensive scientific and technological disciplines, this will result in first-class, second-class and third-class departments, though the nomenclature used to describe them may be less blunt than mine.

Tenure will disappear, perhaps gradually, perhaps overnight. This will result in greater financial flexibility. The Government evidently does not accept the argument that academic staff are entitled to any special protection to enable them to speak their mind. Several factors no doubt lie behind this view: one is the Government's well known dislike of its left-wing critics; but another may be the fact that academics who actually have tenure seldom seem inclined to question conventional wisdom anyway. Other aspects of academic freedom, such as the lecturers' rights to undertake whatever research they wish, and to teach whatever they wish, are also likely to be curtailed in practice. It is the Government which in future will largely determine what is to be researched and what is to be taught, at any rate as far as activities financed by public money are concerned.

The final conclusion which I draw from the documents analysed in this chapter is that before long the environment will require universities to clarify their aims, goals and objectives. I anticipate that this will come about for two reasons. First, university funding from the state is likely to be provided in return for some form of contract (the details of which are not yet clear). As a part of that process, it is possible that the body which commissions services from the universities, i.e. the Government/UFC, may decide on the goals of the operation itself; but even if the contract is only spelt out in very broad terms ('provide a course for 100 historians'), universities may well find it advantageous to show that the goals of their courses are more in tune with the Government/UFC's wishes than are those of University X. In other words, competition is likely to intensify.

A more compelling reason for thinking that goals will have to be clarified is, however, the rapidly growing emphasis on performance indicators. At present most so-called performance indicators relate to unit costs, the number of research students, and similar data which can easily be extracted from existing records. But there are already demands for the effectiveness of teaching to be measured; and when work on that starts in earnest it will surely become apparent that you cannot measure achievement without having clearly defined goals. That, at least, was the conclusion reached by the ETS in Princeton, some twenty years ago.

If I am right in concluding that one of the major demands to be made on universities over the next few years will be the clarification of what they are trying to achieve, then it follows that practical guidance on that point will be of value. The next two chapters will therefore consider the processes by which goals may be clarified: first, by organisations (Chapter 11), and secondly, by individuals (Chapter 12).

Notes

1 Committee of Vice-Chancellors and Principals (1985).
2 Swinnerton-Dyer (1985).
3 Cmnd. 9524 (1985).
4 Cm 114 (1987).
5 Advisory Board for the Research Councils (1987).
6 Education Reform Bill (1987).
7 See various letters to *The Times*, April 1985.

11

Procedures for the Clarification of University Goals by Organisations

The evidence provided in the previous chapter suggests that in the late 1980s British universities will be obliged, by circumstance if not by law, to clarify their goals. The process of determining goals is regarded by most organisations as the first and most important stage of planning, and the aims of this chapter are therefore (1) to review the two principal alternative procedures for planning in higher education, and (2) to describe the nature of the inevitable British compromise in planning.

I hope that this chapter will be useful in providing an understanding of the ways in which society and institutions determine university goals. An understanding of that process will be helpful for those who wish to analyse the goals of a specific institution – something which is dealt with in the next chapter.

The autonomous model

The first planning procedure, or model, which I would like to describe is one which has its origins deep in the past, in the concept of a university as a self-governing community. The system is advocated most vociferously in the United States, but its supporters are found in many democracies. The model is known by a number of different names, such as the administrative sciences or systems analysis or rationalist model. It is essentially a theoretical or ideal model, since it is unlikely that any organisation anywhere conforms to it exactly. Because it is essentially a form of planning which is participative, and appropriate to institutions which are self-governing, I will refer to it here, at the risk of creating yet more jargon, as the autonomous model.

The autonomous planning model consists of the following four stages:

1 Considering and deciding upon the goals of the institution.
2 Considering and deciding upon the means of achieving those goals.
3 Carrying out the functions which are necessary in order to achieve the goals.
4 Evaluating the extent to which the goals have been achieved and reviewing the whole process.

Advocates of this planning model argue that the decisions taken in stage one should be conscious, deliberate and public, rather than intuitive and private. They must take into account a variety of views – those of the principal stakeholders at least, and not just the views of an élite – but the decisions are essentially the decisions of the university, and not of any other organisation; to be precise, the decisions are made by the academic staff or a body representative of academics. Ideally the goals should be expressed in measurable terms, but it is recognised that not everything can be quantified precisely: it is sufficient that independent observers should be able to assess whether the goal has been achieved or not.

Stage two involves consideration of the alternative means which are available to achieve the goals, together with an examination of the costs and benefits of each. It may be necessary to modify some of the goals in the light of a realistic assessment of what can be achieved with finite resources. Once the review is complete, the available resources are allocated.

The third stage, that of carrying out the necessary work, is the most crucial phase of all, and one to which most of a university's time, attention and resources are devoted.

The final stage calls for an evaluation of the extent to which the selected goals have been achieved and for a review of efficiency in the use of resources. Those outputs which can easily be quantified can also be evaluated relatively easily; in the case of goals which cannot easily be quantified the assessment must be more subjective. As a result of the evaluation process, goals may be redefined and the means used to achieve them may be modified. The whole process is therefore circular, in that evaluation (or accountability) provides feedback which modifies the goals established in stage one.

The cycle of stages is repeated on a regular basis, though perhaps not all stages need to be repeated at the same interval. For example, goals could be determined every three years, with an annual evaluation of achievement.

There are, of course, numerous criticisms which can be made of the practicality of the autonomous approach to the planning of universities. For example, stage one appears to assume that agreement on goals within a faculty or a university can be achieved as a result of open, rational discussion among a large number of people. In practice that may not be so: there may be such serious dissension within an institution, or a unit, that agreement on anything but the most anodyne generalisation is impossible. Similarly, at the other end of the process, it is undoubtedly very difficult to evaluate research, for example. How can a paper in *Nature* be compared with a book review in the local evening paper? Both are 'publications', but is one ten times more important than the other, or fifty times? Nevertheless, the autonomous planning model offers certain advantages: for example, it may satisfy the external demand for a justification of the use of scarce resources; it can also satisfy the internal demand for 'industrial democracy' or 'collegiality' and for justice to be seen to be done.

The centralised model

The centralised planning model can safely be claimed to be just as rational as the autonomous or decentralised model: but while the autonomous model may be said to operate from the bottom up, the centralised model operates from the top down. It is closely linked with the concept of manpower planning which was discussed in Chapter 3.

The centralised planning model proceeds through much the same stages as the autonomous model, except that in this case the goals are decided at national rather than institutional level, and are essentially those of the state. The first stage involves the selection of specified goals, which are often economic in character. It is common in the centrally controlled economies of eastern Europe to set up a national plan, often on a five-year basis. This plan will set targets for the output of goods and services. The targets are normally of a fairly basic nature, such as the production of a certain number of houses or lorries; however, there is no reason in principle why the plan should not specify less material goals. For example, one target could be that each town with a population of 100,000 should have a theatre, or that a national ballet company should be established.

It is worth noting that the goals which are selected in the centralised planning model are just as much the product of a series of value judgements as are those selected in the autonomous model. In both cases information from elsewhere is taken into account: in the autonomous system a wise university will note the demand from employers for, say, biologists; and even in the most ruthlessly centralised economies the views of potential students carry some weight.

Once the goals have been established, the activities to be undertaken by universities can be deduced. The main activity will normally be to produce the trained personnel to act as teachers, engineers or whatever. The universities will be instructed accordingly, sometimes in extreme detail, as in the USSR. Changes in the nation's circumstances, such as increased demand for, say, chemical engineers, will require continual adjustments to be made to the plan; and if the system is to work well, speed and flexibility of response will be essential.

Stages three and four of the process are also similar to those in the autonomous model: stage three involves carrying out the functions within the universities concerned; stage four is to evaluate performance and to make any necessary adjustments to the process as a whole. In the centralised model, however, evaluation will be a function of the nation's planning authority rather than of each autonomous institution.

The centralised model also has shortcomings in practice. Not even in the most authoritarian political system does every individual obey every order, and therefore perfect efficiency and effectiveness are never achieved. It is also doubtful whether any state has at present the capacity to collect the necessary data and to adjust its plans sufficiently fast to avoid the kind of mismatches which are well documented in the field of manpower planning.

The British compromise in university planning

It is convenient to conceive of the British system of planning for higher education as following the same four stages as were found in the autonomous and centralised planning models. To recapitulate, the stages are:

1 The determination of goals.
2 Deciding how to achieve the goals; resource allocation.
3 Carrying out the necessary functions.
4 Evaluation.

The previous chapter demonstrated that far-reaching changes are proposed, but for the moment the British system of planning for higher education is a compromise between the two pure forms described above. Stages one, two and four take place both at the national level and within institutions; stages one and two also overlap.

Burton R. Clark has observed that centralised systems of planning for higher education tend to stay centralised, while decentralised systems tend to stay decentralised.[1] In 1982 he predicted that in the foreseeable future the British system, which he characterised as 'mildly decentralised', would certainly not become even as centralised as the French model. However, the tendency since 1945 has been for the British universities to become steadily more influenced by central authority, and the 1987 White Paper and Education Reform Bill provide absolutely no reason to suppose that this process of evolution from a 'bottom-up' system to a 'top-down' form of planning is likely to be reversed. The Leverhulme Inquiry chose to defend autonomy,[2] but there is heavy pressure from the Government for the universities to respond to specified needs.

The framework within which British planning for higher education takes place is pyramidal. At the top of the pyramid stand the Government and the DES. On the next level down (for the moment at least) come the UGC and the NAB; below them are the institutions. The flow of information runs both upwards and downwards. The Government has accepted its responsibility for creating a policy framework (though both the Government and the DES have been roundly criticised for failing to meet this responsibility).[3] The Government and the DES have to take into account the views of a large number of bodies: the UGC, the NAB, the CVCP, the universities, the polytechnics, parents, students and taxpayers. The Government also has to take into account the demands for expenditure on other activities: it is only at the top that a judgement can be made on national priorities, such as the balance between expenditure on universities and hospitals.

The Government, then, decides in broad terms what it wants the universities to achieve and how much money (in total) they are to be given to carry out their tasks; in recent years the Government has chosen to give steadily more detailed indications of its wishes but the policy statements (goals) are still very loosely phrased (defined).

The next stage is for the UGC to divide the financial grants in the best way possible, in the light of its own judgement of the national need; this the UGC is comparatively well placed to do, because its various subcommittees have detailed knowledge of the strengths and weaknesses of each institution. (Incidentally, this subcommittee system will almost certainly continue to be very influential when the UFC is established.) The grants to universities are often accompanied by comments about the activities which the UGC wishes to see developed or reduced. Traditionally the UGC does not give the universities instructions, but in recent years the 'suggestions' have become more and more difficult to ignore; and presumably the UFC will be impossible to ignore. By one means or another the UGC or the DES contrives to control student numbers, particularly in disciplines such as education, medicine and pharmacy.

Finally, as far as goal-setting and resource allocation are concerned, the universities theoretically still have to make their own internal, autonomous decisions on which activities to develop, which to close down and which to continue on level funding. They are expected and allowed to use their own judgement as to what society needs and how best to provide it, but in practice the universities' room for manoeuvre has become increasingly constrained. It is now accepted throughout the system that to set up a new department without UGC approval is politically impossible. There is also massive inertia within the institutions: it is very difficult to persuade a Senate to terminate one activity in order to finance another.

Stages one and two in the British system of planning are therefore a mixture of the centralised and the autonomous procedures. Stage three – carrying out the functions of a university – is largely an internal matter, but it is worth noting that in some instances, such as the provision of sandwich courses, the co-operation of other bodies is needed; and the professional institutions have a powerful influence over perhaps one third of the courses.

It is widely acknowledged that stage four, evaluation, has been largely neglected, but the previous chapter demonstrated that performance evaluation is now inescapable. As in the past, it will take place both internally and externally, but in future the results will be more widely available than hitherto. Some 'performance indicators' are relatively easy to design and to implement, and as a result it seems likely that British universities will soon be able to provide a host of sophisticated analyses of staff:student ratios, research income per head, and similar matters.

Like all compromises, the British system of planning for universities has certain weaknesses. The most obvious shortcoming is that the goals of the system are far from clear. In the 1980s, the Government, the DES and the UGC between them have begun to articulate what they wish to see come about to a far greater extent than in previous decades; however, they still tend to speak in rather vague terms about shifts to science and technology, and co-operation with industry and commerce. Perhaps the proposed system of contracts will be more specific.

Within the universities the arrangements for clarifying goals are also unsatisfactory. As I have demonstrated repeatedly, discussion of goals is notable chiefly by its absence. It is of course true that, within departments, the content of every degree course is debated periodically, often at length and with passion; it is also true that such debates inevitably involve an implicit consideration of the goals and objectives of the course. Nevertheless, explicit consideration of the purpose of university education is rare. What departmental boards, Senates and Councils tend to debate is not goals but the minutiae of course content and resource allocation.

Suggestions for the improvement of the British system of planning for higher education

Almost anyone can suggest a number of ways in which the British system of university planning could be improved. The following suggestions are made on the assumption that what is required is a rationalised mixture of 'top-down' and 'bottom-up' planning.

First, the Government is right, in my view, in its apparent intention to provide a more precise policy framework. This does not involve adopting a five-year plan on the eastern European pattern, but it does involve setting more specific goals than at present. It almost goes without saying that the Government must review higher education as a whole, universities and public-sector institutions together. The Leverhulme Inquiry proposed that to assist this process a policy studies centre should be established.[4] This might be valuable in the long run, but most of the options are already clear, and what is needed is the will to make unambiguous choices. The Leverhulme Inquiry also favoured the creation of an 'overarching body'[5] to co-ordinate the UGC and the NAB; this again seems superfluous if the Government is serious about accepting its responsibility for policy.

Secondly, the universities must be persuaded (or, more likely, obliged) to identify their precise choice of goals. There have already been a number of strong hints that this might come about. As mentioned earlier, the House of Commons Select Committee and the Leverhulme Inquiry have both recommended the adoption of mission statements, and the Jarratt Report is also critical of the lack of clarity on goals. I strongly suspect that those universities, or departments, which can provide a simple statement of what they are trying to achieve, and evidence of the extent of their success, will find themselves at a distinct advantage.

Manpower needs are by no means the whole story when it comes to setting goals, but, from the Government's point of view, manpower needs are currently very important. In recent years several commentators have pointed out that market forces alone are inadequate in ensuring that the manpower needs of a successful economy are met.[6] This does not mean, however, that the necessary improvement can only be effected by moving to a highly centralised system of planning. On the contrary, the necessary improvements can probably be brought about by focusing attention on a few specialist disciplines where rapid increases (or decreases) in the numbers of graduates are required.[7] To achieve the desired result it will be necessary to arrange for better information to be made available to students, so that they will choose their degree courses wisely.

Incentives may also be required to encourage entrants;[8] for some reason which I do not understand, the British seem very reluctant to offer carrots. The incentives are not in themselves difficult to devise or expensive to offer (bearing in mind the cost of *not* meeting manpower needs); but, once again, it requires an act of political will to offer them. Thus the 'problem' of manpower shortages could be alleviated if not solved by adapting the existing system.

Within the universities some means must be found of overcoming the awesome resistance to change. The Jarratt Report's solution is for university Councils to flex their muscles through the more active intervention of lay members; Sir Peter Swinnerton-Dyer (currently Chairman of the UGC), and Lord Robbins had earlier proposed the same solution.[9] However, it is by no means clear that it will be possible to recruit sufficient lay members with the necessary experience, interest and, above all, time, to achieve this result. Nor is it clear that Councils will be able to impose their will: academic staff are adept at avoiding change. The real solution is for the academic staff to come to terms with their existing responsibilities, and this is undeniably a major test of leadership.

This chapter has described a number of ways in which the goals of universities can be clarified at organisational level: (1) through a system of autonomous institutions, using a decentralised model; (2) through a centralised system, with goals being determined outside the institutions; and (3) through the existing British compromise in university planning or an improved version of it. But organisations are made up of individuals, and individuals must make up their own minds about what goals should be pursued: the next chapter provides some assistance in that regard.

Notes

1 Clark (1982), page 195.
2 Leverhulme Report, volume 9 (*The structure and governance of higher education*), page 3. See also the final report (*Excellence in diversity*), page 2.
3 The Jarratt Report is critical of the Government in this respect. *The Times Higher Education Supplement* has criticised the DES; see Times Higher Education Supplement (1985).
4 Leverhulme Report, volume 9 (*The structure and governance of higher education*), page 208.
5 Ibid., page 4.
6 See, for example, Pearson (1985).
7 Ibid., page 195.
8 For useful discussions of this point see Peston (1981) and Lindley (1981).
9 See Swinnerton-Dyer (1984), page 22, and Robbins (1980), page 81.

12

A Procedure for the Clarification of University Goals by Individuals

This chapter is concerned with the selection of university goals by individuals; it is intended to be of practical value to those who are in a position to influence university decisions, such as academic staff and lay members of Councils. Unfortunately, the choice of university goals is a matter on which few individuals are at present equipped to make well founded decisions. Consequently the aim of the chapter is to provide a method of inquiry by means of which anyone who is interested can obtain information, at any given time, about (1) the attitudes towards goals in the environment of universities, and (2) the situation with regard to goals within any particular university.

The method of inquiry consists of a series of questions. Provided you are willing to take the trouble to find out the answers to the questions, you will then have a picture of the explicit and implicit goals of both the environment and the specific university which is of interest. You can then decide, preferably in the light of the material contained in earlier parts of this book, whether or not you are satisfied with the goals which are being pursued, either by the university system as a whole or by one university in particular. If you are not satisfied with the existing goals, you will have to consider how to bring about change. The implementation of change is outside the scope of this book, but a useful starting point would be to study the work of Enderud.[1]

The chapter is divided into two principal sections: the first section lists questions relating to the environment and the second lists those relating to the internal affairs of a university. Please note that the questions relate to *goals* only, and not to such matters as cost-effectiveness or teaching methods.

Anyone who wishes to obtain answers to the questions listed will have to locate published sources of information and conduct a number of interviews: ideally those interviewed should be senior academics and officers of a specific university, together with well informed representatives of national organisations such as the UGC, the DES and the political parties. Depending upon how seriously you pursue the investigation, these tasks will probably involve a significant commitment of time and money, and some comments about the practical problems involved in applying the method of inquiry are made at the end of the chapter. Since the issues involved are so important, I hope that some people at least will be willing to make the effort. It might be sensible, as a starting point, for each university to set up a working party to clarify its own position if it has not done so already.

The questions are framed within a British context, but with relatively small changes they can be made to serve equally well in other national systems.

Questions relating to the goals of the environment

1 What goals has the present Government set for higher education in general and for universities in particular? Has the Government set manpower-planning targets in any specific disciplines? (Likely sources of information: Green Papers; White Papers; UGC/UFC letters; public pronouncements by the Secretary of State.)

2 What means is the Government using for imposing its chosen goals? (Possible means: legislation; financial incentives or 'fines'; exhortation.) Is the Government in the process of reducing or expanding the provision of higher education through universities? Is the Government seeking to weaken university autonomy?

3 What goals are currently being emphasised by the UGC (or UFC)? Are they the same as those favoured by the Government, or is there conflict?

4 What means is the UGC using to impose its goals? In practice, how far can universities afford to ignore the UGC's hopes and expectations?

5 What indicators of performance are currently being used or recommended by the Government and/or the UGC? Do these indicators demonstrate the existence of unconscious or implicit goals other than those overtly recognised?

6 On a national basis, what are the views of the principal university stake-holders? (The stakeholders were listed in Chapter 7.)

Some of these questions are deceptively simple. Few individuals are in a position to answer all of them equally confidently, and some of the answers will, of course, be a matter of judgement.

Questions relating to the goals of a specific university

The British system of university governance is decentralised – whether 'highly' or 'mildly' decentralised is often debated. But in any case, individual universities still retain an element of autonomy, to some extent at departmental level; consequently the questions which must be asked in order to identify the goals of any specific university must of necessity be more detailed than those relating to the environment.

The previous chapter established that planning models can be viewed as having four stages, the process being circular in that evaluation (the fourth stage) feeds back into the first stage and may lead to a revision of the goals. The questions which need to be asked are therefore set out in four groups, of which the first and the last are the most crucial.

Stage one: choosing goals

1 Has the university produced a mission statement? Has the possibility been seriously considered and rejected? If so, why? Are the reasons convincing?
2 Has the university, or any group within it, ever considered drawing up or referring to a catalogue of possible goals such as that provided in Chapter 8?
3 What methods does the university have for testing the views of its stakeholders on a local, rather than a national basis?
4 Can the departments or faculties produce clear statements, on demand, of what they are trying to achieve through their degree courses or other activities? If not, why not?
5 If there are no written goal statements available, at either university or departmental level, what do the senior officers of the university or the departments say they are trying to achieve if pressed to answer? (Preferably, this question should be asked in relation to every degree course.) Also, what are the implied or operative goals? This is by no means easy to discern, but we can ask, for example:

> What courses are being offered by the university?
> What research is it undertaking?
> What facilities, services and activities does it provide for the staff, students and the local community?
> What major academic changes has the university made in the past few years? What was the intention behind those changes? Were they made in response to external or internal pressure?

6 What is the university's attitude – or what are the departments' attitudes – to the major issues discussed in Chapter 9? That is to say:

> Are the degree courses liberal or vocational, broad-based or specialised? And in either case, why? Is it considered desirable that academic staff should have had industrial or professional experience?
> Does the university offer sandwich courses?
> What is the attitude towards research? Is every member of staff expected to undertake it? To what extent is pure or applied research preferred? Why?
> Is there any overt policy on teaching style, or on academics making public statements on controversial issues? What is the justification for the policy? If there is no overt policy on these issues, what are the 'unwritten laws'? Are there any staff who ignore the policy/unwritten laws?

7 What level of agreement is there, within the university or within each department, on the explicit or implicit goals? Is the university in conflict with any major stakeholder group on any major issue?

What individual or group effectively makes the decisions about the university's goals or about activities which imply goals? (The actual decision-maker is not necessarily the same as the theoretical decision-maker.) Is Senate or Council dominant when it comes to determining goals or activities which imply goals?

Stage two: choice of methods and resource allocation

In the first stage of planning, goals are identified; in the second stage the most efficient and effective means of achieving each goal is selected. The second stage is therefore not critical in any analysis of goals, but a consideration of the decisions reached by a university in the second stage will certainly shed further light on the operative or implicit goals of the institution. The questions which follow are therefore intended to facilitate not a complete analysis of the second stage of planning but an analysis which will provide information on the intended outcomes of a university's activities.

1　In recent years, which activities have been given more resources? Why?
2　Which activities have had resources taken away? Why?

Much more could be said about the implicit goals which are revealed by a study of the decision-making process. For example, a Senate, or Council, which consistently refuses to distinguish between weak and strong departments in the allocation of resources is surely telling us something about its attitude towards excellence – but to find out exactly *what* it is telling us it may be necessary to undertake extensive inquiries.

Stage three: carrying out the necessary functions

The third stage of the planning process involves performing the functions which are necessary to achieve the various goals; this stage constitutes much of the university's day-to-day work. An analysis of what the university is actually doing, in terms of courses offered, research undertaken etc., has already been suggested in the questions relating to stage one.

Stage four: evaluation (accountability)

The following questions apply:

1　If there are explicit goals, what information is being gathered about the extent to which each goal is being achieved? (This question will make more sense, perhaps, after you have read the next chapter.)
2　If there are no explicit goals, what performance indicators are being used by the university? What do they tell us about the implicit goals of the institution?

3 Specifically, what assessment is the university carrying out of the effectiveness of its teaching? For example, how satisfied are the students, when graduating, that their needs have been met? What is their opinion of the education they received, five years after graduation, or ten? Is the university collecting this information? If not, why not?

4 How satisfied are employers with the graduates they recruit from this university? What proportion of graduates are unemployed?

5 Does the university measure the intellectual and attitudinal changes which have occurred in the students during their years at the unversity? If not, why not?

6 What performance indicators are used to monitor research? Does the university attempt to measure the social and scientific value of research, as opposed to the financial value of grants and contracts?

7 How does the university evaluate the performance of its staff (in all categories)? What arrangements does the university have for appraisal and staff development? Are the arrangement adequate?

8 How does the university evaluate its achievements in the various forms of public service?

The lists of questions given above are clearly not exhaustive, and asking any one of them is likely to generate a number of supplementary questions.

Consideration of the results of the inquiry

The procedure which is described above can be carried out with varying degrees of enthusiasm, but even a perfunctory analysis would require quite a large amount of work. In order to obtain an adequate cross-section of views it is necessary to interview a substantial number of members of the university (and possibly MPs, local employers, etc.); it is also necessary to select the right individuals to interview, and unless the researcher is a long-serving member of the institution under review, an experienced adviser will be a great asset. My own experience suggests that this work can be undertaken successfully by a single individual, and there are some advantages in that procedure: one person then has an overview of all the evidence. On the other hand, it may well be more convenient for the task to be managed by a group of researchers: this will be particularly likely if it is intended to analyse the goals of every course. In any event, before embarking on the study, the researcher(s) should consider whether it is necessary to adapt or refine the basic method, depending on the circumstances. For example, it may well be necessary to draw up a revised list of questions for semi-structured interviews. Ideally, an inquiry should have the full support and approval of the university's Vice-Chancellor and other senior officers.

Assuming the procedure is completed, the researcher(s) will then be faced with a mass of information. It may be helpful to refine this information into a draft mission statement for the university as a whole (if such a document does not exist already), or to modify an existing mission statement in the light of what has been learnt about operative goals; the information could be further refined to provide goal statements for individual departments or degree courses. Such a procedure may appear to be daunting, but in fact it is fairly straightforward, and an example of how the result might look is provided in the next chapter.

With the aid of a mission statement you can then explore a number of interesting lines of thought, such as: is this university likely to be in conflict with the Government of the day? And other similar issues.

Finally, anyone who bravely embarks on the kind of inquiry which I have described in this chapter has to ask himself three further questions:

1 How satisfied are you, the questioner, with the clarity of the goals of the university or of the departments within it?
2 How satisfied are you that they are the right goals?
3 If you are not satisfied, on either count, what are you going to do about it?

With rare exceptions, such as those who hold the office of Vice-Chancellor or Chairman of Council, there is little that one individual can do to alter the course of any university; and even for those in positions of authority, the implementation of change demands leadership qualities of a high order. For example, suppose that the inquirer wished to influence an 'ivory-tower' university towards adopting a more vocational/applied emphasis in teaching and research. To achieve any significant progress it would probably be necessary to persuade Council to follow the recommendation of the Jarratt Report and assert itself as the governing body of the university. Council would have to insist on specifying the university's goals in detail, in discussion with Senate, and the staff would have to be persuaded (or required) to adopt the desired vocational/applied emphasis. It would be necessary to set up a system of rewards for links with industry and commerce and penalties for the dragging of feet. My own view, based on the example of universities such as Aston and Salford in the years after 1981, is that change of this order could be brought about, but that it would be more likely to be achieved with the aid of external pressure than by the force of internal argument alone.

Note

1 See Enderud (1980). The Leverhulme Report volume 3 (*Agenda for institutional change in higher education*) is also relevant, particularly the paper by John L. Davies and Anthony W. Morgan.

13

An Example of a
Mission Statement

At this point, or even earlier, readers may be forgiven for thinking that, having heard so much about mission statements, it was high time an example was provided. This chapter is intended to remedy that deficiency.

The mission statement set out in this chapter is *not*, I must emphasise, a document issued by any real university; it is not even my analysis of the goals of a real university. What I have done, simply by way of example, is to draw up a mission statement for the kind of university with which I am most familiar. It follows that my imaginary institution has a bias towards vocational courses and has close connections with industry and commerce; it offers sandwich courses. I do not, of course recommend that all universities should follow the same pattern: what I do recommend is that each university should make up its mind about what it is trying to do. Is it sensible, for example, for some of the newer universities to try to compete with Oxbridge in terms of research? Or should they (what a dreadful thought) seek to concentrate on teaching?

With relatively little adjustment, the first part of the mission statement could be made to apply to almost any university. There is nothing surprising in that: the charters of most universities are similar in their wording. But the goals for individual departments may well differ quite sharply, both within universities and between universities.

Mission statements often cover much more than 'mission', which is normally defined as the university's purpose encapsulated in a few sentences. American mission statements commonly incorporate goals for the university as a whole, together with goals for individual departments, and sometimes objectives for individual courses. The example which follows has been prepared along these lines: it proceeds through a list of goals in relation to students generally, and goals in relation to society, to a set of goals for one department (business administration) and one degree course within that department (a bachelor's degree in business administration). The mission statement therefore conforms with the recommendations of the Leverhulme Report, the Jarratt Report, and the 1985 Green Paper, all of which call for the establishment of 'objectives' for each department. Just as the mission statement as a whole relates to no real university, the sections dealing with business administration relate to no actual department. True, I have had the opportunity of studying two such departments in detail (at the University of Bath in England, and at Northeastern University in Boston, USA). However, neither department would thank me for in any way implying that this is a portrait of their current or past aims and objectives. The description is one drawn from my imagination, for the purpose of illustration only.

As mentioned earlier, the Green Paper and the Jarratt Report both laid stress not only on the clarification of purpose but on performance evaluation. The question of how to assess performance is one which deserves a book in itself, and I have no intention of going into any detail on the subject. However, I thought it would be useful to give some indication, in brackets after each goal statement, of the performance indicator(s) (PI) which would be appropriate in evaluating success. Some further comments on evaluation will be made at the end of the chapter.

A mission statement for the University of Nowhere

Introduction

The University's central concern is knowledge: its preservation, transmission, creation and application.

Knowledge is preserved within the University Library, within the memory of computers, and by other physical means such as the establishment of archives. Knowledge is also stored within the minds of members of the University.

Knowledge is transmitted through teaching and writing.

Knowledge is created through research. Scholarship is the mastery of existing knowledge, a process which is essential for effective teaching and which can in itself provide new insights.

Knowledge is applied by members of the University to both internal and external problems.

In order to achieve its overall aims, the University has identified certain goals in relation both to students and to society at large. These goals are specified below, together with (in brackets) the means by which the level of achievement is tested in each case.

Goals relating to students

In the list of goals which follows, the order is not an order of importance.

Through the courses offered, and through the more general experience of being a member of the University community, the University seeks to enable students to acquire the following:

1 A knowledge of one or more academic subjects, particularly in connection with preparation for a career. At undergraduate level the knowledge will be

more broadly based than at postgraduate level. (PI: course work; examinations; surveys of employers' opinions after a period of employment.)

2 A broad acquaintance with the major features of a number of important areas of knowledge outside the student's main subject of study: for example, engineering students should learn something about history, literature, the arts and politics. To some extent this knowledge will be acquired by taking advantage of extra-curricular activities and opportunities. (PI: surveys of graduates' and employers' opinions.)

3 The ability to communicate effectively in speech and writing. (PI: course work; examinations; surveys of employers' opinions.)

4 The ability to weigh evidence and evaluate facts and ideas critically. (PI: course work; examinations; surveys of employers' opinions.)

5 The ability to undertake self-directed learning. (PI: course work; surveys of graduates' and employers' opinions.)

6 Self-confidence and the ability to analyse one's own talents, interests, emotions, and weaknesses. (PI: surveys of graduates' opinions.)

7 A personal set of values and moral principles. (PI: surveys of lecturers' and graduates' opinions.)

8 The ability to form satisfactory personal relationships with others. (PI: surveys of graduates' opinions.)

9 The ability to work with others. (PI: surveys of employers' opinions.)

10 The ability to apply knowledge in order to solve practical problems. (PI: surveys of employers' opinions.)

11 The ability to cope with change. (PI: surveys of graduates' and employers' opinions.)

12 The ability to make sound career decisions. (PI: surveys of graduates' opinions, at intervals.)

13 The ability to find rewarding uses for leisure time. (PI: surveys of graduates' opinions.)

14 Respect for the truth. (PI: surveys of employers' opinions.)

15 Respect for the law and the democratic process. (PI: surveys of employers' opinions.)

16 An appreciation of the value of scholarship and research. (PI: surveys of graduates' opinions.)

17 An awareness of social issues and a sense of social responsibility. (PI: surveys of employers' and fellow students' opinions.)

18 An awareness of the needs of industry and commerce (to be inculcated, as far as possible, through direct experience). (PI: surveys of employers' opinions.)

19 An awareness of the value of sport and physical recreation. (PI: participation rates.)

In addition, the University seeks to provide an environment within which the students' experience of university life will be satisfying, rewarding and pleasant.

Goals relating to society

The University's aims in relation to society are as follows:

1 To assist in the preservation of knowledge, through scholarship, publications, libraries, museums, information retrieval systems, and other means. (PI: data on numbers of publications, library stock, museum support, etc.)
2 To disseminate such knowledge as is needed to achieve the University's goals in relation to students. (PI: as for student-related goals.)
3 To discover new knowledge through research, both pure and applied. (PI: data on volume and value of research grants and contracts; assessment of the social and financial value of research results; patents, consultancies.)
4 To apply knowledge to the solution of practical problems in industry, commerce, and society at large. To do so both by invitation, as in contract research, and spontaneously, through individual members of the University acting as social critics. (PI: reports of research results; publications.)
5 To provide services for the surrounding community, through the provision of lectures, concerts, plays, exhibitions and other means. (PI: data on the number and variety of services offered. Surveys of the level of satisfaction within the surrounding community.)
6 To identify individuals with skills which are needed by society; to develop those skills, and to certify the level of achievement of each student. (PI: data on intake quality as revealed by 'A' level scores etc.; degree classifications; measurement of 'value added'; attraction rates for masters' and doctoral students; completion rates for research degrees.)
7 To offer opportunities for study to students from overseas. (PI: data on the number, origin and degree classifications of overseas students.)
8 To provide continuing-education courses. (PI: data on the number and variety of courses offered. Surveys of the level of satisfaction among clients.)

Subsidiary goals

In order to achieve its goals, both in relation to students and in relation to society, the University will seek:

1 To recruit students of high ability and high potential.
2 To recruit staff of high quality.
3 To obtain resources which are adequate for the fulfilment of all other goals.

Goals for the Department of Business Administration

1 The Department of Business Administration's principal goal is to meet the needs of industry and commerce. The primary needs of business organisations are for trained personnel and for research which will improve their

effectiveness and efficiency; comment and advice are also needed. (PI: degree classifications; employment rates; surveys of employers' opinions; number and value of research grants and contracts; publications.)

2 In order to meet the need for trained personnel, and by so doing to assist in the maintenance and growth of national productivity, the Department will offer the following courses:

> Bachelor's degree in business administration
> Master's degree in business administration
> Post-experience courses.

The courses are intended to train the mind through studying business. In all courses the emphasis will be on the development of skills, and on the acquisition of knowledge, directly related to the problems of practising managers; any learning about management is only valid if tested in action. The aims will be to attract students of high ability who have the potential to become the top managers of the future. Close links will be established between the Department of Business Administration and the technological Departments in the University in order to equip students to cope with rapid technological change. Through the award of degrees (classified at first-degree level), the Department will certify the level of skill which has been achieved by each student.

3 In order to meet the need for research which is relevant to solving the problems of industry and commerce, the Department will undertake the following activities:

> Supervision and training of research students, organised so as to provide a strong methodological base for research which is relevant to the problems of practising managers.
> Consultancies by individual members of academic staff, or by teams of staff if appropriate.

Goals for the bachelor's degree course in business administration

The undergraduate course in business administration is a four-year full-time course which includes a total of one year spent in industry or commerce. It is designed to prepare students for managerial and administrative careers in industry and commerce, and to provide professional training in such fields as accountancy, management services, marketing and personnel management. It seeks to achieve these aims through a programme of broadly based, interdisciplinary study.

The goals of the course are to equip students with certain skills and to instil certain attitudes; these skills and attitudes are listed below. The goals are divided into three categories: key goals, major goals, and subsidiary goals. The order of items within each category is not significant. [In fact it corresponds broadly with their position in the catalogue of goals provided in Chapter 8.]

Key goals

The goals which are regarded as most important for the undergraduate course in business administration are to equip students with:

1 The ability and disposition to weigh evidence, to evaluate facts and ideas critically, and to think rationally. (PI: course work; examinations, surveys of employers' opinions.)
2 The ability to apply knowledge in order to solve practical problems. (PI: surveys of graduates' and employers' opinions.)
3 A willingness to assume responsibility; leadership skills. (PI: surveys of employers' opinions.)
4 An awareness of the needs of industry and commerce and an awareness of how managers make decisions in practice (to be obtained by the student through direct experience). (PI: surveys of employers' opinions.)

Major goals

Other major goals for the course are to develop in students the following abilities and attitudes:

1 A deep and detailed knowledge of a selection of the following subjects: [Here would follow a long list of the academic options offered by the Department, e.g. marketing, business law, use of computers, etc.]. (PI: course work; examinations; surveys of employers' opinions.)
2 The ability to comprehend through listening, reading and doing. (PI: course work; examinations.)
3 The ability to speak and write clearly, correctly, fluently. (PI: course work; examinations.)
4 The ability to organise ideas and to present them effectively, particularly in discussion. (PI: practical tests; course work; examinations.)
5 The ability to form prudent judgements and to make decisions; the ability to analyse and synthesise. (PI: surveys of graduates' and employers' opinions; course work, examinations.)
6 A willingness to question orthodoxy and to consider new ideas. (PI: course work; examinations; surveys of employers' opinions.)
7 Imagination in formulating new hypotheses and ideas. (PI: course work; examinations; surveys of employers' opinions.)
8 Respect for the truth. (PI: surveys of employers' opinions.)
9 The ability to undertake self-directed learning. (PI: course work; examinations; surveys of graduates' and employers' opinions.)
10 Knowledge of one's own talents, interests, emotions and weaknesses. (PI: surveys of graduates' opinions.)
11 Self-confidence. (PI: surveys of graduates' and employers' opinions.)
12 The ability to co-operate. (PI: practical tests; surveys of employers' opinions.)
13 A personal set of values and moral principles. (PI: surveys of lecturers' and graduates' opinions.)

14 The ability to cope with change. (PI: surveys of graduates' and employers' opinions.)
15 The capacity to learn from experience. (PI: surveys of graduates' and employers' opinions.)
16 A motivation towards accomplishment. (PI: surveys of graduates' and employers' opinions; psychological testing.)
17 Initiative, energy, persistence, self-discipline. (PI: surveys of employers' opinions.)
18 Resourcefulness in coping with crises. (PI: surveys of employers' opinions.)
19 The ability to negotiate and a willingness to compromise. (PI: practical tests; surveys of employers' opinions.)
20 An awareness of social issues and a sense of social responsibility. (PI: surveys of employers' and fellow students' opinions.)
21 Knowledge of, and respect for, the law. (PI: course work, examinations; surveys of employers' opinions.)
22 The ability to make sound career decisions. (PI: surveys of graduates' opinions.)
23 Adaptability. (PI: surveys of employers' opinions.)

Subsidiary goals
The course is also intended to develop the following qualities:

1 An awareness of the history and contemporary features of technology. (PI: course work; examinations.)
2 Intellectual curiosity. (PI: project work.)
3 An understanding of the limitations of science and philosophy. (PI: course work; examinations.)
4 Conscientiousness of inquiry and accuracy in reporting the outcome of inquiries. (PI: course work; examinations.)
5 An awareness of the value of scholarship and research. (PI: course work; examinations.)
6 Spontaneity. (PI: surveys of graduates' and employers' opinions.)
7 A capacity for empathy. (PI: surveys of lecturers' and employers' opinions.)
8 Readiness to seek advice. (PI: surveys of employers' opinions.)
9 Knowledge of the major political philosophies. (PI: course work; examinations.)
10 Knowledge of governmental institutions and procedures. (PI: course work; examinations.)
11 Knowledge of current affairs. (PI: course work; examinations.)

Comments on the mission statement for the University of Nowhere

The mission statement provided above illustrates a number of interesting points. In the first place, it is simply a summary of intentions: it says very little about means. The choice of means is a matter for a university's decision-making bodies, and it requires a combination of top-down and bottom-up planning. The academic staff within each department will have the clearest idea of what means should ideally be adopted to achieve the detailed goals, and they will have to ask for the appropriate resources; but, realistically, the final decision on resource allocation can only be made at the centre, and that decision may involve some compromise with the ideal.

Another point worth noting is that the list of goals for the undergraduate degree concentrates on goals which the *course* seeks to achieve: it says nothing about that side of education which comes (we hope) from the very fact of attending a university and participating in the communal life.

Finally, the list of performance indicators illustrates a very significant fact: it is that the level of achievement of many of the goals cannot be fully assessed while the student is at the University. Some goals, such as the ability to solve practical problems, and resourcefulness in coping with crises, can only be properly tested during subsequent employment. Indeed it may well be impossible to devise *any* satisfactory means of establishing the extent to which a degree course has developed those qualities. You can obtain a student's subjective assessment of changes in himself, together with the employer's assessment of the ex-student's level of ability in each case; but how can you tell what the level of ability would have been if the student had never taken the course at all?

So – that is how a mission statement might look. Apart from drawing some conclusions from the book as a whole, which will be the subject of the next and last chapter, I think I have said as much on the subject of mission statements as I reasonably can. It is now for each reader to decide whether the advantages of having such a document, either at university or departmental level, are sufficient to justify the effort of producing it.

14

Conclusions and Recommendations

Introduction

This chapter sets out the conclusions which I have drawn from the contents of the book as a whole; I also make some recommendations for action based on my conclusions. Critics might argue that the making of recommendations should be left to committees, and that to try to be a one-man Leverhulme, so to speak, is over-ambitious. I can only say that, in my opinion, anyone who writes a book of this length and scope without including some recommendations at the end of it is lacking either in courage or in perspicacity.

The overall aim of the book has been to assist readers to decide what the goals of a university should be. To achieve that aim, the book provides the means whereby an individual can:

(1) obtain an overview of the range of possible goals for a university;
(2) find out what goals are preferred by stakeholders, and by society at large; and
(3) find out what the goals of a particular university actually are at any given time.

Conclusions drawn from Part 1

Part 1 provides the philosophical and historical frame of reference which is needed for an informed consideration of university goals.

Chapter 1

The first chapter draws attention to the distinction between a university's mission, its goals and its objectives. It is not always easy to move logically from mission to goals to objectives; there are also difficulties in measuring the extent to which goals have been achieved. However, the evidence suggests that such problems do not constitute a valid excuse for failing to clarify purpose. The risk that organisations may concentrate upon objectives which can easily be measured, at the expense of those which cannot, is in my view a more legitimate source of concern.

Chapter 2

Chapter 2 surveys philosophy as a source of ideas about what the goals of a university should be. Two main ideas are identified which have recurred periodically over the centuries. The first of these ideas is the vocational philosophy of higher education: this embodies the belief that society needs trained manpower and that higher education should therefore prepare students for the world of work. The second idea is the liberal, or liberal arts philosophy: adherents of this view argue that the trained mind can be applied to any activity. The study of philosophy also reveals that, for better or for worse, science cannot resolve disputes about the purpose of university education.

Chapter 3

Chapter 3 examines three approaches to the analysis of universities in order to find out what light they shed on the actual or potential goals of such institutions.

The first viewpoint considered is that of organisation theorists. Universities, it appears, are unsatisfactory organisations: they are sometimes described as organised anarchies, having ambiguous goals and weak governmental systems.

In the immediate post-war years, the British nation (like many others) invested heavily in the establishment of universities, with hopes of a correspondingly high return in the shape of economic growth. Clearly the growth has been nothing like as great as was hoped, but economists have demonstrated that universities still offer a good return on investment for society and an even better return for the average individual.

A third approach to the analysis of universities' purpose is that provided by the concept of manpower planning. This technique views universities primarily as a mechanism for producing a highly trained work-force. Whatever virtues this approach may have in theory, it proves difficult to apply in practice; the techniques work better in the centrally planned economies of the eastern bloc than in the democracies of the west. The rigid application of central control involves a loss of individual liberty which is unacceptable in this country; on the other hand, failure to take any account of manpower needs will clearly lead to waste. This is therefore one area in which the usual British compromise has much to commend it.

Chapter 4

Chapter 4 considers what the goals of British universities have been, historically speaking, and identifies the landmarks in the history of British higher education.

The historical review in this chapter makes it clear that British universities have never been swift or flexible in responding to changing needs; some would claim that this is their great virtue. In the nineteenth century, the refusal of Oxford and Cambridge to train middle-class students for industry led directly to the establishment of new universities. In the years after the Second World War, even more new universities became necessary because the existing ones simply could not cope with the demand.

The massive growth in government investment in the universities has led to a steady (but by no means commensurate) growth in the Government's desire to influence the universities. The establishment of the binary policy was a direct outcome of this desire for greater central control over higher education. The announced intention of introducing a system of contracts is a further indication of the same tendency.

Major investigations into higher education, such as that conducted by Lord Robbins in the 1960s, or the Leverhulme Inquiry in the 1980s, have devoted surprisingly little attention to questions of purpose. The Robbins Report did review the overall aims of higher education, in a very English, amateur way, but its conclusions can scarcely be regarded as a blueprint for the rest of the twentieth century. The Leverhulme Inquiry did not begin with a consideration of goals at all, but it did conclude by arguing that institutions should make their intentions clear in the form of mission statements, to be agreed with the funding body.

The main conclusions of Chapter 4 are that, in the post-war period particularly, there has been a large expansion in the number of British universities, principally with the aim of increasing economic growth. For much of the time this growth was 'demand led' – that is to say, the aim was to allow students who were qualified for higher education to take courses in subjects of their own choice. To a large extent the consequences which this demand-led growth would have on the volume and nature of research were either ignored or were assumed to be beneficial. The age-old debate about the vocational or liberal emphasis of degree courses continued, and a lesser debate about whether courses should be broad-based or specialised began. Perhaps the most significant post-war trend was, however, the Government's gradually increasing determination to control the way in which public money is spent.

Conclusions drawn from Part 2

The main aims of Part 2 are to determine the extent to which stakeholder groups have formally considered what the goals of British universities should be, and to identify areas of actual or potential disagreement, both within and between groups.

Chapter 5

Chapter 5 reviews the American approach to university goals with the aim of identifying good practice in this context. The legacy of such systems as PPBS and MBO is that most American universities are well aware of the need to clarify their goals; in some instances they are under a legal obligation to produce mission statements. As a result, a large amount of research has been undertaken in the USA, both to analyse the range of possible goals and to develop techniques for measuring opinions on what the principal goals should be.

Study of the American experience is valuable because it reveals certain pitfalls to avoid, and also identifies a number of practices which British universities would do well to emulate. The pitfalls include pompous mission statements, which are simply window-dressing, and over-elaborate questionnaires; among the more valuable features of American practice are a recognition of the fundamental importance of purpose and a willingness to discuss it openly.

It is worth repeating that in the late 1960s the Educational Testing Service at Princeton started out by concentrating on evaluation, but it soon became clear to the researchers that in order to assess the level of success it was first necessary to identify an organisation's goals. In the 1980s the British Government has shown great interest in performance indicators, but, so far, no commensurate awareness of the importance of clarifying purpose.

Chapter 6

Chapter 6 is concerned with the British approach to university goals. Research reveals that very few British universities can produce a formally agreed statement of purpose; most can only quote a few words from their charter, and several Registrars considered it odd to be asked even for that. The response from Cambridge University – ten words in Latin from the time of Edward VI – would be amusing if it did not make one reflect on the attitudes which have done so much damage to British universities in recent years. I cannot help feeling that if the universities had taken the trouble to produce mission statements some time ago, they might not have ended up in their present predicament.

Given the attitude of senior university officers, it is not surprising to find that only a small amount of research into the goals of British universities has hitherto been undertaken. Most academic staff seem to take the view that every educated person knows what a university is, just as every child knows what an apple is; further definition is considered superfluous. Such an attitude might be acceptable if universities occurred naturally, as apples do; but, since universities are man-made structures which consume large volumes of public funds, the attitude is fundamentally unsound. It can be argued that universities should be judged not by what they say (or fail to say), but by what they do, and that it is naive to expect complex organisations to produce simplistic statements of aims. It can equally well be argued that it is naive to suppose that universities can go on expecting to receive large sums of public money without being prepared to justify their existence to laymen; and since the universities, when attacked in 1981, found few lay defenders, the latter argument seems to me the more convincing. In a period when universities are once again suffering a reduction in resources, the continued failure to address the question of purpose, with the same rigour as other intellectual issues are addressed in universities, seems positively perverse.

Chapter 7

Chapter 7 reviews the opinions of the principal stakeholder groups on what the goals of a university should be. The evidence which is assembled in this chapter shows that few stakeholder groups have given much formal consideration to the matter. This is scarcely surprising, particularly in view of the universities' own failure in this respect. In some instances it is possible to deduce a group's views on goals from statements made publicly about university activities, such as teaching, research, or links with industry. Many such opinions are critical of the universities. It has to be remembered, however, that satisfied customers are less likely to speak up than are the disenchanted.

The overall position with respect to stakeholders' opinions suggests that it would be helpful to have available an analysis of the whole range of possible goals for universities, so that interested parties could choose which goals to support and which to reject. Such an analysis is provided in Chapter 8.

Chapter 8

Chapter 8 provides a classified list of goals for British universities. The catalogue is intended to be of value in analysing the goals which universities have adopted, consciously or unconsciously; it also enables interested individuals (or groups) to familiarise themselves with the range of possible goals and to choose the ones which they believe should be given the greatest emphasis.

Few of the goals which are listed in the catalogue are likely to surprise the reader. The value of the list lies not in the unfamiliarity of the contents but in having an analysis easily to hand. The catalogue is not considered exhaustive. It does not purport to be a list of all conceivable goals; it is simply a classified summary of those goals which have been given substantial emphasis in recent years, either in the relevant literature or in practice.

It is worth pointing out in this context that it is relatively easy to select goals; it is harder to identify the means of achieving those goals, harder still to carry out the necessary work, and in some cases it may be impossible to establish whether the goal has been achieved. For example, how can we ever prove that a degree course has developed in a student the capacity to cope with change? It may be possible to measure the extent to which a graduate and his employers believe that he can cope with change, but it is clearly never going to be possible to compare that level of ability with the level which would have existed had the graduate not taken the course at all.

Chapter 9

Chapter 9 discusses six areas of controversy in the field of university goals, in order to clarify the underlying issues. The six controversial topics are:

Teaching: whether degree courses should be liberal or vocational; and whether they should be broad-based or specialised.

Research: whether research is an essential function of a university or not; and whether it should be pure or applied.

The role of academic staff: whether a lecturer should argue a particular point of view, or should allow students to form their own conclusions; and, in relation to society, whether a lecturer should adopt a passive 'civil servant' role, or be an active critic and an instigator of change.

These six issues were selected because they were judged to be the most important areas of controversy in the mid 1980s; disagreements about them are essentially disagreements about the underlying goals. Chapter 9 summarises the main thrust of the argument on either side of the issues. No attempt is made to resolve the long-standing debate on these topics. Indeed on some of them there perhaps can be no 'right' answer: many observers would argue that degree courses should be both vocational *and* liberal, and that both pure and applied research are essential for the well-being of society. The intention in this chapter is therefore to identify the most likely areas of conflict, both within stakeholder groups and between groups, so that some form of agreement or working compromise may be reached before the conflicts become too damaging. Anyone who has worked in a university for very long will know that internal disputes can sometimes have serious consequences.

The last section of Chapter 9 summarises the results of some research which I undertook to measure attitudes towards the six controversial issues. To my mind, the most interesting findings are the overall distaste for indoctrination, and the fact that Conservative MPs are strongly opposed to the idea that academic staff should function as social critics, seeking to bring about change.

Conclusions drawn from Part 3

The main aim of Part 3 is to provide practical assistance to those who wish to determine what the goals of universities actually are, what they could be, and what they should be.

Chapter 10

In Chapter 10 I describe the universities' environment in the late 1980s. During the 1980s, important and strongly held views on goals have been expressed in such publications as the Jarratt Report, the 1987 White Paper on higher education, and others. The conclusions which I draw from these publications are:

1 The age of academic autonomy is over, in the sense that universities will no longer be free to spend their block grants as they think best; instead, the Government will probably buy services through a system of contracts.

2 Student numbers will be controlled by the Government in the interests of the economy. (At the moment, it seems likely that the participation rate will be increased.) The Government will try to shift the balance of teaching towards more vocational courses and will aim to increase the proportion of students studying science and technology.

3 Research will be funded on a much more selective basis.

4 Tenure will be abolished, with implications for academic freedom.

5 Universities will be obliged, by circumstances if not by legislation, to provide explicit statements on their overall aims and on the goals of specific courses.

Personally, having read the documents referred to in Chapter 10, in rapid succession, I am left with one overwhelming impression. It is that, insofar as politicians and businessmen think about universities at all, they are thoroughly disenchanted with them. In the very near future, universities will surely be forced to pay much more attention to the wishes of 'the environment' and will be much less free to arrange their affairs as the academic staff think best.

One other point strikes me very forcibly. It is the absence of any significant protest from the millions of university graduates. They, of all people, are intelligent enough to read the newspapers and they must be aware of the changes being thrust upon the universities from outside. And yet there are virtually no objections being raised by these graduates. I can only conclude that if the universities have not convinced the very students who pass through their hands that the status quo is worth preserving, they stand little chance of convincing anyone else.

Chapter 11

One of the aims of the book is to assist individuals, or groups, to analyse the operative goals of a particular institution, or the goals preferred by the universities' environment, at any given time. In order to carry out such an analysis it is necessary first to understand the ways in which society and the universities reach decisions about goals. Chapter 11 therefore examines the procedures by which university goals can be clarified by organisations. This involves consideration of three planning models: a system in which planning is carried out by autonomous institutions; a centralised system (the eastern European model); and the inevitable British compromise.

Making suggestions for improvements in planning techniques is relatively easy: the difficult task is to effect change. It is almost impossible to over-emphasise the resistance to change which exists within British universities: academic tenure, and the refusal to close down any existing activity, are but two aspects of this inertia. In the past it has sometimes proved easier to establish new universities from scratch than to adapt existing ones; bringing about any significant change constitutes a severe test of leadership.

It is probably because of the recognition that a debate about goals may involve change that the debate is so seldom attempted. In the past, commentators have sometimes despaired of finding a solution to this problem, and have restricted themselves to diagnosing a state of 'organised anarchy' in universities. But there is in fact a solution: it is for academic staff (in particular) to come to terms with their responsibilities and to give the question of purpose the same degree of attention which they devote to their academic specialisms.

Chapter 12

Chapter 12 is essentially practical. It provides a method of inquiry by means of which readers can familiarise themselves with the attitudes towards university goals which exist at any given time. The method of inquiry is in two parts. The first part enables readers to identify the goals which are preferred by groups in the universities' environment – groups such as the Government, the UGC or the CBI. The second part enables readers to analyse the operative goals of a specific university; that is the first step in deciding whether you are happy with the present state of affairs.

Chapter 13

Chapter 13 provides an example of a mission statement (for an imaginary university); the statement includes a list of goals for one department (Business Administration), and for one undergraduate degree course within that department.

The analysis of the goals of the degree course illustrates the point that the extent to which some goals have been achieved cannot be measured at all; the success in achieving certain other goals can only be assessed years after the course has finished.

Recommendations

Even those readers who have skipped judiciously must surely have gathered by now that my own conviction is that British universities have done themselves no favours by repeatedly failing to articulate their mission, goals and objectives. Until quite recently, academic staff have assumed that everyone knows what a university is for, and that society will be prepared to go on providing whatever resources the academics think are needed. In the late 1980s the universities are paying the price for these delusions. But it may not be too late to repair some of the damage, and the recommendations set out below are intended to assist in that process. To some extent the recommendations overlap; they are listed in order of importance, but that order does not necessarily constitute the sequence in which I would like to see them implemented.

1 *In future, the goals of universities should be discussed much more fully and directly than has been the case in the past.*

The evidence presented in earlier chapters shows that even some major stakeholder groups have not considered what the goals of universities should be; individuals within the groups may have views, but the groups as a whole have not pronounced on the issue in any formal sense. That is not a satisfactory state of affairs, given the large investment of human and other resources in universities, but to some extent it can be explained by the absence of suitable material on which a debate could be based. This book is an attempt to remedy that deficiency – which is not to say that it constitutes an exhaustive treatment of the subject, merely that it provides a basis for discussion. As a taxpayer (if in no other capacity), I would personally like to see all major stakeholder groups giving formal consideration to the question of university goals as soon as possible. Among the stakeholders, of course, I include the Government; in other words I would like to see a broad national policy developed in respect of the (higher) education system as a whole; within that policy universities could then, with the agreement of the UGC or UFC, decide on their diversified roles. Furthermore, I would like to see a debate which was focused *directly* on goals: that is to say, it should be conducted not in terms of course content, for example, but in terms of the skills to be developed or the attitudes to be instilled through the teaching of a particular course. To date, most of the discussion has been indirect, and there are two problems about that: one is that not all participants will be aware of the goals implicit in any degree course, and therefore confusion and misunderstandings may arise; the other problem is that such discussions fail to consider the university experience as a whole – and most observers would agree that there is more to being a student than completing a course of study. The only advantage in avoiding the overt discussion of goals is that staff can continue to pursue goals which may differ greatly without the possibility of disagreement degenerating into personal antagonisms.

If this first recommendation of mine (for more direct discussion of goals) were put to a Senate for debate, I have no doubt that numerous objections would be raised to the implementation of it, so it is worth considering the chief of such objections to see how convincing they are.

In the first place, the choice of goals is a value judgement, and the evidence suggests that in recent years many individuals have become increasingly uncomfortable with value judgements of all kinds. In the context of university goals, making a value judgement may involve not only choosing a goal (which some people find difficult), but also defending that choice by means of rational argument (which some people find impossible). Science cannot help in such debates; reliance upon tradition may be considered embarrassingly old-fashioned; and the use of intuition may be considered either undignified or feeble-minded. All of these are reasons for not discussing goals overtly. The main argument on the other side is that if academic staff, in particular, do not choose and defend their goals, the Government shows every sign of being willing to do it for them. Indeed it may already be too late to have any choice in the matter.

Another reason why the discussion of goals is sometimes avoided, by academic staff particularly, is that it may lead to unwelcome conclusions. It may lead, for example, to the realisation that change is long overdue. This may lead, in turn, to the disturbing suggestion that Dr X's course is no longer needed – but then what is to become of Dr X? And next year, what is to become of the rest of the department? It is often tempting to remain silent rather than face these painful dilemmas; tempting, but scarcely praiseworthy.

A third deterrent to the consideration of goals is the feeling which can be sensed in some quarters that to try to *do* something to a student is vaguely immoral or even indecent. The idea of moulding students' attitudes smacks of thought control, manipulation, the fascism of the right or the left. My own research (reported briefly in Chapter 9) demonstrates how strong is the view that students should be allowed to make up their own mind about controversial issues. It is scarcely surprising therefore that many academics feel uneasy about spelling out in detail, even amongst themselves, what changes they seek to effect in those they teach. But it can equally well be argued that degree courses will inevitably change students – and should not students be made fully aware of the changes which academic staff hope to bring about? There is surely a need to give students more detailed information about goals and objectives, to avoid mis-understandings and to minimise wastage.

Finally, for those who are determined not to discuss the matter, there is always the excuse that it is in any case impossible to obtain agreement on goals and that the subject is therefore best ignored. Some commentators have argued that 'no single list of agreed university objectives can be drawn up unless it is couched in such general terms as to have no precise meaning.'[1] This difficulty is acknowledged by the Americans, who refer to it as the 'motherhood and apple pie' problem: in other words, there is a danger that goal statements will be phrased in such bland and generalised terms that no one will wish to disagree with them; they are therefore useless. However, it is hard to believe that these conceptual difficulties are more serious than other major obstacles which are daily tackled, and tackled successfully, in many areas of university life. The idea that differences of opinion within a university cannot be resolved by rational discussion does not say much for the intellectual powers of the staff, and it is therefore an idea which universities might do well to avoid propagating.

In short, I can find no convincing arguments against the prompt implemen-tation of my first recommendation.

2 *Every university should be obliged (by law if necessary) to produce a mission statement, to be agreed with the UGC. The statement should include a list of goals for each department and for each degree course, and should state the performance indicators which will be used to measure success.*

My second recommendation presupposes that the present relationship between the universities and the UGC will remain largely unchanged after the introduc-tion of the UFC; that assumption may be false, but I possess no crystal ball. In the last few years the possibility of drawing up mission statements has been mentioned with increasing frequency in the literature on the management of British universities.[2] Nevertheless, the suggestion that my second recommendation should be imposed by law is made because I consider it unlikely that it will be put into effect otherwise. Perhaps the risk of some severe financial penalty imposed by the UGC or UFC might serve equally well, but nothing less would. Essentially the same recommendation (apart from the phrase about performance indicators) was made by the House of Commons committee on education in 1980,[3] and again in volume 9 of the Leverhulme Report;[4] but no obvious action has been taken as a consequence.

Ideally, of course, the institution's mission statement and the departmental goals should be seen as the first stage in a four-stage cycle of activity in what might be termed 'the organised university' (as opposed to an 'organised anarchy'). In the second stage of the cycle, the decision-making bodies of the organised university would consider the various ways and means of achieving the goals, would choose the most cost-effective means, and would allocate resources. In the third stage, to which universities devote most of their time and effort, the staff would carry out the necessary functions, such as teaching and research. And to complete the cycle, there would be regular evaluation to assess the extent to which the goals were being achieved.

Unfortunately, as we have seen, British universities have a remarkable history of refusing to examine their reasons for existence. In 1973, in their famous text on *Planning and management in universities*, Fielden and Lockwood stated that: 'Ideally, we might have recommended a system in which the first task would be to set and obtain agreement upon objectives. We decided against that approach because we believe most universities would not be prepared to implement it at this time.'[5] In 1978 Norris quoted that statement in his book *The effective university* and asked rather plaintively, 'Has the time now arrived for setting and obtaining agreement upon objectives; for the setting of priorities for different research and teaching projects in each institution and monitoring their performance through research publications, patents and graduates entering industry and commerce etc.?'[6] Norris was right to ask a question rather than to make an affirmative statement, because the time had clearly not arrived in 1978 any more than in 1973. In the late 1980s there has been some movement towards the clarification of purpose and the evaluation of performance, but I strongly suspect that anyone who believes that universities will adopt my second recommendation willingly is still guilty of unjustified optimism.

3 *Induction courses for new lecturers should provide an introduction to the theory and practice of university goals.*

Since the goals of a university are fundamental to its activities, it follows that new lecturers should be acquainted with the explicit or implicit goals of the institution which they have joined as soon as possible. This process will become very much easier if recommendation 2 is implemented. A general grounding in the theory of goals is also desirable.

4   *A catalogue of goals should be made available to all academic staff in universities, and should become a basic tool of their trade. The catalogue should also be made available to all other members of the university.*

It would be nice to think that every member of academic staff was reviewing the aims and objectives of his own teaching and research at regular intervals – perhaps annually. A catalogue of goals would be useful for that purpose (and one is, of course, provided in Chapter 8). The catalogue will also be valuable wherever the content of a degree course is being formally reviewed, or a new course is contemplated. I would encourage academic staff to enlarge and refine the catalogue whenever possible: perhaps one member of each department could be appointed to collate all such suggestions.

By this stage it goes almost without saying that a catalogue of goals is an asset to other members of the university too: students, for example, can use it to help them to decide what they want from a university education; lay members of Council can use it to inform their decisions on budgeting.

5   *The Committee of Vice-Chancellors and Principals should set up a working party to devise a manual of good practice in relation to goals.*

In 1984/85 the CVCP set up a committee, under the chairmanship of Professor P. A. Reynolds, to examine ways and means of maintaining academic standards. The end result of that exercise was useful, if not perfect, and much the same process could be undertaken, with advantage, in relation to goals.

The CVCP has recently begun to pay greater attention to public relations. In that context, the value of a clearly defined set of goals for each institution, together with convincing proof that they were being achieved in a cost-effective manner, can scarcely be overestimated. I fear that, in the eyes of some observers, the absence of such statements of intent, with accompanying proof, is regarded either as a mark of incompetence or as a tacit admission of failure.

6   *More research into university goals should be undertaken as soon as possible.*

Chapter 6 reveals that research into university goals in a British context is notable chiefly for its paucity. I was once intrigued to find an entry on university goals in a register of current research – intrigued because such indications of interest are very rare. So I turned to the appropriate page, only to find my own name and address. There is, however, no shortage of interesting and valuable work which could be undertaken, and I have made some suggestions elsewhere.[7]

Final conclusion

When it comes to accepting carefully considered recommendations, universities have a poor record; this is true even when the advice comes from highly prestigious committees, so what chance have the opinions of a presumptuous university administrator? I offer, as examples of sadly neglected recommendations, the fate of the Robbins Report's argument that expansion in student numbers should be linked to a broadening of the content of degree courses. Or, as another example, take the question of staff development. Ten years ago an attempt was made to persuade universities to improve their arrangements for the training of staff;[8] but in 1985 the Jarratt Committee was still complaining that staff development in universities was neglected (paragraph 5.5). History therefore suggests that the recommendations listed in this chapter will also be largely ignored. If so, does it matter?

The evidence, again, suggests that it does matter. My final conclusion is that the failure of British universities to determine their goals with precision is intellectually unacceptable; more to the point, it has become politically disadvantageous – possibly even disastrous. Universities would therefore be well advised to clarify what they are trying to do, to set out their goals in writing, and, where possible, to measure how effective they are in achieving the selected goals; such steps should be taken for the most cynical reasons of self-preservation if for no other. It is my firm conviction that unless universities take this action they will increasingly leave themselves exposed to their enemies and will deny their friends the means with which to defend them.

Notes

1 Dunworth and Cook (1975).
2 See, for example, the articles in volume 9 number 3 of the *International Journal of Institutional Management in Higher Education*, November 1985.
3 House of Commons (1980).
4 Leverhulme Report, volume 9 (*The structure and governance of higher education*), pages 200 and 201.
5 Fielden and Lockwood (1973), page 113.
6 Norris (1978), page 50.
7 Allen (1986), page 252.
8 Piper and Glatter (1977).

Some Quotations

During the course of the research which underpins this book, I came across a number of quotations which seemed to me to be worth recording. Some of them give pause for thought; others, in the circumstances, provided me with a certain amount of grim amusement.

What is education for?

Sir Keith Joseph – apocryphal?

At present, opinion is divided about the subjects of education.

Aristotle

One of the commonest areas of disagreement among educational theorists concerns what education should be for.

Paul Nash

. . . throughout its history, higher education in Britain has been backed by no simple and unambiguous view of the purposes of education.

Maurice Kogan

There seems to be little real agreement about what a university is for.

N. J. Entwistle and K. A. Percy

. . . universities do not exist for their own sakes, as daffodils and sparrows and mice do: they have a purpose.

Eric Ashby

Our patrons have the right to ask what universities stand for . . .

Eric Ashby

Having been at the University, and received there the taste and tincture of another education, I saw that there were things in this world of which I never dreamed; glorious secrets, and glorious persons past imagination. . . . We studied to inform our knowledge, but knew not for what end we so studied. And for lack of aiming at a certain end we erred in the manner.

Thomas Traherne

Almost any educated person can deliver a lecture entitled 'The Goals of the University'. Almost no one will listen to the lecture voluntarily.

Michael D. Cohen and James G. March

Finally, an institution that cannot articulate its purposes is forever vulnerable to the outside world on which it ultimately relies for its existence.

Derek C. Bok

References

Ackoff, Russell L. (1981). *Creating the corporate future*. Chichester: John Wiley and Sons.

Advisory Board for the Research Councils. (1987). *A strategy for the science base*. London: Her Majesty's Stationery Office.

Allen, Michael. (1979). *University resource allocation*. (M.Ed. dissertation – copy lodged in the Library of the University of Bath.)

Allen, Michael. (1986). *The goals of British universities*. (Ph.D. thesis – copy lodged in the Library of the University of Bath.)

Annan, Lord. (1983). Was Robbins wrong? *A.C.U. Bulletin of Current Documentation*, 61, December, 11–15.

Ansoff, H. Igor. (1979). *Strategic management*. London: Macmillan.

Ashby, Eric. (1966). *Technology and the academics*. London: Macmillan.

Ashby, Eric. (1974). *Adapting universities to a technological society*. London: Jossey-Bass.

Ashby, Eric. (1976). Tradition and modernity in universities. In McMurrin, Sterling M., editor, *On the meaning of the university*. Utah: University of Utah Press.

Ashley, Janette C., Tinsley, Dillard B., Lewis, John H., and Arnold, Danny R. (1981). MBO in the university – beware the pitfalls. *Journal of the National Association of Women Deans*, 44, Spring, 10–15.

Ashworth, John M. (1982). Reshaping higher education in Britain. *Journal of the Royal Society of Arts*, CXXX, 5315, October, 713–729.

Association of Commonwealth Universities. (1981). *Commonwealth universities yearbook*. London: The Association of Commonwealth Universities.

Association of University Teachers. (1979). *The universities' contribution to the nation*. London: Association of University Teachers.

Association of University Teachers. (1982). Britain needs its universities. *AUT Bulletin*, 102, October, 3–4.

Association of University Teachers. (1983). Leaner and fitter research? *AUT Bulletin*, III, October, 10–12.

Bacon, C., Benton, D., and Gruneberg, M. M. (1979). Employers' opinions of university and polytechnic graduates. *The Vocational Aspect of Education*, XXXI, 80, 95–102.

Balderston, Frederick E. and Weathersby, George B. (1972). *PPBS in higher education*. Berkeley, California: University of California.

Ball, Christopher. (1983). Action or firm answers must counter the criticism. *The Times Higher Education Supplement*, 14 October, 12–13.

Barnes, W. H. F. (1973). Finance and control of universities: basic principles. In Bell, R. E. and Youngson, A.T., editors, *Present and future in higher education*. London: Tavistock.

Barnett, Correlli. (1979). Technology, education and industrial and economic strength. *Journal of the Royal Society of Arts*, CXXVII, 5271, February, 117–139.

Baron, Bernard. (1978). *The management approach to tertiary education – a critical analysis*. London: University of London Institute of Education.

Beard, Ruth M., Healey, F. G. and Holloway, P. J. (1970). *Objectives in higher education*. London: Society for Research into Higher Education Ltd.

Bevan, John. (1983). The structure and funding of higher education in the public sector in the eighties and nineties. *Journal of the Royal Society of Arts*, CXXXI, 5324, 438–453.

Beverton, Ray and Findlay, Geoffrey. (1982). Preserving quality and vitality. *The Times Higher Education Supplement*, 19 March, 12.

Birch, Derek W. and Calvert, John R. (1977). Performance indicators in higher education: a comparative study. *Educational Administration*, 5, 2, 15–29.

Blaug, Mark. (1982). Book review. *Studies in Higher Education*, 7, 2, 169–170.

Bloom, Benjamin S. *et al*. (1956). *Taxonomy of educational objectives. Handbook I: cognitive domain*. London: Longmans.

Blume, Stuart. (1982). Customer–contractor principle comes under criticism. *The Times Higher Education Supplement*, 19 March, 12.

Bok, Derek C. (1973). *The President's report, 1971–1972*. Cambridge, Massachusetts: Harvard University.

Bok, Derek C. (1974). *On the purposes of undergraduate education*. Cambridge, Massachusetts: American Academy of Arts and Sciences.

Bok, Derek C. (1978). *The President's report, 1976–1977*. Cambridge, Massachusetts: Harvard University.

Bolton, Brian. (1986). Quality assurance and quality control of a new engineering curriculum. *Assessment and Evaluation in Higher Education*, 11, 3, autumn, 181–191.

Booth, Clive. (1983). A war of independence. *The Times Higher Education Supplement*, 9 December, 16.

Bowen, Howard R. (1977a). *Investment in learning*. London: Jossey-Bass.

Bowen, William G. (1977b). *Report of the President*. Princeton: Princeton University.

Bowen, William G. (1979). *Report of the President*. Princeton: Princeton University.

Bradley, Peter. (1983). *Undue influence – pressures on the universities*. London: The Centre for Contemporary Studies.

Brecht, Arnold. (1959). *Political theory*. Princeton, New Jersey: Princeton University Press.

Brennan, John and Percy, Keith. (1975). Sociological perspectives on teaching and learning in higher education. *Higher Education Bulletin*, 3, 2, Spring, 107–126.

Brubacher, John S. (1978). *On the philosophy of higher education*. London: Jossey-Bass.

Burgess, Tyrell. (1972). Resource planning in polytechnics. *Further Education Staff College Reports*, 5, 9, 40–45.

Burgess, Tyrell. (1979). New ways to learn. *Journal of the Royal Society of Arts*, CXXVII, 5271, 143–157.

Burgess, Tyrell. (1981). Book review. *Studies in Higher Education*, 6, 2, 190–191.

Burloiu, Petre. (1980). Methodology of educational planning – Romanian experience. *Higher Education in Europe*, V, 1, 32–37.

Buss, Allan R. (1975). Systems theory, generation theory, and the university: some predictions. *Higher Education*, 4, November, 429–445.

Butler, Dennis George. (1980). The institutional goals use survey: an examination of the use and impact of institutional self-study information in California colleges and universities. *Dissertation Abstracts International*, 41/10-A, 4302.

Caine, Sir Sydney. (1969). *British universities – purpose and prospects*. London: The Bodley Head.

California State University, Los Angeles. (1981). *General catalog*. Los Angeles: California State University.

Campbell, Duncan D. (1975). Determining the university's goals: the setting of the problem. *Canadian Journal of Higher Education*, 5, 1, 53–64.

Cane, Alan. (1971). Rothschild urges cut in Council funds. *The Times Higher Education Supplement*, 26 November, 1.

Carnegie Commission on Higher Education. (1973). *The purposes and the performance of higher education in the United States*. London: McGraw-Hill.

Carter, Charles. (1980). *Higher education for the future*. Oxford: Blackwell.

Carter, Charles. (1983). Great expectations. *The Times Higher Education Supplement*, 4 November, 11.

Chaplin, Maud. (1978). Philosophies of higher education, historical and contemporary. In Knowles, Asa S., editor, *The international encyclopaedia of higher education*. London: Jossey-Bass.

Child, Dennis, Cooper, H. J., Hussell, C. G. I., and Webb, P. (1971). Parents' expectations of a university. *Universities Quarterly*, 25, 4, 484–490.

Clark, Burton R. (1979). *The Japanese system of higher education in comparative perspective*. (Yale Higher Education Research Group working paper Y HERG – 33.) New Haven, Connecticut: Institution for Social and Policy Studes, Yale University.

Clark, Burton R. (1982). A cross-national view. In *Leverhulme Report*, volume 3. Guildford: Society for Research into Higher Education.

Cm 81 (1987). *Review of the University Grants Committee*. London: Her Majesty's Stationery Office.

Cm 114 (1987). *Higher education – meeting the challenge*. London: Her Majesty's Stationery Office.

Cmnd. 9524 (1985). *The development of higher education into the 1990s*. London: Her Majesty's Stationery Office.

Cohen, Michael D. and March, James G. (1974). *Leadership and ambiguity – the American College President*. London: McGraw-Hill.

Collier, K. G. (1983). Book review. *Journal of Further and Higher Education*, 7, 1, 99–103.

Colorado State University. (1982). *Pattern for the eighties*. Fort Collins, Colorado: Colorado State University.

Committee of Vice-Chancellors and Principals. (1970). *University development in the 1970s*. London: Committee of Vice-Chancellors and Principals of the universities of the United Kingdom.

Committee of Vice-Chancellors and Principals. (1972a). *Report of an enquiry into the use of academic staff time*. London: Committee of Vice-Chancellors and Principals of the universities of the United Kingdom.

Committee of Vice-Chancellors and Principals. (1972b). *The function of the university – teaching and research*. (Report of a conference convened jointly by the Committee of Vice-Chancellors and Principals and the Association of University Teachers.) London: Committee of Vice-Chancellors and Principals of the universities of the United Kingdom.

Committee of Vice-Chancellors and Principals. (1978). *Financial arrangements for universities*. London: Committee of Vice-Chancellors and Principals of the universities of the United Kingdom.

Committee of Vice-Chancellors and Principals. (1980). *Research in universities*. London: Committee of Vice-Chancellors and Principals of the universities of the United Kingdom.

Committee of Vice-Chancellors and Principals. (1981). *Universities and industry*. London: Committee of Vice-Chancellors and Principals of the universities of the United Kingdom.

Committee of Vice-Chancellors and Principals. (1984). *Development of a strategy for higher education into the 1990s*. London: Committee of Vice-Chancellors and Principals of the universities of the United Kingdom.

Committee of Vice-Chancellors and Principals. (1985). *Report of the Steering Committee for efficiency studies in universities*. (The Jarratt Report.) London: Committee of Vice-Chancellors and Principals of the universities in the United Kingdom.

Committee of Vice-Chancellors and Principals. (1986). *The future of the universities*. London: Committee of Vice-Chancellors and Principals of the universities of the United Kingdom.

Confederation of British Industry. (1982). CBI submission to the Leverhulme Programme into the future of higher education. *CBI Education and Training Bulletin*, 12, 3, September, 26–31.

Cook, T. G., editor. (1973). *Education and the professions*. London: Methuen.

Crequer, Ngaio. (1981). More cuts would close universities. *The Times Higher Education Supplement*, 13 November, 2.

Crequer, Ngaio. (1983). The binary system – from both sides. *The Times Higher Education Supplement*, 16 December, 5.

Crequer, Ngaio, and Jones, Felicity. (1982). DES climbs down over quotas. *The Times Higher Education Supplement*, 17 September, 1.

Croham Report. (1987). See Cm 81.

Daily Telegraph. (1984). Not enough attention given to education. *The Daily Telegraph*, 23 June, 2.

Dainton, Sir Frederick. (1981). *British universities: purposes, problems and pressures*. Cambridge: Cambridge University Press.

Dancy, John. (1981). The laying of a moral foundation. *The Times Higher Education Supplement*, 24 July, 12.

David, Peter. (1981a). Report on the fifth higher education conference held at Lancaster University. *The Times Higher Education Supplement*, 11 September, 5.

David, Peter. (1981b). Sir Keith in an old battlefield. *The Times Higher Education Supplement*, 25 September, 8.

David, Peter. (1982). Cultivation scarce in the multiversity. *The Times Higher Education Supplement*, 21 May, 30.

Davies, John L. (1976). Management by objectives in higher education institutions. *Paper presented to the OCED–IMHE General Conference*.

De Landsheere, Viviane. (1977). *Evaluation in education: international progress*. Oxford: Pergamon Press.

Department of Education and Science and the Scottish Education Department. (1978). *Higher education into the 1990s – a discussion document*. London: The Department of Education and Science.

Department of Education and Science. (1980). *Press notice on research into what is expected of higher education*, dated 29 September 1980. London: Department of Education and Science.

Department of Education and Science. (1983a). *Curriculum 11–16 – towards a statement of entitlement*. London: Her Majesty's Stationery Office.

Department of Education and Science. (1983b). *Through government eyes*. (Press release.) London: The Department of Education and Science.

Department of Education and Science. (1986). *Statistical bulletin 14/86*. London: The Department of Education and Science.

Dunworth, John and Cook, Rupert. (1975). Can universities be made more efficient? *The Times Higher Education Supplement*, 22 August, 11.

Ebel, Robert L., Noll, Victor H., and Bauer, Roger M. (1969). *Encyclopaedia of educational research*. London: Collier-Macmillan. Fourth edition.

Education Reform Bill. (1987). London: Her Majesty's Stationery Office.

Educational Testing Service. (1979). *Institutional Goals Inventory – comparative data*. Princeton, New Jersey: Educational Testing Service.

Educational Testing Service. (1981). *Notes: ETS college and university programs*. Princeton, New Jersey: Educational Testing Service.

Edwards, E. G. (1982). *Higher education for everyone*. London: Spokesman University Paperbacks.

Eggleston, John. (1983). Research into higher education in England. *Higher Education in Europe*, VIII, 1, January–March, 66–75.

Elton, Lewis. (1981). Can universities change? *Studies in Higher Education*, 6, 1, 23–32.

Elton, L. R. B. (1983). Book review. *Journal of Further and Higher Education*, 7, 2, 124–127.

Enderud, Harald. (1980). Administrative leadership in organised anarchies. *International Journal of Institutional Management in Higher Education*, 4, 3, November, 235–253.

Entwistle, N. J. and Percy, K. A. (1970). Educational objectives and student performance within the binary system. *Paper presented at the Sixth Annual Conference of the Society for Research into Higher Education*.

Entwistle, N. J. and Percy, K. A. (1973). Critical thinking or conformity? An investigation of the aims and outcomes of higher education. *Paper presented at the 9th Annual Conference of the Society for Research into Higher Education*.

Entwistle, N. J., Percy, K. A., and Nisbet, J. B. (1971). *Educational objectives and academic performance in higher education*. Lancaster: University of Lancaster Department of Educational Research.

Eurich, Neu P. (1981). *Systems of higher education in twelve countries*. New York: Praeger.

Evans, Keith. (1978). *The development and structure of the English educational system*. London: Hodder and Stoughton.

Fenske, Robert H. (1978). Using goals in research and planning. *New Directions for Institutional Research*, 19, 1–63.

Fenske, Robert H. (1981). Setting institutional goals and objectives. In Paul Jedamus *et al.*, *Improving academic management*. London: Jossey-Bass.

Fielden, John. (1969). *Analytical planning and improved resource allocation in British universities*. London: University of London Press.

Fielden, J. and Lockwood, G. (1973). *Planning and management in universities*. London: Chatto and Windus for Sussex University Press.

Financial Times. (1982). The educated unemployed. (Leading article.) 21 January, 12.

Fincher, Cameron. (1972). Planning models and paradigms in higher education. *Journal of Higher Education*, 43, December, 754–767.

Fincher, Cameron. (1978). The lust for efficiency: a downhome story of the implications of zero-based budgeting. In Fenske, Robert H. and Staskey, Paul, editors, *Research and planning for higher education*. Montreal: The Association for Institutional Research.

Finniston, Sir Monty. (1983). Education – for what? *Journal of the Royal Society for Arts*, CXXXI, 5323, June, 366–378.

Flather, Paul. (1982a). SDP proposes review of universities. *The Times Higher Education Supplement*, 16 July, 3.

Flather, Paul. (1982b). The Merrison remedy; protect and survive. *The Times Higher Education Supplement*, 18 June, 8.

Flather, Paul. (1982c). Who'll put the fizz into research? *The Times Higher Education Supplement*, 19 March, 10.

Flather, Paul. (1984a). Sir Keith reassures humanities. *The Times Higher Education Supplement*, 20 July, 3.

Flather, Paul. (1984b). Survey shows intolerance. *The Times Higher Education Supplement*, 1 June, 1.

Florida State University. (1979). *Mission statements*. Gainesville: State University System of Florida.

Foot, Michael, Kinnock, Neil, and Whitehead, Philip. (1981). *The Labour Party and higher education*. (Statement issued to University of Manchester Communications Office.) London: The Labour Party.

Footman, Roy. (1982). Government policy? *Conference of University Administrators' Newsletter*, 30, March, 4–9.

Fowler, G. T. (1982). May a thousand flowers bloom: the evolution of the higher education system and of institutions within it. *New Universities Quarterly*, Spring, 122–144.

Fulton, Oliver, Gordon, Alan and Williams, Gareth. (1980). Higher education and manpower planning: a comparison of planned and market economies. *Education Policy Bulletin*, 8, 1, 83–113.

Geddes, Diana. (1981). Bankruptcy and closures: the grim future that is facing our universities. *The Times*, 30 March, 12.

Grant, Nigel. (1985). Higher education in the Soviet Union. In Jacques, David and Richardson, John T. E., editors, *The future of higher education*. London: SRHE and NFER–Nelson.

Green Paper. (1985). See Cmnd. 9524.

Green, V. H. H. (1969). *The universities*. London: Penguin.

Gross, Edward and Grambsch, Paul V. (1968). *University goals and academic power*. Washington, D.C.: American Council on Education.

Hall, Phoebe, Land, Hilary, Parker, Roy, and Webb, Adrian. (1975). *Change, choice and conflict in social policy*. London: Heinemann.

Halsey, A. H. (1979). Are the British universities capable of change? *New Universities Quarterly*, 33, 4, 402–416.

Halsey, A. H. (1981). Will decay follow the last decade? *The Times Higher Education Supplement*, 16 October, 11.

Halsey, A. H. (1985). The idea of a university: the Charles Carter lecture 1984. *Oxford Review of Education*, 11, 2, 115–132.

Halsey, A. H. and Trow, M. A. (1971). *The British academics*. London: Faber and Faber.

Hamelman, Paul W., editor. (1972). *Managing the university: a systems approach*. New York: Praeger.

Handy, Charles B. (1979). The challenge of industrial society. *Journal of the Royal Society of Arts*, CXXVII, 5271, February, 131–139.

Hansard. *Parliamentary debates*. London: Her Majesty's Stationery Office.

Hartley, Harry J. (1968). *Educational planning, programming, budgeting – a systems approach*. New York: Prentice Hall.

Hirst, Paul. (1983). Bias in teaching. *The Times*, 25 October, 13.

Hobson, Peter. (1982). Book review. *Journal of Educational Administration*, XX, 2, 232–233.

Hogg, Sarah. (1982). Think-tank's chief. *The Sunday Times*, 7 March, 3.

Horowitz, Morris A. (1978). Manpower planning: overview. In Knowles, Asa S., editor, *The international encyclopaedia of higher education*. London: Jossey-Bass.

House of Commons. (1980). *Fifth report from the Education, Science and Arts Committee, session*

1979/80 – the funding and organisation of courses in higher education. Volume I. London: Her Majesty's Stationery Office.

Hoyle, Eric. (1979). Evaluation of the effectiveness of educational institutions. *Proceedings of the Eighth Annual Conference of the British Educational Administration Society*, September, 159–178.

Hutton, Geoffrey. (1972). *Thinking about organization.* London: Tavistock Publications. Second edition.

Immegart, Glenn L. and Pilecki, Francis J. (1977). *An introduction to systems for the educational administrator.* London: Addison-Wesley.

Indiana University. (1981). *Guidelines for planning and development.* Bloomington: Indiana University.

Institute of Manpower Studies. (1984). *Competence and competition – training and education in the Federal Republic of Germany, the United States and Japan.* London: National Economic Development Office.

International Bureau of Education. (1980). *Education goals.* Paris: United Nations Educational, Scientific and Cultural Organisation.

Jadot, Jean. (1981). Survey of the state-of-the-art and likely future trends of university management in Europe. *International Journal of Institutional Management in Higher Education*, 5, 1, March, 49–78.

Jarman, T. L. (1963). *Landmarks in the history of education.* London: John Murray.

Jarratt Report. See Committee of Vice-Chancellors and Principals. (1985).

Jaspers, Karl. (1965). *The idea of the university.* Edited by Karl Deutsch; with a preface by O. L. Zangwill. London: Peter Owen Ltd.

Jobbins, David. (1983). Union hears opposition views. *The Times Higher Education Supplement*, 17 May, 2.

Jobbins, David. (1984). Thatcher sets new task for universities. *The Times Higher Education Supplement*, 2 March, 1.

Johnstone, Bill. (1984). University opposes technology institute. *The Times*, 3 September, 2.

Jones, J. C. (1967). The designing of man-machine systems. In Singleton, W. T., editor, *The human operator in complex systems.* London: Taylor and Francis.

Jones, John. (1979). Students' views of the roles of a university. *Higher Education*, 8, 513–524.

Joseph, Sir Keith. (1983). *Letter to the Chairman of the University Grants Committee.* London: Department of Education and Science.

Kearney, Hugh. (1973). Universities and society in historical perspective. In Ben, R. E. and Youngson, A. T., editors, *Present and future in higher education.* London: Tavistock.

Kerr, Clark. (1973). *The uses of the university.* Cambridge, Massachusetts: Harvard University Press.

Kirst, Michael. (1975). The rise and fall of PPBS in California. *Phi Delta Kappan*, 56, April, 535–538.

Kogan, Maurice. (1983). Mad axemen. *The Spectator*, 21 October, 10.

Kogan, Maurice and Boys, Christopher. (1983). *Expectations of higher education: a summary of the DES funded project (1980–1983).* Uxbridge: Department of Government, Brunel University.

Kraft, Richard H. P. and Latta, Raymond F. (1972). Introduction to the systems approach in educational planning and management. *Educational Technology*, February, 5–8.

Krathwohl, David R., Bloom, Benjamin S., and Masia, Bertram B. (1964). *Taxonomy of educational objectives. Handbook II: affective domain.* London: Longmans.

Kwiatowski, Stefan. (1983). Book review. *Higher Education*, 12, 4, August, 463–471.

Labour Party. (1973). *Higher and further education*. London: The Labour Party.

Labour Party. (1983). The Labour Party's discussion document on education after 18. *AUT Bulletin*, January, 104, 5–6.

Labour Party. (1986). *Education throughout life*. London: The Labour Party.

Laycock, M. J. A. (1979). *Institutional self-evaluation: the NELP goals inventory*. London: North East London Polytechnic.

Leicester, Leicestershire and Rutland University College. (1920). *An appeal*. Leicester: The University College Committee.

Leverhulme Report. (1981 onwards). Consists of ten monographs and a final report, various editors, all published by the Society for Research into Higher Education. Details as follows:

1. *Higher education and the labour market.*
2. *Access to higher education.*
3. *Agenda for institutional change in higher education.*
4. *The future of research.*
5. *The arts and higher education.*
6. *Professionalism and flexibility in learning.*
7. *Accountability or freedom for teachers?*
8. *Resources and higher education.*
9. *The structure and governance of higher education.*
10. *Response to adversity.*

Final Report *Excellence in diversity.*

Liberal Party. (1977). *Higher education.* (Study paper no. 9.) London: Liberal Party Publication Department.

Liberal Party. (1984). *Press release on higher education policy*. London: The Liberal Party.

Lindley, Robert. M. (1981). The challenge of market imperatives. In *Leverhulme Report*, volume 9. Guildford: Society for Research into Higher Education.

Lockwood, Geoffrey and Davies, John. (1985). *Universities: the management challenge*. Windsor: SRHE and NFER–Nelson.

Lowe, John. (1973). The other side of the binary system. In Bell, R. E. and Youngson, A. T., editors, *Present and future in higher education*. London: Tavistock.

MacLure, J. Stuart. (1973). *Educational documents, England and Wales, 1816 to the present day*. London: Methuen.

Mager, Robert F. (1984). *Preparing instructional objectives*. London: Pitman. Third edition.

Management Today. (1984). Education's hard lessons (editorial). *Management Today*. May, 3.

Manchester Polytechnic. (1974). *Statements on development – number one: policy for development*. Manchester: Manchester Polytechnic.

Marris, Robin. (1984). The great British university miracle. *The Times Higher Education Supplement*, 6 April, 14–15.

Martin, Brian. (1984). Academics and social action. *Higher Education Review*, 16, Spring, 2.

Maynard, Alan. (1983). Book review. *Journal of Further and Higher Education*, 7, 1, Spring, 93–96.

McKie, Robin. (1981). Flexibility is strength for both sides. *The Times Higher Education Supplement*, 30 October, 9.

McMurrin, Sterling M., editor. (1976). *On the meaning of the university*. Utah: University of Utah Press.

McVoy, Edgar C. (1978). Manpower planning: role of international agencies. In Knowles, Asa S., editor, *The international encyclopaedia of higher education*. London: Jossey-Bass.

Meynell, Hugo A. (1976). On the aims of education. *Proceedings of the Philosophy of Education Society of Great Britain*, X, 79–97.

Middlemas, Keith. (1977). *The pursuit of pleasure – high society in the 1900s*. London: Gordon and Cremonesi.

Minogue, Kenneth R. (1973). *The concept of a university*. London: Weidenfeld and Nicolson.

Moberly, W. (1949). *The crisis in the university*. London: SCM Press.

Moodie, Graeme C. and Eustace, Rowland. (1974). *Power and authority in British universities*. London: Allen and Unwin.

Moore, Peter G. (1984). Universities: their role in a changing economic structure. *Journal of the Royal Society of Arts*, CXXXII, 5337, 605–618.

Morris, Vera, Woodhall, Maureen, and Westoby, Adam. (1977). *The planning of higher education – the social demand*. (Open University course ED322, block 11.) Milton Keynes: The Open University Press.

Mountford, Sir James. (1966). *British universities*. London: Oxford University Press.

Mullen, Michael. (1974). Management by objectives in higher education. *Journal of College and University Personnel Association*, 25, October/November, 52–67.

Nash, Paul. (1975). Philosophy of education. In *Encyclopaedia Britannica*, 15th edition, 6, 408–412.

National Union of Students. (1981). *The future of the universities*. London: National Union of Students.

Newman, John Henry. (1959). *The idea of a university*. With an introduction by George N. Shuster. Garden City, New York: Image Books.

Niblett, W. Roy. (1981). Robbins revisited. *Studies in Higher Education*, 6, 1, 1–12.

Norris, Graeme. (1978). *The effective university – management by objectives approach*. London: Saxon House.

Nosow, Sigmund and Clark, Frederick R. (1976). *Goals, aims, objectives – Duquesne university, a case study*. Atlantic Highlands, New Jersey: Humanities Press.

O'Hea, Anthony. (1981). Implications of university economies. *The Times*, 24 March, 13.

O'Leary, John. (1981). Need for better contacts. *The Times Higher Education Supplement*, 30 October, 9.

O'Leary, John. (1982). Reform or die warns Waldegrave. *The Times Higher Education Supplement*, 19 November, 1.

Ortega y Gasset, Jose. (1946). *Mission of the university*. London: Routledge and Kegan Paul.

Owen, Tom. (1980). The University Grants Committee. *Oxford Review of Education*, 6, 3, 255–278.

Page, G. Terry and Thomas, J. B. (1977). *International dictionary of education*. London: Kogan Page.

Parkes, Edward. (1981). *Grant for 1981/82 and guidance for succeeding years*. (Circular letter 10/81.) London: University Grants Committee.

Parkes, Sir Edward. (1983). *Address to the Committee of Vice-Chancellors and Principals, 28 September 1983*. London: Committee of Vice-Chancellors and Principals of the universities of the United Kingdom.

Passmore, John. (1984a). A moral tale. *The Times Higher Education Supplement*, 6 July, 13.

Passmore, John. (1984b). The case for civic celibacy. *The Times Higher Education Supplement*, 13 July, 14.

Pearson, Richard. (1985). The demands of the labour market. In Jacques, David and Richardson, John T. E., editors, *The future of higher education*. London: SRHE and NFER–Nelson.

Pennsylvania State University. (1980). *Agenda for action for the Pennsylvania State University.* University Park, Pennsylvania: The Pennsylvania State University.

Percy, K. A. and Brennan, J. L. (1977). What do students want? An analysis of staff and student perceptions in British higher education. In A. Bonboir, editor, *Instructional design in higher education.* London: European Association for Research and Development in Higher Education.

Perkins, James A. (1973). *The university as an organization.* London: McGraw-Hill.

Peston, Maurice. (1981). Higher education policy. In *Leverhulme Report,* volume 9. Guildford: Society for Research into Higher Education.

Peterson, Richard E. and Uhl, Norman P. (1977). *Formulating college and university goals – a guide for using the Institutional Goals Inventory.* Princeton, New Jersey: Educational Testing Service.

Phillips, Sir David. (1986). Research in a modern society: a UK view. *Journal of the Royal Society of Arts,* CXXXIV, 5364, November, 819–831.

Pickup, A. J. (1976). Aims, objectives and evaluation in vocational education. *Coombe Lodge Reports,* 9, 10, 301–306.

Piper, David Warren and Glatter, Ron. (1977). *The changing university – a report on the staff development in universities programme 1972–4.* London: National Foundation for Educational Research.

Polczynski, James J. and Thompson, A. Gray. (1980). Determinants of successful Management by Objectives implementation efforts within higher education. *International Journal of Institutional Management in Higher Education,* 4, 3, 255–270.

Pope, J. A. (1979). The role of universities in a changing technologically based industrial society. *Journal of the Royal Society of Arts,* CXXVII, 5278, September, 610–626.

Premfors, Rune and Ostergren, Bertil. (1975). *Systems of higher education: Sweden.* New York: International Council for Educational Development.

Pritchard, Malcolm. (1983). Book review. *Journal of Further and Higher Education,* 7, 2, Summer, 119–123.

Rice, A. K. (1970). *The modern university – a model organization.* London: Tavistock Publications.

Robbins, Lord. (1963). *Higher education report.* (Cmnd. 2154.) London: Her Majesty's Stationery Office.

Robbins, Lord. (1980). *Higher education revisited.* London: Macmillan.

Robbins, Lord. (1981). I am truly shocked by UGC policy. *The Times Higher Education Supplement,* 16 October, 13.

Roizen, Judith and Jepson, Mark. (1985). *Degrees for jobs.* Windsor: SRHE and NFER–Nelson.

Romney, Leonard. (1978). *Measures of institutional goal achievement.* Boulder, Colorado: National Centre for Higher Education Management Systems.

Ross, Murray G. (1976). *The anatomy of academe.* London: McGraw-Hill.

Royal Society of Arts. (1982). *The future of technological higher education in Britain.* London: The Royal Society for the encouragement of Arts, Manufactures and Commerce.

Sanderson, Michael, editor. (1975). *The universities in the nineteenth century.* London: Routledge and Kegan Paul.

Scott, Peter. (1981a). Inheritance of the Robbins/Crosland era. *The Times Higher Education Supplement,* 7 August, 24.

Scott, Peter. (1981b). The wrong side of the binary tracks. *The Times Higher Education Supplement,* 21 August, 32.

Scott, Peter. (1982a). 'Public' purposes and 'private' values. *The Times Higher Education Supplement,* 20 August, 24.

Scott, Peter. (1982b). More questions posed than answers found. *The Times Higher Education Supplement*, 19 March, 10.

Scott, Peter. (1983a). Building a better tomorrow. *The Times Higher Education Supplement*, 5 August, 24.

Scott, Peter. (1983b). Hopes and fears of twenty years. *The Times Higher Education Supplement*, 28 October, 10.

Scott, Peter. (1983c). Degrees of expert knowledge. *The Times Higher Education Supplement*, 12 August, 32.

Scott, Peter. (1983d). A lot of research for a little money. *The Times Higher Education Supplement*, 27 May, (iv).

Scott, Peter. (1983e). A broken treaty with the State? *The Times Higher Education Supplement*, 26 August, 24.

Scruton, Roger, Ellis Jones, Angela and O'Keeffe, Dennis. (1985). *Education and indoctrination*. London: The Sherwood Press.

Silcock, Bryan. (1984). The strangling of science. *The Sunday Times*, 5 February, 72.

Silver, Harold. (1981). *Expectations of higher education: some historical pointers*. Reading: Brunel University.

Silverman, David. (1970). *The theory of organisations*. London: Heinemann.

Social Democratic Party. (1982). The Social Democratic Party election programme for education and training. *AUT Bulletin*, October, 102, 11.

Social Democratic Party. (1983). *The SDP's white paper on education and training*. London: The Social Democratic Party.

Standing Conference of Employers of Graduates. (1982). *Submission to the Leverhulme programme*. London: The Standing Conference of Employers of Graduates Limited.

Startup, Richard. (1979). *The university teacher and his world*. Westmead, Hampshire: Saxon House.

State University of New York at Albany. (1977). *Mission, programs and priorities for action*. Albany, New York: State University of New York.

Strickland, Geoffrey. (1982). The future of higher education: a Conservative view. *New Universities Quarterly*, Spring, 113–121.

Swinnerton-Dyer, Sir Peter. (1983). *Letter to all Vice-Chancellors and Principals on the development of a strategy for higher education into the 1990s*. London: University Grants Committee.

Swinnerton-Dyer, Sir Peter. (1984). *Lecture to PA Technology*. London: The University Grants Committee.

Swinnerton-Dyer, Sir Peter. (1985). *Planning for the late 1980s*. (Circular letter 12/85.) London: University Grants Committee.

Taylor, William, editor. (1984). *Metaphors of education*. London: Heinemann Educational Books.

Teichler, Ulrich, Hartung, Dirk and Nuthmann, Reinhard. (1981). *Higher education and the needs of society*. London: National Foundation for Educational Research.

Temple, Charles M. (1973). Management by objectives at the University of Tennessee. *Intellect*, 102, November, 98–100.

Thomas, Allen and Taylor, Ernest. (1974). *The organization and the outside world*. (Open University Systems Management course, unit 6.) Milton Keynes: The Open University Press.

Thomas, Raymond. (1980). Corporate strategic planning in a university. *Long Range Planning*, 13, 70–78.

Thomas, R. E. (1978). Higher education and the national economy. *Paper presented to the C.I.P.F.A. seminar*, 13 April.

Times, The. (1984). Campus and the market (editorial). *The Times*, 15 August, 11.

Times Higher Education Supplement. (1982a). The metaphor of structure. *The Times Higher Education Supplement*, 1 October, 32.

Times Higher Education Supplement. (1982b). The research jungle. *The Times Higher Education Supplement*, 19 March, 32.

Times Higher Education Supplement. (1983a). Robbins to Leverhulme. *The Times Higher Education Supplement*, 27 May, (i)–(iv).

Times Higher Education Supplement. (1983b). The Leverhulme verdict. *The Times Higher Education Supplement*, 27 May, 32.

Times Higher Education Supplement. (1983c). His master's voice. *The Times Higher Education Supplement*, 16 September, 28.

Times Higher Education Supplement. (1983d). Universities of industry? *The Times Higher Education Supplement*, 20 May, 28.

Times Higher Education Supplement. (1984a). Manpower's 'broad steer'. *The Times Higher Education Supplement*, 9 March, 1.

Times Higher Education Supplement. (1984b). Too much and too little (editorial). *The Times Higher Education Supplement*, 30 March, 32.

Times Higher Education Supplement. (1984c). Flaws in the fightback. *The Times Higher Education Supplement*, 2 March, 28.

Times Higher Education Supplement. (1984d). A post-Robbins mould? *The Times Higher Education Supplement*, 16 March, 32.

Times Higher Education Supplement. (1984e). How the UGC goes about its job. *The Times Higher Education Supplement*, 4 May, 11.

Times Higher Education Supplement. (1984f). Universities would like to see stronger, broader schools. *The Times Higher Education Supplement*, 4 May, 11.

Times Higher Education Supplement. (1984g). The limits of hierarchy. *The Times Higher Education Supplement*, 23 March, 32.

Times Higher Education Supplement. (1984h). The great debate. *The Times Higher Education Supplement*, 14 September, (i)–(iv).

Times Higher Education Supplement. (1985). The poverty of planning. *The Times Higher Education Supplement*, 3 May, 36.

Toyne, Peter. (1985). Mission and strategy: a case study of North East London Polytechnic. *International Journal of Institutional Management in Education*, November, 9, 3, 323–328.

Truscott, B. (1943). *Redbrick university*. London: Faber and Faber.

Turner, John D. and Rushton, James. (1976). *Education for the professions*. Manchester: Manchester University Press.

Turney, Jon. (1982). Universities contribute mere 5% to research. *The Times Higher Education Supplement*, 26 November, 3.

Turney, Jon. (1983). Ask the engineers. *The Times Higher Education Supplement*, 18 March, 8.

Universities Statistical Record. (1987). *University statistics 1986/87*. Cheltenham: Universities Statistical Record.

University Grants Committee. (1981). *Circular letter 10/81*. London: The University Grants Committee.

University Grants Committee. (1984). *A strategy for higher education into the 1990s*. London: Her Majesty's Stationery Office.

University of Aston in Birmingham. (1981). *Academic plan revision: July 1981*. Birmingham: The University of Aston.

University of Bristol. (1984). University of Bristol response to the UGC questionnaire. *University of Bristol Newsletter*, 14, 14, 1–5.

University of Cincinnati. (1977). *The mission, goals and objectives of the University of Cincinnati*. Cincinnati: University of Cincinnati.

University of Kansas. (1981). *Missions and goals*. Lawrence, Kansas: The University of Kansas.

University of Kent. (1983). *A place at Kent: notes for applicants to the Faculty of Social Sciences*. Canterbury: University of Kent.

University of Kentucky. (1981). *Five-year plan, 1981–1986*. Lexington: University of Kentucky.

University of Leicester. (1981). *Jubilee year 1981–82, souvenir programme*. Leicester: University of Leicester.

University of Maryland (1980). *A plan for action*. Baltimore: The University of Maryland.

University of Ulster. (1984). *Mission statement*. Coleraine: The University of Ulster.

University of Wales. (1964). *Report of the University Commission*. Cardiff: University of Wales.

Urwin, K. (1969). What is a university? *AUT Bulletin*, January, 24–28.

Veblen, T. (1918). *The higher learning in America*. New York: W. B. Huebsch.

Verma, Gajendra K. and Beard, Ruth M. (1981). *What is educational research?* London: Gower.

Washington State University. (1978). *Planning for quality*. Pullman, Washington: Washington State University.

Weathersby, George B. (1979). A review of the state and role of planning in contemporary higher education institutions. *Paper presented to the Organisation for Economic Co-operation and Development Conference*, Paris, 20 August.

Weaver, Toby. (1982). Education for capability. *Higher Education Review*, 14, 3, Summer, 68–72.

Weaver, Toby. (1983). Looking at the memoirs. *The Times Higher Education Supplement*, 11 November, 14.

White Paper. (1987). See Cm 114.

Williams, Gareth. (1972). The politics of long-range planning in education. *Further Education Staff College Reports*, 5, 9, 16–22.

Williams, Gareth. (1983). On the mathematics of student numbers. *The Times Higher Education Supplement*, 18 November, 13.

Winstead, Philip C. (1978). Using Management by Objectives as a planning tool. *Paper presented at the conference on Academic Planning sponsored by the Higher Education Research Institute, Inc.*, Newport Beach, California, June 13–15.

Wiseman, T. P. (1981). University cuts. *The Times*, 25 November, 13.

Wojtas, Olga. (1984). UGC accused over pharmacy threat. *The Times Higher Education Supplement*, 24 August, 5.

Wolfle, Dael. (1978). Manpower planning: role of government. In Knowles, Asa S., editor, *The international encyclopaedia of higher education*. London: Jossey-Bass.

Woods, R. G. and Barrow, R. St C. (1975). *An introduction to philosophy of education*. London: Methuen and Co.

Wyatt, J. F. (1981). Ortega y Gasset's 'Mission of the university': an appropriate document for an age of economy? *Studies in Higher Education*, 6, 1, 59–69.

Wyatt, J. F. (1982). Karl Jaspers' *The idea of the university*: an existentialist argument for an institution concerned with freedom. *Studies in Higher Education*, 7, 1, 21–34.

Young, David. (1984). Coping with change: the new training initiative. *Journal of the Royal Society of Arts*, CXXXII, 5335, June, 449–459.

Supplementary Bibliography

The following books and articles have not been referred to directly in the text but have been found to be particularly useful as background reading. They may be of interest to other researchers in this field and are therefore listed here.

Argyris, Chris. (1970). Resistance to rational management systems. *Innovation*, 10, 27–35.

Balderston, Frederick E. (1974). *Managing today's university*. London: Jossey-Bass.

Barnathy, Bela H. (1973). *Developing a systems view of education*. Belmont, California: Fearon.

Barzun, Jacques. (1969). *The American university*. Oxford: Oxford University Press.

Beard, Ruth. (1979). *Teaching and learning in higher education*. London: Penguin Books.

Calvert, John R. (1980). Relative performance of educational institutions. *Proceedings of the Eighth Annual Conference of the British Educational Administration Society*, September, 179–192.

Calvert, John R. (1981). Institutional performance assessment under conditions of changing needs. *International Journal of Institutional Management in Higher Education*, 5, 3, 237–249.

Campbell, Duncan Darroch. (1973). An empirical approach to the inference and classification of university goals: the University of Alberta. *Dissertation Abstracts International*, 35/04-A, 2000.

Carter, Charles F. (1972). The efficiency of universities. *Higher Education*, 1, February, 77–90.

Davies, Digby and McHugh, Royton. (1976). *The role of objectives*. (Open University course E321, unit 7.) Milton Keynes: The Open University Press.

Dennison, W. F. (1980). The education audit as a monitor of institutional effectiveness. *Proceedings of the Eighth Annual Conference of the British Educational Administration Society*, September, 192–199.

Dobson, Lance, Gear, Tony, and Westoby, Adam. (1975). *Management in education: some techniques and some systems*. Milton Keynes: Open University Press.

Edwards, E. G. (1975). *The relevant university*. Bradford: The University of Bradford.

Eggleston, John. (1980). Educational objectives in the 1980s. *Prospects*, X, 3, 294–302.

Lumsden, Keith G. (1974). *Efficiency in universities: the La Paz papers*. London: Elsevier Scientific Publishing Company.

Royal Society of Arts. (1983). Education for capability – summary of a symposium held at the Society's House on Tuesday 7th December 1982. *Journal of the Royal Society of Arts*, CXXXI, 5325, August.

Schools Council. (1981). *The practical curriculum*. London: Methuen Educational.

Sizer, John. (1982). Institutional performance assessment under conditions of changing needs. *International Journal of Institutional Management in Higher Education*, 6, 1, March 17–28.

Smith, R. A. (1977). On the third realm – once more – against PPBS in education. *Journal of Aesthetic Education*, 11, October, 5–8.

Index

The Society for Research into Higher Education

The Society exists both to encourage and co-ordinate research and development into all aspects of Higher Education, including academic, organisational and policy issues; and also to provide a forum for debate, verbal and printed. Through its activities, it draws attention to the significance of research into, and development in, Higher Education and to the needs of scholars in this field. (It is not concerned with research generally, except, for instance, as a subject of study.)

The Society's income derives from subscriptions, book sales, conferences and specific grants. It is wholly independent. Its corporate members are institutions of higher education, research institutions and professional, industrial, and governmental bodies. Its individual members include teachers and researchers, administrators and students. Members are found in all parts of the world and the Society regards its international work as amongst its most important activities.

The Society discusses and comments on policy, organises conferences and encourages research. Under the Imprint SRHE & OPEN UNIVERSITY PRESS, it is a specialist publisher, having some 40 titles in print. It also publishes *Studies in Higher Education* (three times a year) which is mainly concerned with academic issues, *Higher Education Quarterly* (formerly *Universities Quarterly*) which will be mainly concerned with policy issues, *Research into Higher Education Abstracts* (three times a year), and a *Bulletin* (six times a year).

The Society's committees, study groups and branches are run by members (with help from a small staff at Guildford), and aim to provide a forum for discussion. The groups at present include a Teacher Education Study Group, a Staff Development Group, a Women in Higher Education Group and a Continuing Education Group which may have had their own organisation, subscriptions or publications (e.g. the *Staff Development Newsletter*). The Governing Council, elected by members, comments on current issues; and discusses policies with leading figures, notably at its evening Forums. The Society organises seminars on current research for officials of DES and other ministries, an Anglo-American series on standards, and is in touch with bodies in the UK such as the NAB, CVCP, UGC, CNAA and the British Council, and with sister-bodies overseas. Its current research projects include one on the relationship between entry qualifications and degree results, directed by Prof. W. D. Furneaux (Brunel) and one on questions of quality directed by Prof. G. C. Moodie (York). A project on the evaluation of the research standing of university departments is in preparation. The Society's conferences are often held jointly. Annual Conferences have considered 'Professional Education' (1984), 'Continuing Education' (1985, with Goldsmiths' College), 'Standards and Criteria in Higher Education' (1986, with Bulmershe CHE), 'Restructuring' (1987, with the City of Birmingham Polytechnic) and 'Academic Freedom' (1988, the University of Surrey). Other conferences have considered the DES 'Green Paper' (1985, with the *Times Higher Education Supplement*), and 'The First-Year Experience' (1986, with the University of South Carolina and Newcastle Polytechnic). For some of the Society's conferences, special studies are commissioned in advance, as 'Precedings'.

Members receive free of charge the Society's *Abstracts*, annual conference Proceedings (or 'Precedings'), *Bulletin and International Newsletter* and may buy SRHE & OPEN UNIVERSITY PRESS books at booksellers' discount. Corporate members also receive the Society's journal *Studies in Higher Education* free (individuals at a heavy discount). They may also obtain *Evaluation Newsletter* and certain other journals at a discount, including the NFER *Register of Educational Research*. There is a substantial discount to members, and to staff of corporate members, on annual and some other conference fees.